COPING

WITH

CHEMOTHERAPY

AND RADIATION

Daniel Cukier, M.D., FACR, Frank Gingerelli, M.D.
Grace Makari-Judson, M.D., and Virginia E. McCullough

McGraw·Hill

New York Chicago San Francisco Lisbon London Madrid Mexico City
Milan New Delhi San Juan Seoul Singapore Sydney Toronto

Library of Congress Cataloging-in-Publication Data

Coping with chemotherapy and radiation / Daniel Cukier . . . [et al.].
     p.   cm.
   ISBN 0-07-144472-6 (book : alk. paper)
    1. Cancer—Chemotherapy—Popular works.   2. Cancer—Radiotherapy—Popular
works.   I. Cukier, Daniel.

   RC271.C5C675   2004
   616.99′4061—dc22   2004017956

*We wish to dedicate this book to the many
patients and their families whom we have worked
with over many years.*

3 4 5 6 7 8 9 10 11   FGR/FGR   0 9 8 7 6 5

ISBN 0-07-144472-6

McGraw-Hill books are available at special quantity discounts to use as premiums and sales promotions, or for use in corporate training programs. For more information, please write to the Director of Special Sales, Professional Publishing, McGraw-Hill, Two Penn Plaza, New York, NY 10121-2298. Or contact your local bookstore.

The information contained in this book is intended to provide helpful and informative material on the subject addressed. It is not intended to serve as a replacement for professional medical advice. Any use of the information in this book is at the reader's discretion. The author and publisher specifically disclaim any and all liability arising directly or indirectly from the use or application of any information contained in this book. A health care professional should be consulted regarding your specific situation.

This book is printed on acid-free paper.

Contents

Acknowledgments vii

A Word to Professionals ix

Introduction xi

PART 1 **The Purpose of Radiation Treatment
and Chemotherapy 1**

1 **The Basics of Radiation Therapy and Chemotherapy 3**

How Is Cancer Thought to Develop? 3

How Does Radiation Treatment Work? 4

Treatment Planning 5

Consulting with Your Radiation and Medical
Oncologists 7

Treatment Procedure for Radiation Therapy 9

Basics of Chemotherapy 15

Other Treatments 19

Support Staff 21

Current Treatment 21

2 **Side Effects of Radiation and Chemotherapy 23**

Radiation: Some Things Haven't Changed 23

Treatment to the Head and Chest 25

Treatment to the Upper Abdomen 27

Treatment to the Lower Abdomen 27

How Radiation Affects the Skin 28

Side Effects Common to Both Radiation and
Chemotherapy 28

Reproductive and Sexual Issues 32

Side Effects of Chemotherapy 33

Long-Term Side Effects of Chemotherapy and Radiation 40

3 **Diet, Lifestyle, and Emotional Concerns 45**

Diet and Cancer 45

Lifestyle Changes 55

Emotional Concerns 60

Motivation for Change 64

The Truth Is Essential 64

Spirituality 65

When Treatment Ends 65

PART 2 **Cancer Treatment: Radiation Therapy and
Chemotherapy 67**

4 **Cancers Most Commonly Treated with Radiation and
Chemotherapy 69**

Bladder Cancer 69

Brain Cancer 75

Breast Cancer 79

Cancer of the Cervix 99

Colorectal Cancer 102

Esophageal Cancer 108

Head and Neck Cancer 114

Hodgkin's Disease 119

Lung Cancer 124

Myeloma (Multiple Myeloma) 129

Non-Hodgkin's Lymphoma 134

Ovarian Cancer 138

Pancreatic Cancer 140

Prostate Cancer 142

Skin Cancer 154

Testicular Cancer 157

Uterine Cancer 160

5 **If Cancer Has Spread 165**

Metastasis to Bones 166

Metastasis to the Brain 170

Metastasis to the Chest 173

Metastasis to the Lymph Nodes 174

Metastasis to the Skin 177

Metastasis to the Spine 179

If Cancer Has Spread and Treatment Stops Working 181

6 **More Treatments for Cancer 183**

Bone Marrow Transplantation 183

Other Anticancer Substances 185

Gene Therapy 186

Monoclonal Antibody Therapy 189

Genetic Predisposition and Preventing Cancer 190

Looking to the Future 191

7 **Treating Pain 193**

Why Is Cancer Painful? 193

Pain Relief Medications 194

Treating the Disease 196

Pain Assessment 197

Additional Strategies 198

PART 3 Other Issues in Cancer Treatment 199

8 **Diagnostic Testing 201**

Choosing the Test to Use 202

Review of Test Results Prior to Treatment 202

Testing During Treatment 203

Testing After Completion of Radiation Therapy and
Chemotherapy 203

Types of Tests 203

9 **Frequently Asked Questions About Cancer and
Treatment 223**

Glossary 239

Additional Resources 245

Index 249

Acknowledgments

Countless people have inspired us to make this updated and expanded book a reality, particularly Michele Pezzuti at McGraw-Hill Trade. We also wish to acknowledge the countless efforts of physicians and nurses, medical support staff, social workers, and clergy. These professionals offer cancer patients and their families the best treatments available, practical support, emotional sustenance, and hope. In addition, we thank our families for enriching our lives with their love and support.

A Word to Professionals

Our goal in writing this book is to help cancer patients and their families and loved ones understand radiation treatment and chemotherapy. We believe that patients are better able to cope with their illnesses and the recommended medical treatments when they are given comprehensive information about both. Therefore, we've written the book in a style that laypeople can easily understand. Where the use of medical terminology is unavoidable, we have tried to explain the concepts in a way that the average reader can grasp. The brief discussions of issues other than radiation treatment and chemotherapy are approached in the same way.

It is our hope that the many professionals who work with cancer patients and their families will discuss in greater detail the issues we've raised. While physicians directly involved in cancer treatment try to attend to the emotional concerns of their patients, we know that many other practitioners are involved as well. Clinical social workers often establish a close therapeutic relationship with patients and their families. Hospital oncology nurses and home-care nurses frequently advise patients and help them cope with the physical and emotional side effects of treatment. Dietitians may be involved in planning nutritional programs for patients.

No matter which profession we practice, we all want to provide quality care to our patients and help alleviate their fear and anxiety as well. Offering concise, easy-to-comprehend information about the treatment they are undergoing is one way we can achieve this.

The radiation dose schedules and chemotherapy protocols vary somewhat among different treatment centers. Much depends on the patient's clinical picture as well as their doctors' experiences with treatments and their results for patients. Thus, the treatments described in this book are only general guidelines that give readers ideas about what they can expect.

Introduction

More than likely, if you are reading this book, you either have cancer yourself or are close to someone who does. You already may have been referred to a facility for treatment, following a series of diagnostic tests and consultations with your doctors. The past few days or weeks have been traumatic, and now you're about to begin radiation treatment, chemotherapy, or both, and you surely have dozens of questions about what lies ahead. You may be feeling lonely and frightened, too, as you prepare to cope with the treatment you will be undergoing in the coming weeks.

This book was written to provide cancer patients and their loved ones with the information they need to cope with radiation treatment and chemotherapy. (Only those cancers most commonly treated with radiation and chemotherapy are discussed here. Because pediatric cancer is a specialized field with unique issues, it is not included.) Our goal is to make the course of your treatment a little easier by providing you with basic knowledge. You'll know why and, just as important, how the treatment is done. You'll know what to expect at the time of treatment, you'll be prepared for the most commonly experienced side effects, and you'll know about effective ways to alleviate them.

Your own physician has probably told you what to expect, but after you left his or her office, you may have thought of many more questions. Of course, you also may be going through the natural adjustment period when you learn to accept your illness and make decisions about the treatment options that have been recommended for you. Because treatment usually begins as soon as possible after cancer is diagnosed, you may have little time to prepare psychologically. Because a diagnosis of cancer is an emotionally powerful event, this book explores the normal emotional ups and downs you may experience during the course of your treatment. It also offers advice about sorting through your feelings about your illness and its effect on your body, as well as its impact on your relationships with family and friends. The information included here will serve a twofold purpose. First, it will fill many gaps in the information you already have, and then it will help you form the questions you want to ask your doctor or your treatment team.

The ability to cope with cancer and its various treatments varies greatly from person to person. Having the support of family members and other loved ones is crucial during this period, but, by the same token, no disease puts stress on a family quite like cancer does, and family relationships are often stretched to the limit. Some families grow closer; others are torn apart. However, helping the patient and family members is an essential element of your physician's job. Office staff, nurses, and social workers also provide support.

Medical oncologists treat and provide follow-up care over a period of weeks, months, or years. They and their staff typically help patients deal with side effects, lifestyle adjustments, nutrition, and other issues. After treating cancer patients for many years, we have learned that well-informed patients tend to go through treatment and recover more easily than those who understand less about their situations. Furthermore, many remarkable recoveries occur every day, even among patients whose cancer is in an advanced stage. So while statistics may be important when discussing overall outlook with a patient, we emphasize that *an individual's response to treatment determines the final outcome.*

Radiation Therapy, Chemotherapy, and Their Side Effects

In order for you to understand how radiation treatment and chemotherapy work, the first chapter of this book will explain why one or both of these treatments is performed and take you step-by-step through treatment planning. In the case of radiation treatment, the equipment may look forbidding, even though the treatment itself is painless. You also may be afraid of the idea of radiation being directed to your body. Similarly, patients often are afraid of the potential debilitating effects of chemotherapy, not to mention the side effects, such as hair loss. Chapter 1 is designed to help alleviate your fears and answer initial questions you may have about treatment procedures.

The side effects of radiation therapy and chemotherapy are generally predictable and, most important, they are almost always manageable. You will be less fearful after you have read Chapter 2 and learned what symptoms you may expect to experience and at approximately what point during treatment they are likely to appear. Most side effects of radiation occur in the general area of the body receiving the treatment. For example, radiation directed to the prostate gland may cause urinary tract symptoms because of the proximity of the urinary bladder to that organ. While some symptoms are unavoidable, changes in diet, specific medications, and some adjustments in lifestyle can alleviate others.

In the case of chemotherapy, extensive research has helped to define the likelihood of a particular side effect occurring with each chemotherapy drug or combination. For example, it is well-known which chemotherapy drugs are very likely to result in nausea or vomiting, which are associated with only mild nausea, and which generally do not cause nausea at all. As part of your treatment plan, you may receive medicines to *prevent* nausea rather than waiting for it to happen and receiving a prescription to deal with it after the fact. After the first treatment, if this medicine worked well, it will be continued. If it did not work well, additional medicines will be recommended with the goal of eliminating any nausea.

The Growing Role of Supportive Therapies

The conventional therapies for cancer—surgery, chemotherapy, and radiation—are considered primary treatments. In a technical sense, these treatments are done to a person and for a person and are administered in a clinical setting by a variety of professionals. However, today we know that patients can do much on their own behalf to improve their quality of life during treatment. For example, we generally believe that maintaining a positive psychological outlook can be a powerful tool for recovery. However, it is unrealistic to assume that anyone diagnosed with cancer will be able to maintain a positive attitude all the time. Your treatment team may recommend support groups or psychological counseling to provide a place to share your doubts, fears, and hopes. In addition, you may find it helpful to seek religious or spiritual support.

The importance of a patient's attitude and coping skills have begun to be recognized in recent years. Some studies have shown that breast cancer patients who participate in support groups appear to have a better prognosis. Some research suggests that techniques that help a patient relax may create subtle biological changes that can boost the immune system and help the body to fight off the invading cancer. These techniques include special breathing techniques, meditation, yoga, guided imagery (visualization), self-hypnosis, and prayer. The effect on cancer patients of spiritual intervention, such as prayer, whether individual or in large gatherings, is also currently being studied. Trying to maintain a positive attitude, setting goals for each day, and carrying on the will to live are all important.

Dietary changes can also make patients more comfortable during treatment and enhance the effectiveness of the therapy. These are generally considered supportive therapies, used in conjunction with conventional cancer treatments.

Clearly, traditional treatments remain the mainstay of cancer therapy. So, while supportive therapies are extremely helpful, we don't believe that cancer patients should rely *only* on special diets, alternative medicine, support groups, or counseling. There is no evidence that these methods are effective when used alone. However, because much is still not known about the body's ability to fight the disease, any technique that potentially boosts the immune system can only help and never hurt. Therefore, we recognize the importance of these treatments for some patients when used along with conventional therapies.

It is crucial, however, that you share with your doctor information about any additional therapies you may be pursuing or considering. This is especially important for herbal remedies or supplements, as these may interfere with cancer treatments or medications. (See Chapter 3.) Remember that you and your team need to be partners in your care.

Living with Cancer

A patient's illness can not be viewed as separated from the rest of his or her life, and so part of your treatment team's role is to advise you about your day-to-day life during treatment. Chapter 3 is devoted to a discussion of lifestyle issues, including a discussion of diet. The food you eat may have a considerable effect on your body's ability to fight cancer. Certain foods may make some cancer symptoms and side effects of treatment worse, while other foods may help alleviate side effects. This chapter offers suggestions about cooking, food selection, and the timing and size of meals. There is increasing research on the benefits of exercise in cancer patients and how it may reduce fatigue and improve mood. We also discuss sexuality, sleep and rest issues, and social relationships.

Emotional Concerns

Two patients with the same disease in the same stage may have totally different reactions and side effects, depending on their perception of their conditions. Their ability to function during the course of radiation treatment or chemotherapy may be profoundly affected by the presence or absence of depression and anxiety. Fear about the future, questions about the possibility of recovery, financial concerns, and special pressures on relationships represent the kind of issues with which cancer patients must contend. For some patients, support groups are the answer; other patients choose individual psychotherapy to help them cope; still others rely on spiritual counselors, family, or friends for support. Chapter 3 discusses the profound emotional issues that invariably accompany a diagnosis of cancer.

Radiation Treatment and Chemotherapy for Specific Cancers

Radiation treatment and chemotherapy programs vary greatly, depending on the kind of cancer being treated. In addition, individual factors such as age and overall physical condition are taken into consideration, too. The length of radiation treatment (weeks or months) and doses also vary among treatment centers and according to the patient's clinical picture. The length of chemotherapy treatment and chemotherapy doses are standardized for each particular cancer, but exact doses are calculated for individual patients based on their height and weight. In this book, chemotherapy drugs and other medications are listed using their generic names first, followed by the brand name in parentheses. Physicians commonly use the generic names, while the brand name is how the drug is advertised.

Chapter 4 is designed to help you learn about radiation treatment and chemotherapy for your specific cancer. An entire section is devoted to each type of cancer for which these therapies are commonly recommended. In addition, we discuss specific expected side effects and ways to treat them. In those cancers for which chemotherapy and radiation treatments are administered concurrently, a treatment-team approach is essential, and that topic is covered as well. Each section also discusses diet and lifestyle issues and some emotional concerns that typically accompany particular cancers. However, we urge you to read the introductory chapters that provide more general information before turning to the individual sections.

We believe that it is important for physicians to be as positive as possible when discussing treatment and the possibility of cure. Therefore, without being unrealistically cheerful, we attempt to describe the origin and staging of particular cancers as concretely as possible, knowing that when patients are able to get a clear understanding of their disease, the fear of the unknown is often greatly reduced. This lays the groundwork for patients to gain a sense of control over the condition and not simply be helpless observers. To that end, we've included as much information as possible to help you understand the origin and course of your particular cancer.

The statistics concerning the incidence of certain cancers, the effectiveness of treatments, and cure rates for various cancers change often. An individual's specific prognosis depends on many variables, most of which are beyond the scope of this book. Therefore, for most of the cancers we discuss, it is nearly impossible to provide meaningful cure or long-term survival statistics because what is valid today might not be valid tomorrow. The outlook for your particular case should be discussed with your own doctors.

If Cancer Has Spread

Cancer may *metastasize*, or spread, beyond its original site, and if this occurs, radiation therapy and/or chemotherapy are often used to control the disease, rather than cure it. This is known as *palliative* treatment, and it is primarily used to control pain and limit the damage caused by uncontrolled disease affecting various organs. Chapter 5 describes the specifics of radiation treatment delivered to the parts of the body most likely to be treated for metastatic cancer. We also describe the situations in which chemotherapy is used as palliative treatment and to help individuals live longer. In addition, we discuss side effects and relevant diet and lifestyle issues.

An individual with metastatic cancer is similar to a person who has other types of chronic diseases, such as diabetes. As such, they may continue to need treatments to keep the cancer under control. The focus changes from trying to cure the cancer to getting back to day-to-day activities so that the patient can live *despite* the cancer.

No other area of cancer treatment is changing more rapidly than chemotherapy. Research today is identifying new drugs and new combinations. Most exciting, however, is the discovery of new *targeted treatments*, which are directed against a specific molecular abnormality unique to the growth mechanism of the cancer cell. These treatments have fewer side effects. These drugs will probably not replace chemotherapy, but work best in combination with chemotherapy. Many authorities believe that targeted therapies may be the wave of the future. These therapies and other treatments are discussed in Chapter 6.

Handling Pain

Chapter 7 discusses pain, the most dreaded symptom of cancer. Radiation treatment can alleviate much of the pain caused by certain cancers, and it is often given for this purpose. Chemotherapy is helpful in controlling pain by shrinking cancer at sites that may be pressing on nerve endings. However, many cancer patients may also need medications. The vast majority of patients will have their pain well controlled by treating the underlying cancer; by the optimal use of medication, including narcotics; and by the occasional use of other strategies, such as nerve blocks. Cancer specialists know how to use medications judiciously and can prescribe them individually or in combination, thereby minimizing their side effects.

Because you are part of your treatment team, you should play a role in deciding which medication you prefer and, in effect, take charge of your own problem with pain. This book will answer your questions about pain-relieving medications and their side effects. We also talk about possible addiction to these drugs, a concern of many patients.

There is simply no reason to suffer discomfort and pain in silence. If one drug or combination of medications isn't effective, then talk with your doctors about trying others. The physical stress of unrelieved pain can make treatment more difficult, and it may also affect the way in which patients are able to cope with their illness. Therefore, it is important for you to know that the pain you experience can and should be relieved.

Diagnostic Testing

A variety of tests are used to diagnose cancer, monitor progress of the treatments used, and to follow up after treatment is completed. It is likely that during the coming years you will be undergoing on a regular basis various x-ray tests and the newer diagnostic tests using non–x-ray technology. We've included a description of these tests in Chapter 8 so that you will understand why they are administered and what each procedure will be like. In the future, tests may be done that may help predict how the cancer is likely to behave and may help patients and doctors decide on the best treatments.

The Multidisciplinary Approach to Cancer Treatment

You may or may not have heard the terms *multidisciplinary approach* or *treatment-team concept* in cancer treatment, but in recent years, these ways of formulating and managing treatment plans have become an important part of the cancer "picture." The multidisciplinary approach involves combining the different treatments with the goal of enhancing survival rates and reducing the risk of cancer recurrence as much as possible. Using the treatment-team approach, cancer specialists—that is, surgeons, radiation oncologists, and medical oncologists—work together to formulate a specific treatment plan for each patient.

In practical terms, we believe that the best treatment decisions are made when these specialists can communicate together. One means to that end is the treatment-planning conference, at which they will carefully review all the diagnostic testing results and pathology slides.

In general, you can view surgery and radiation therapy as *local* treatments that affect the specific area of the cancer. Chemotherapy and hormone treatments are *systemic* treatments, meaning that they travel through the bloodstream for the purpose of affecting cancer cells that may have spread outside of the initial area. In some cases, such as in breast and colon cancer, these treatments are given as *adjuvant*, or extra, treatments for early-stage patients even when it is not definitively known that the cancer has "escaped" out of the region of the primary site. Adjuvant treatments are recommended because research has shown positive results. In other words, chemotherapy or hormonal treatments have, over time, been shown to reduce recurrence and improve survival rates in a significant percentage of patients.

Once in the bloodstream, the particular chemotherapy drug attacks circulating cancer cells and destroys them before they become established in other organs, such as the lungs, the liver, or the bones (common sites of metastatic disease). We have learned that this preemptive treatment works best, rather than waiting until detectable tumor masses have developed and then addressing them after the fact.

In the early days of cancer therapy, surgery was the only treatment available. Basically, doctors thought that cutting it all out offered the best chance for achieving a cure. However, this meant that patients often went through extensive and sometimes deforming surgeries. Unfortunately, even with these radical surgeries, cancer often came back in the same spot or in distant sites in the body. Today, many types of cancer surgery are less extensive because we are able to add other treatments such as radiation and chemotherapy. In some situations, surgery is avoided altogether.

Your team of cancer specialists determines the sequence of treatments. For example, if a patient has locally advanced breast cancer, the team may determine that the most advantageous treatment is a course of chemotherapy first, followed by surgery and then radiation. Or to take a different example, a patient with head and neck cancer may receive concurrent radiation and chemotherapy, followed by surgery.

The multidisciplinary approach is a rapidly evolving area of cancer treatment, which involves seeking opinions from the different cancer specialists before making treatment decisions and undergoing any of the procedures.

When faced with the news that they have cancer, many individuals believe that they must have it removed, one way or another, as soon as possible. They may feel pressured about starting treatment because of the emotional issues involved with this disease. Well-meaning family members may urge that treatment begin right away. However, in situations in which more than one option is available, it is most important to investigate options and feel comfortable with treatment decisions, which is why we recommend getting more than one opinion.

Clinical Trials

Before making a final decision on your treatment, be sure to ask if you are eligible to participate in any clinical trials. In some cases, clinical trials are important means of determining the best treatments for different cancers. Clinical trials have their own language or designations, and as such they are defined in terms of phases: Phases I, II, or III.

In *Phase I trials*, a new drug is tested to determine the best dose and learn about the side effects. These studies are limited to smaller numbers of patients, usually with more advanced disease, whose cancers have progressed despite receiving standard drugs. *Phase II trials* look at efficacy of new treatments. *Phase III trials* compare one or more new treatment strategies with a standard one. These tend to be very large studies available at cancer centers, but sometimes are also available through a physician's office. These studies represent excellent opportunities for some cancer patients, because often patients have a chance to receive a drug before FDA approval makes it generally available. Drugs used in clinical trials are often provided at no cost to the patient.

When they enter a study, a cancer patient does not know if a specific treatment will turn out to be better than a standard treatment and if he or she will directly benefit from the treatment. In addition, some new treatments or combinations of strategies may turn out to have more side effects than anticipated. However, most patients in clinical trials are followed more closely then average and are given additional tests. Sites that actively participate in clinical trials are more in tune with state-of-the-art treatments.

Currently, there are excellent opportunities to participate in clinical trials looking at sequencing chemotherapy, radiation, and surgery in the treatment of a number of cancers. The implications of participating in a clinical trial are worth considering. For example, clinical trials provide an individual with the opportunity to be part of potentially landmark cancer research. As an example, think about the first women who participated in the early trials that looked at breast-conserving therapy. Up to that point, mastectomy was the standard surgery, and these women acted courageously when they agreed to try new treatments. But, thanks to those women, newly diagnosed patients today have a choice. See the Additional Resources to find websites that include information about clinical trials.

Your Right to Know

It's unfortunate but true that some patients and family members are afraid to ask questions, sometimes because they fear the answers. Some patients are afraid to ask questions that might make them appear stupid, but when it comes to cancer treatment, there is no such thing as a stupid question.

We're often asked such questions as "Will radiation and chemotherapy make my hair fall out?" or "Will I become radioactive because of the radiation therapy?" Medical oncologists might hear numerous questions about the fear of being "poisoned" by chemotherapy. Similarly, patients may have an underlying fear that radiation treatment will kill them, usually because they know about the extensive fatalities at Hiroshima and Nagasaki. Are these stupid questions? Not at all. They are valid questions that deserve answers. In our experience, patients have questions about everything from hair loss to sleep disturbance and sexuality. Therefore, we've included a chapter at the end of the book that answers many of the most frequently asked questions about cancer treatments. It is best, though, to make your own list of questions to take with you when you go in to see your cancer specialist.

We also know that patients may want to know if radiation treatment or chemotherapy are last-ditch efforts or if, on the other hand, the treatments are recommended because chances of recovery are good. Naturally, patients are concerned about being bedridden and incapacitated, and they may wonder if treatments other than chemotherapy or radiation treatment could be effective. In addition, family members may be frightened when their loved one has no appetite or shows signs of depression. Each of these issues is discussed in appropriate chapters which, when taken together, help patients and their families cope. Share any fears and concerns with your treatment team. Be partners in your care.

The Patient Is in Charge

In our view, it is absolutely essential that all cancer patients understand the disease process taking place. Patients must see themselves as part of the treatment team, and they must demand to be fully supported in the effort to ease them through treatment and restore their health. As a patient, you are entitled to know what is considered the standard of care in treating any given cancer. This book can be your resource.

If you are dissatisfied with your treatment center, speak to your referring physician and speak to friends or relatives who have undergone cancer therapies. An open attitude with your treatment team, including all the support staff, is very important; confrontation is almost always counterproductive. If you're dissatisfied at any point, clearly communicating your needs and expectations is the first step to resolving the problem. Keep in mind that you choose your physicians and support services and that it is up to you to take an active part in decisions affecting your recovery.

A Word About the Future

Research into new treatments for cancers of all types is ongoing. Improved surgical techniques; new chemotherapeutic, hormonal, and biologic agents; and advances in radiotherapeutic technology continue to increase the length of survival. However, cure rates for cancer remain modest. The greatest improvement in cure rates results from early detection. You have no doubt heard public service announcements about the importance of early detection for common cancers such as those occurring in the breast, colon, and the prostate gland. Mammography, colonoscopy, and blood screening tests for prostate cancer continue to help save lives. Sophisticated testing now is enabling physicians to detect small rectal and colon cancers that have cure rates above 90 percent. The average size of a breast cancer at the time of diagnosis today is significantly smaller then the size of a tumor diagnosed ten years ago. In addition to early diagnosis strategies for the general population, we are trying to predict which family members may need increased surveillance, so they can be identified for specific screening and prevention strategies.

Too many individuals fail to consider the enormous impact early detection has on survival rates. Too often the news about cancer sounds remote or not particularly positive. However, the outlook for early detection continues to improve, and every member of your family stands to benefit from this current research work.

Clearly, scientists are working hard to try to find a cure for all cancers. We also are attempting to make the treatments more tolerable, to achieve cure with less invasive surgery, more directed radiation, and finding and using drugs that will affect cancer cells and leave normal cells alone. We are aware that prevention is better than cure. But until we discover the most effective ways to prevent cancer, the focus will remain on detecting cancer at the earliest stages so that treatments will have the highest likelihood of success.

PART 1

THE PURPOSE OF RADIATION TREATMENT AND CHEMOTHERAPY

WE DESIGNED THIS section to introduce you to the
medical terminology and concepts used in cancer
treatment and to explain the rationale for using radiation
therapy, chemotherapy, and other treatments. Our goal is
to present essential information that will help you
through this difficult time in your life. In order to better
understand the treatment plan recommended by your
oncology team, we suggest reading the chapters in the
order presented.

1

The Basics of Radiation Therapy and Chemotherapy

The use of radiation for diagnostic and treatment purposes was a revolutionary step in the evolution of medicine. Without it, we wouldn't be able to diagnose numerous conditions and diseases, and we wouldn't be able to treat cancer with radiation. Therapeutic radiation takes the technology one step further and allows us to treat cancer in various organs without opening up the body. For some kinds of cancer, radiation may be used as the primary treatment, and, for other cancers, it is used in conjunction with surgery and/or chemotherapy. Radiation therapy is known as a *local* treatment.

Chemotherapeutic agents are specific medications that circulate through the blood for the purpose of destroying the cancer cells. Because these agents can affect cancer cells anywhere in the body, chemotherapy is referred to as a *systemic* treatment. For some cancers it is the primary or only treatment. Under other circumstances, it is one treatment in a total plan and may be given either before or after surgery or radiation, or given concurrently, meaning that patients receive radiation and chemotherapy in the same time frame. Because we now are able to detect some cancers in earlier stages, an aggressive combined treatment approach often has been found to be more effective than using only one or another treatment.

How Is Cancer Thought to Develop?

Cancers begin as a cluster of cells multiplying in an out-of-control manner, unlike the body's normal cycle of cell destruction and replenishment. Particular abnormal genes (*oncogenes*) that influence this uncontrolled growth have been identified in some cancer cells. Scientists believe that once a cluster of cancer cells has arisen in an organ, a step-by-step progressive pattern in cancer growth and spread follows. At first, the body's immune system resists the growth of the invader, a process that may go on for years. Once the battle tips in favor of the cancer, though, local growth proceeds. At some point, and this point is thought to vary among cancers as well as individuals, the cancer spreads locally into surrounding tissues.

The next step is for cancer cells to attach themselves to and penetrate the neighboring blood-vessel and lymph-vessel walls; once this occurs, the cancer cells enter the bloodstream and the lymph system. Cells traveling in the lymph system settle in the lymph nodes. The cancer cells then travel throughout the body via the lymph system pathways, but must reattach to and penetrate the vessel wall at a distant site. The organs into which these cells settle are generally those richly endowed with blood vessels and with nutrient materials. Thus, the bones, the liver, the lungs, and the brain are common sites to which cancers commonly spread, or *metastasize.*

How Does Radiation Treatment Work?

The effects of radiation on tissues and their cells are very complex. For the sake of simplicity, the principles can be explained as the ability of radiation to injure DNA, the genetic material in the nucleus of the cell. The results of the biochemical effects, which do not make the body radioactive, is to either destroy the cell or alter its metabolism so as to hinder its ability to function normally.

Radiation may be administered in the form of gamma rays or x-rays (as discussed later). They differ only in their origin, but not in their ultimate biological effects. Radiation therapy is administered to those cancers in which there is a selective ability for the radiation to destroy cancer cells while allowing the adjacent normal cells to repair themselves from the injury.

The treatment course for some cancers is relatively long in order to allow for normal tissue repair and to minimize permanent injury. In other words, relatively small doses given over a long period of time allow for normal tissues to recover at the expense of the cancer cell. Proper nutrition and a patient's mental state may also help the body repair tissues. (These issues will be discussed later in this book.) The daily dose must also be great enough to destroy the cancer cell while sparing the normal tissues. This balancing act is fundamental to radiation therapy. When chemotherapy, which also harms normal tissues, is used in combination with radiation, the balance can be even harder to achieve.

Patients often ask why some cancers may be destroyed by radiation while others don't respond to this treatment. Simply stated, cancer cells vary in their sensitivity to destruction by x-rays. This sensitivity largely depends on the origin of the cancer. For example, the usual skin cancer is generally more sensitive, meaning more easily destroyed, by radiation than a cancer originating in the lung.

Sensitivity may also vary in the same cancer site. One patient with cancer of the uterus may respond much better to radiation than another patient with the same cancer because the uterus contains more than one cell type. Each cell type varies in its ability to be destroyed by radiation therapy. Thus, cancer cells arising from the lining of the uterine cavity are more sensitive to radiation than those arising from its muscle cells. As a result, a relatively small amount of radiation may be necessary to effectively treat one patient, whereas much higher doses are necessary for another.

In addition, cancer cells in the same tumor may vary in their sensitivity to radiation depending on their location in the mass. Generally, the outer areas of the tumor are more sensitive. This is related to the amount of oxygen reaching the cancer. The peripheral regions are better oxygenated and are destroyed more easily than tumor cells at the center.

When we talk about resistance, we mean the opposite of sensitivity. Some cancers, such as melanoma (a less common but very serious type of skin cancer), are usually resistant to radiation therapy and little or no benefit is achieved by using it.

Treatment Planning

The decision to use radiation therapy for your cancer is arrived at after consultations by the pathologist, internist, surgeon, medical oncologist, and the radiation oncologist, all of whom may be part of your treatment team. Some cancers respond better to surgical treatment or chemotherapy. Nowadays, improvement in cancer survival often involves treatments that combine surgery, radiation, and chemotherapy. But each situation is tailored to the individual patient. In addition to the type and location of the cancer, your age and general physical condition guide the choice of treatment procedures used.

Organs are composed of different cell *types*; each type can lead to a different cancer. For example, cancer cells arising from the air sacs of the lungs lead to a different type of cancer than those arising from the bronchial tubes. The cell type provides the information that allows a radiation oncologist to predict the tumor's response to radiation and a medical oncologist to predict the response to chemotherapy. Thus, a prognosis, or educated opinion, is possible about the probable effectiveness of radiation therapy and/or chemotherapy.

The individual cancer cell type may vary in its ability to spread. This degree of aggressiveness is referred to as *cell grade*.

We also look at the extent to which the cancer is present. Is it *localized*, meaning limited to the organ of origin, or has it metastasized? The evaluation of the extent of the cancer is referred to as the *stage* of the tumor. This involves using various diagnostic x-ray tests (see Chapter 8). CT scans, MRIs, PET scans, bone scans, ultrasound examinations, and simple x-ray tests are often used to assess the entire clinical picture. Obviously, the goal is to correctly treat the tumor while minimizing any negative effects on the surrounding normal tissues.

Radiation oncologists use the three parameters of grade, type, and staging to evaluate how much radiation will be necessary and for what period of time. This is known as the *dose-time relationship* of treatment. The dose levels and length of treatment are guidelines. The treatment schedules have been developed based on the cumulative experience of major treatment centers, using large numbers of patients. However, every person's case is different, and your treatment dose and time may vary from those described here.

Your doctors (radiation oncologist and/or medical oncologist or surgeon) are not treating your cancer as an isolated event. They generally work closely with the referring physician before and during your treatment, jointly evaluating the impact of the therapy on your entire medical condition. For example, other diseases and disorders may coexist with cancer, or you may have medical problems that could be aggravated by radiation therapy and/or chemotherapy. Obviously, these conditions must be carefully monitored.

In addition to delivering treatment, your oncologists are also responsible for treating the side effects of the treatments with appropriate medications and strategies. For example, your nutritional status is monitored, and you will be given advice about certain foods that should be avoided and those you should be sure to include in your diet (see Chapter 3). In other words, your oncologists are involved with your overall well-being during and after your treatment.

Consulting with Your Radiation and Medical Oncologists

A radiation oncologist is a physician who is specially trained in not only the science but also the art of administering radiation treatments. A radiation oncologist is trained to evaluate which patients may undergo radiation therapy by determining if the tumor will respond to radiation. A medical oncologist is a physician who has the same training as your internist, plus additional specialty training in the diagnosis and treatment of cancer. Medical oncologists oversee the use of medications to treat cancer, such as chemotherapy, hormone treatments, or immunotherapy. Many medical oncologists are also trained in hematology, which is the study of blood diseases and cancers of the blood cells.

When you and your family members first meet with your radiation or medical oncologist, tell him or her what you already know about your illness. We generally ask patients what they understand about their disease and then tell them that by the time they leave the office they should have a complete understanding of their cancer and the proposed treatments. You should leave your first appointment knowing that you are part of the treatment team.

Write down your questions before your office visit, because the issues you want to discuss might slip your mind when you're actually in the office. This is understandable because the first visit is often emotionally charged for both you and your family members. If you think of additional questions when you are back home, call the physician and get your answers. Remember that information will alleviate your fear and anxiety and, therefore, boost the therapeutic effect of your treatment.

Don't be afraid to ask your doctors about the likely outcome of your disease. Such issues should be dealt with realistically, and the response should be based on current statistics for the specific cancer and its stage. However, it is just as important to discuss individual variation. In our own practices we've seen patients cured, even when, according to the statistics, the outlook was grim. As Norman Cousins wrote in his book *Head First*, "Don't deny the diagnosis, just the verdict that is supposed to go with it."

Although no special preparation is necessary before these first visits to the oncologist's office, we have found that the better-prepared patients generally get more from the visit. As part of your preparation, it's important to have your medical records available. These include previous history and medical examinations related to the cancer and other conditions and any available x-rays and pathology reports. If the biopsy that was found to contain cancer was not done at the same hospital or office where you are going for radiation or chemotherapy treatments, the oncologist will likely request that the actual slides be sent over for review. (This allows for a second opinion.) If you can't personally obtain these, then make sure they have been sent to your oncologist's office beforehand. This will save considerable time.

During an initial consultation with a radiation oncologist, he or she will review the pathology report and all x-ray tests available, and evaluate and determine an appropriate field (portal) of treatment. Assuming the patient agrees to proceed with treatment, this is drawn on the skin with indelible ink. This ink may wash off with time, but patients are instructed not to scrub at the marks when showering or bathing.

A *simulator machine* will ensure that the portal will include the cancer and its potential areas of spread. This phase of treatment planning is known as simulation. Thus, the treatment process is set up, checked, and rechecked to guarantee that the actual treatment will be as precise as possible. Technical staff, who often deliver the actual radiation therapy, will work in conjunction with you and your treatment team to make sure any questions about the treatment plan are resolved.

During the initial visit with a medical oncologist, your complete medical history will be taken and you'll be given a complete physical examination. Be sure to bring in a list of all the medications you take as well as any over-the-counter drugs and supplements. Your height and weight will be measured, as these are important in calculating drug doses. The medical oncologist will ask questions about any past and present medical problems and treatments, symptoms that are bothering you, and your current level of activity. Because there may be so much to digest, a family member or friend can serve as an extra pair of ears during an initial consultation and a written list of questions will be valuable.

As you discuss your condition with your physicians, bear in mind that treatment plans for cancer can't be isolated from a person's age, general physical condition, or even his or her psychological makeup. An older person who is suffering from cancer in addition to having an underlying chronic health problem—a lung condition, for example—will be treated differently than a person twenty years younger with a similar cancer but without other physical disabilities or medical conditions. Although there's no universally accepted definition of quality of life, you and your doctors certainly consider the concept when making treatment decisions, including radiation dose levels, size of treatment areas, length of treatment, and chemotherapy drugs and doses.

Your radiation oncologist will probably be involved in your case for an average of two to eight weeks. The time to build a comfortable relationship with this person is at the beginning of treatment. Your family doctor will take over your care at some point, although the radiation oncologist will see you to follow up treatment results and to evaluate side effects. He or she will order diagnostic tests if necessary.

Your medical oncologist may be involved in your care for five years or longer, because medical oncologists are also interested in the medical concerns of cancer survivors. They will work with your family doctor to suggest the best strategies for staying well. They have a good perspective on what ongoing health monitoring is important for you, keeping in mind your prior cancer diagnosis and treatment. It is also helpful to stay in contact with your medical oncologist in the event that new advances in cancer care may be relevant to you. If it is not possible or practical to continue to see your medical oncologist, be sure your family doctor sends him or her updates on how you are doing and any questions or concerns that arise about your health.

Treatment Procedure for Radiation Therapy

Radiation treatments are painless. However, depending on the location, the cumulative effects may result in discomfort or pain in the area. Although patients are afraid they will feel intense heat, there is no heat, light, or sound associated with the treatment. The fact that treatment is silent may produce anxieties of its own, but the information in this book may help alleviate any anxieties you have.

The patient lies on a treatment couch for a few minutes. The treatment equipment unit you see is mostly shield and/or circuitry. The area subject to the treatment is known as the *treatment field,* and a beam of predetermined size passes through other tissue to the desired site. The exact length of time depends on body size, the location of the tumor, and the size of the area being treated.

You are able to breathe normally during treatment. This is surprising to some patients, but ordinary breathing does not significantly alter the position of the organs. Physical restraints are generally not used unless a patient is disoriented and unaware of his or her surroundings, therefore lacking normal judgment. Young children, senile older persons, and severely ill patients may require some immobilization devices or tranquilizers.

Today's treatment rooms look pleasant and cheerful. Often, soothing music will be playing or can be turned on at your request. In general, every effort is made to keep you comfortable and relaxed. Patients are usually relieved after the first treatment because they see how painless and easy the actual treatments are.

If you are too ill to travel on your own, then you will need to arrange for friends, relatives, or an ambulance service to take you to the radiation therapy facility. Naturally, if you're already a patient in the hospital, you will go to the facility by direct in-hospital transportation.

You may wonder whether you may drive home after the first or subsequent treatments, and you may also be concerned about feeling ill after the first treatment. Except where there is a physical disability that precludes driving, it is likely that you will be able to drive yourself home after the first treatment and usually after subsequent treatments. There is no need to make special arrangements. (However, those having radiation therapy to the brain are advised to have someone available to drive them home, because, by virtue of the cancer itself, these patients are at risk for a sudden onset of new symptoms. Chapter 5 explains this further.)

Portals vary in size, depending on the staging of the tumor and a person's body size and shape. A heavier person will require a longer daily treatment time than will a small person because of the greater amount of tissue present between the skin surface and the tumor. However, the treatment plan remains the same. Treatment times average just a few minutes, and individual variation results from the variables discussed above.

Treatments may be administered through both the front and the back of the body, or as a single treatment through the front, back, or side. Alternatively, multiple-angle treatments are sometimes necessary, as well as rotation of the machine around the body. Some patients require a combination of these different treatment approaches. The directions and angles depend on the particular clinical situation and are determined by your radiation oncologist.

As a rule, treatments are given five consecutive days each week, and the entire treatment course lasts several weeks. On average, the treatment course will vary from two to eight weeks. You will receive a total dose of radiation, which is the accumulation of daily doses. The concept of daily doses is medically known as *fractionation*. The neck, chest, abdomen, and pelvis (soft tissues) generally can't tolerate more than 900 to 1,000 units per week, 180 to 200 units per day. The bones of the arms and legs can easily tolerate daily doses of 250 to 300 units. (Radiation units are technically designated as *grays* or *centigrays*.) More rapid treatment may lead to severe short- or long-term side effects. Conversely, lower doses, delivered in a longer course, may result in decreased effectiveness of radiation therapy. Thus, there is an optimal dose and time schedule for treating various types of tumors.

The length of treatment courses and the radiation doses have been established through extensive clinical trials. Modification of the established times and doses may be necessary due to a person's general physical condition, or if problems arise because of complications with the cancer itself or the side effects of radiation.

Following an initial consultation, a letter is mailed to the doctors on your treatment team to summarize your condition, describing the treatment plan and expected side effects and making recommendations for further tests, if indicated. Periodic letters and telephone calls follow during the treatment course when indicated. Depending on their condition, patients are usually examined by the radiation oncologist many times a week or on an "as needed" schedule.

After radiation therapy is completed, a discharge letter is mailed to your various doctors describing the side effects, possible problems, progress, and recommendations. Many radiation oncologists, we among them, see patients for one or more follow-up visits after treatment is completed. Remaining problems and side effects may be addressed, and patients have an opportunity to ask additional questions. In our experience, follow-up visits help patients feel less abandoned and more able to make the transition from radiation treatment back to their everyday lives. Medical oncologists, internists, or family physicians will continue to provide additional medical and emotional support.

New Techniques and Procedures in Radiation Therapy

Radiation treatment has evolved over many decades. At one time, more than thirty years ago, the cobalt machine was high-energy and up-to-date equipment. This was simply a shielded housing that contained a radioactive source of co60. There was a little opening that would allow the radiation to be emitted and thereby treat the patient. A device called a *collimator*, placed below the opening, allowed us to change the size of the field that we wanted to treat, and at that time, we could make only square or rectangular treatment fields. We could modify the shape slightly by adding blocks of lead on a plastic tray below the collimator. To determine the treatment time, we had to use graphs and charts and we used a slide rule for necessary calculations. Patients were usually treated from only two directions because calculating dose and time for multiple fields was cumbersome, time consuming, and not very accurate using charts, graphs, and slide rules. Because we used only two fields or directions, the normal tissue in front and behind the tumor received almost the same dose as the tumor.

The development of high-energy linear accelerators and the use of computers allowed significant advancements. They gave us the ability to perform the very complex calculations required to determine the dose and time to treat with multiple fields. In addition, computer technology led to the development of the CT scan. The CT scan gives us a cross-sectional picture every three to five millimeters. To understand the images a CT scan produces, think of a bologna sausage with an olive in the center. We can't see the olive until we slice the baloney. Each slice is a cross section of the bologna, just as each CT scan picture shows a cross sectional slice of the patient.

With a CT scan and computer-generated treatment plans we gained the ability to see the tumor in relationship to the normal surrounding organs. This information is key to determining what dose each would receive. Another new development, *3-D conformal radiation therapy*, allows us to shape the beam with poured lead blocks to conform to a more optimal treatment area. As a result, we are able to lower the dose to normal tissue and increase the dose to the tumor.

Knowledge begets knowledge. Computers became faster and the manu-facturers of the linear accelerators produced multiple-leaf collimators. These have multiple fingers that can shape the radiation beam into any shape. These two further developments lead to *intensity-modulated radiation therapy* (IMRT). Essentially, IMRT is a progression of conformal treatments. These advanced treatment planning systems, combined with computer-controlled linear accelerators, enable us to deliver multiple fields, each with a different shape and each field with a different dose, thereby optimizing the tumor dose and minimizing normal tissue dose. For example, we can set the computer to deliver 200 centigrays to the tumor and keep the dose to a nearby organ to less than 10 percent of the tumor dose. The computer will then calculate how many fields, the shape of each field, and the dose to each field.

IMRT is not indicated for most radiation treatments. It focuses the beam on a confined area and most times we not only want to treat the tumor but we also want to treat the surrounding area because cancerous tumors have invasive tentacles into the adjacent tissue.

On other hand, early prostate cancer lends itself well to IMRT. The can-cer is usually confined to the prostate gland, a relatively small organ, and we must deliver a high dose while sparing the rectum and bladder.

Radiosurgery

Stereotactic *radiosurgery* or *gamma knife* is another technique used in certain circumstances. These are essentially the same procedure except that the for-mer utilizes a linear accelerator and the latter a co60 machine to produce the radiation. They have a specialized collimator that produces a pinpoint-sized beam and are coupled to a high-speed computer. It incorporates CT scan images and generates a treatment plan that delivers a very high dose to a small area by directing this pinpoint beam through many angles. It is useful only when we want to treat a relatively small tumor, two to three centimeters, with a high dose.

Radiosurgery and gamma knife have been around for at least a decade and are most commonly used to boost radiation doses to metastatic tumors occurring in the brain either before or after whole-brain radiation. They can also be useful in treating small primary brain tumors. However, this procedure has limited use in other parts of the body.

We had high hopes for the general application of these techniques when they were first introduced, but, unfortunately, they have not lived up to our expectations, perhaps because we were unrealistic in our assessment of their value.

High-Intensity Iridium After-Load Device

This device is basically a coil of wire in a shielded casing, with a high-energy iridium source at the tip. If you've ever seen a Roto-Rooter sewer snake you can understand how a high-intensity after-loading device works. An image of the tumor is incorporated into a treatment planning system and a treatment plan is generated. High-speed computers then guide us as we insert needles or catheters into the tumor as prescribed by the treatment plan, and the radioactive tip of the wire is inserted into the catheter. Under computer control the radioactive wire passes through the area to be treated and makes stops along the way and delivers the prescribed dose to the tumor volume. This is a great way to deliver high doses quickly to a tubular structure such as the trachea or bronchus.

Permanent Implants

Permanent implant is a technique in which sealed radioactive sources are inserted directly into the tumor or the organ we want to treat. Men with localized prostate cancer are frequently treated with this technique. Needles are inserted into the prostate, guided by ultrasound, and *radioactive iodine* or *palladium seeds* are passed through the needles and implanted into the prostate. This technique allows us to deliver a high dose to a concentrated area, while sparing the surrounding organs, such as the rectum or bladder, from excessive radiation.

Basics of Chemotherapy

As previously stated, chemotherapy agents are medications that travel through the bloodstream and act against rapidly dividing cells. It is referred to as *systemic treatment* because it circulates through the bloodstream. Cancer cells grow and divide rapidly, but some normal cells also divide rapidly, and hence, may be temporarily affected by the chemotherapy drug. For example, when the agents circulate through the bloodstream they may affect normal blood cells, hair cells, and cells that line the mouth and intestinal tract. Side effects such as hair loss or nausea may occur for this reason.

Chemotherapy drugs are given in different *schedules*. Each time the drug or combination of drugs is given, it is called a *cycle*. Some may be given once every three weeks, while others are given once every two weeks or once a month. Some that are in pill form may be given daily with days off to provide a break. So, a twenty-one-day schedule means that you would get cycle number one on the first day and cycle number two on the twenty-first day and so on. Chemotherapy may cause a reduction in the white blood cells, perhaps hitting a low in two weeks; however, they may rebound back to normal by the third week, in time for the next treatment. Chemotherapy schedules are carefully designed to allow crucial normal cells enough time to recover, while repeating the treatment soon enough so that the cancer cells do not recover.

Some cancers are very sensitive to one chemotherapy drug, but not sensitive to others. Certain cancers may not be sensitive to a particular drug at a lower dose but may be sensitive to the same drug at higher doses. Sometimes cancers may start out being sensitive to a particular chemotherapy drug, but, after several treatments, the cancer cells develop resistance to that drug, thereby rendering it ineffective. If that is the case, the medical oncologist will alter your treatment and change to a different chemotherapy drug.

How Are Chemotherapy Drugs Administered?

Chemotherapy most commonly is given intravenously, or directly into a vein. Sometimes the intravenous medication is given over a short period of time, meaning in a matter of a few minutes; at other times, it is diluted into fluids and given over one to three hours. A few chemotherapy drugs are given as a *continuous infusion*, which means that the medication is given continuously, over five days, for example. Continuous infusion chemotherapy may require hospitalization.

Other chemotherapy drugs may be given as an injection in the muscle (*intramuscular*), under the skin (*subcutaneous*), or into an artery (*intraarterial*). On occasion, the chemotherapy may be given directly into the tumor (*intralesional*), directly into the spinal canal (*intrathecal*), or into body cavities, such as the space between the lungs (*intrapleural*) or in the abdomen (*intraperitoneal*). Fortunately, some medications may be in pill form, which is most convenient because the patient may take them at home. (Chapter 4 will explain which chemotherapy agents are administered for specific cancers.) A few medications may be given at home through an infusion pump, which is a device about the size of a portable tape player. It can be worn on a belt or a strap and delivers chemotherapy into a venous access device (see below). In the past, chemotherapy was most frequently given in the hospital, but today only certain medications for certain diagnoses must be given in the hospital. Most are given in outpatient clinics or the doctor's office.

Behind the scenes, much goes on to make sure that the chemotherapy drugs are delivered safely. Your medical oncologist calculates the dose you will be given based on standard, recommended amounts, using calculations that include your body weight and height. These calculations are double- and often triple-checked by the pharmacist who is mixing the chemotherapy and by the nurse who is giving the chemotherapy. Nurses in medical oncology settings are specially trained to administer chemotherapy.

For intravenous treatments, it is important that there is a vein big enough to receive the chemotherapy injection. If the vein is too small, or if it is hard to get into, then the chemotherapy agent may irritate the vein or otherwise cause discomfort. If having good enough veins is a problem, then a semi-permanent catheter called a *venous access device* may be recommended. These catheters are placed by a surgeon, usually under local anesthesia in an outpatient procedure, into a large vein in the chest area. The catheter can remain in place indefinitely and is generally painless. Most patients actually view them as a convenience, as blood tests and all intravenous treatments may be given through them, meaning that they no longer need to be "stuck" every time they come to the office for treatment.

Patients who will be having treatments for just a few months may prefer to have the veins in their hands used for intravenous treatments, but most patients needing treatment for longer periods of time prefer venous access devices. When any "foreign body" is introduced to the body there is a slight risk of infection and in this case, a slight risk of developing a clot in the catheter. You will be given recommendations about minimizing these risks. Several types of catheters may be used, based on what your oncologist thinks is best suited for your treatment. These catheters may be left in place for several months or even for over a year. However, they are usually removed once your treatment plan is completed.

When More Than One Treatment Is Needed

Sometimes, chemotherapy is given at the same time as radiation to enhance the effects of radiation on the cancer, in which case it may be given on a daily or weekly basis. In Chapter 5 you will find a discussion of the kinds of cancers for which this may be recommended.

Cycles of chemotherapy may be given prior to surgery. For example, in certain breast and rectal cancers, or head and neck cancers, the preoperative chemotherapy is given to shrink the tumor and allow for less-extensive surgery. In the case of breast cancer, preoperative chemotherapy may allow some women who might otherwise need a mastectomy, to have breast-conserving therapy. Similarly, it may allow patients with a rectal cancer to forgo the need for a colostomy, and patients with head and neck cancer may be able to keep their voice box.

Chemotherapy is also one of the main treatments for blood cancers such as leukemia and lymphomas (tumors of the lymph glands), where it is often associated with high cure rates. Certain lymphomas and leukemias are cured with the use of chemotherapy alone. In other lymphomas, adding a course of radiation treatment is very important. Generally, surgery has less of a role in the treatment of these cancers.

When cancer has metastasized, chemotherapy is the major treatment. Radiation and surgery are less successful in these situations, because it is likely that the tumor has spread through the bloodstream to reach the distant site. Although chemotherapy may not lead to cure in these situations, it may extend life and improve quality of life for many patients, despite the fact that the cancer remains. When chemotherapy is given to patients with advanced, metastatic disease, it is particularly important to carefully examine the advantages and weigh them against the potential side effects. In these situations, chemotherapy may help to relieve symptoms caused by the cancer, such as pain and breathing difficulties.

Combination Treatment

Chemotherapy agents may be given alone as single agents or in combination to maximize the benefits. Because more than one hundred different chemotherapy drugs are in use today, with even more in the pipeline, many possible combinations exist. Combination chemotherapy results from extensive research examining the best ways to combine drugs. There may be two drug combinations (*doublets*), three drug combinations (*triplets*), or several drugs being given together. The combinations have been carefully studied so that the side effects do not affect the same organs. In other words, the combinations are designed in such a way so that a particular side effect is not more severe just because two drugs are used. As when we use a single agent, the schedules for combination chemotherapy are important because we want to maximize the benefit while allowing ample time for normal tissues to recover. Sometimes, chemotherapy may need to be delayed to allow for recovery of normal white blood cells or other normal tissues.

Although some side effects are predictable, the severity of a given side effect may differ among individuals. People who are otherwise healthy generally tolerate chemotherapy better than someone who is ill enough to be bedridden. One patient may experience little or no nausea after receiving treatment, while another may experience vomiting. Because a major focus of cancer research today is symptom management, clinicians give considerable attention to making treatments easier to tolerate.

As a result of extensive research, your likelihood of experiencing nausea or vomiting with a particular combination of drugs can be estimated and your oncologist may order medications that prevent these side effects. If you experience no nausea following treatment, then for the next treatment, these drugs could be cut back. On the other hand, if you experience some nausea or vomiting, then either the drugs will be increased or new drugs will be added. So, if you have some difficulty with the first cycle, then modifications will likely make the next cycle more tolerable. Some side effects, such as nausea, predictably appear after each dose; and if it can be minimized after cycle one, then it should be relatively well controlled for the duration of treatment.

Other side effects may differ from cycle to cycle. Numbness or tingling in the fingertips is one such side effect. However, it is important to discuss the appearance of these symptoms with your oncologist so that modifications may be made in your treatment. Part of the severity of side effects depends not only on the drugs but also on the health of the person receiving the drugs.

As a result of the increasing attention to treating symptoms, side effects are more effectively managed today. Many individuals continue to work and pursue their usual activities while receiving chemotherapy, taking only the time off needed for treatments. However, others prefer to work on a limited basis, and still others need a leave of absence from their jobs or businesses. You need to do what helps you get through your treatments.

Other Treatments

Besides chemotherapy, other treatments are considered systemic therapies because they circulate through the bloodstream and affect cancer cells anywhere in the body. These include hormonal agents, immunotherapy (drugs that act on the immune system, thereby allowing the body to "fight" the cancer), monoclonal antibodies, and targeted therapies (see Chapter 6). Your medical oncologist may also recommend that these be included in your treatment plan.

Hormonal Treatments

Hormonal agents are extremely useful in the treatment of certain cancers, such as breast and prostate cancer, both of which may be influenced by naturally occurring hormones. When tested, many breast cancer tumors are found to be sensitive to the effects of estrogen or progesterone because of the presence of estrogen or progesterone receptors. When this is the case, the tumor may respond to treatments that inhibit the ability of those hormones to stimulate cancer growth. In prostate cancer, androgens may stimulate tumor growth. Thus, using a drug that inhibits androgen production may be an important component of treatment for this cancer.

Targeted Therapies

These therapies include some of the newest cancer treatments. Unlike chemotherapy that indiscriminately affects both cancer and normal cells, these treatments target specific molecular abnormalities unique to the cancer cells. Although hormone agents are considered targeted therapies, other new agents may target certain *tumor growth factors*, substances that stimulate the growth of the tumor. These agents specifically target only those cells that are found to have the receptor. Tamoxifen is an example of this kind of treatment, and is targeted against estrogen receptors. Newer agents for breast cancer treatment also include trastuzumab (Herceptin), which targets breast cancers that have too much of the *Her-2 neu protein* that is associated with the potential for rapid growth. Only about 20 percent of all breast cancers have excessive amounts of this protein on their surface, so it is used only in selected patients.

Imatinib (Gleevec) is another example of a newer drug that is a targeted treatment. Its target is the molecular abnormality associated with chronic myelogenous leukemia, making imatinib responsible for dramatic improvement in the prognosis for these patients. The monoclonal antibody, rituximab (Rituxan), targets CD20 protein, an abnormality on lymphoma cells, and has contributed to significantly prolonging the benefit of chemotherapy for these patients.

Other new targeted treatments against *epidermal growth factor* are being studied for use in treating colorectal cancer, lung cancer, and other solid tumors. These agents may be used alone or with chemotherapy.

Antiangiogenesis Therapy

Cancerous tumors rely on *angiogenesis*, the formation of a new blood supply, to grow. Antiangiogenesis drugs inhibit the formation of new blood vessels to the tumor, thereby preventing its growth and spread. These drugs are most effective when used in combination with chemotherapy. The use of antiangiogenesis drugs is a rapidly expanding and very promising area of oncology.

Support Staff

A team of specialists support the radiation oncologist in delivering radiation therapy. Radiation physicists accurately determine the radiation doses and precisely assess the risk of injury to normal tissues. Radiation physicists use their critical expertise in medical computer technology to assist in treatment planning.

Radiation oncologists operate the complex treatment machines, position the patient for treatment, and verify that treatments are precisely reproduced daily. They combine their technical and scientific skill with compassionate, hands-on involvement with the patient.

Oncology nurses have made working with cancer patients their nursing specialty. They have received extensive training in order to deal with the multitude of concerns of patients, including such things as fears about treatment, controlling side effects, changing dressings, and intravenous feedings.

These disciplines are an integral part of today's radiation treatment, and you should feel free to ask questions about the role each of these specialists will play in your care.

In a medical oncologist's office, there may be nurse practitioners or physician's assistants who help patients manage symptoms. There may also be nurses who are specially trained to deliver chemotherapy. These nurses administer the drugs and also can answer your questions about these medications. The chemotherapy drugs are often mixed and prepared by specially trained pharmacists who may review the treatment plan and doses. Other important support staff include a social worker, chaplain, nutritionist, and physical therapist. You may or may not need the services of these professionals, but we suggest asking about their availability.

Current Treatment

At one time, radiation therapy caused more severe side effects than it does today. Much technological progress has been made over the past decades, and new advances in radiation therapy have contributed to improvement in the cure rates for many cancers. Still, your apprehension is normal and expected, and you should not be satisfied until all your concerns are addressed and your questions answered. Your radiation oncologist is there to help you during your treatment course, and we urge you to ask about all aspects of your treatment.

The term *chemotherapy* often is associated with debilitating side effects. Thanks to a strong focus on managing symptoms, side effects can be minimized today. Many patients are surprised by how well they feel after receiving their initial treatments. However, both chemotherapy and radiation are very involved and often need to become the priority for a period of time. Cancer treatment is not easy, but your treatment team is there to help you get through it.

You have a right to feel both physically attended to and emotionally supported during the course of your treatment. The technicians working with you and your radiation or medical oncologists should be available to answer questions and help you understand your treatment. Remember that the nurses administering the chemotherapy can answer questions about what to expect after receiving a particular chemotherapy drug. If, at any time, you believe that you're not being given the kind of information and help you need, then by all means speak up!

This advice applies to family members, too. If a loved one is undergoing any cancer treatment, you may be better equipped to ask questions and retain information than your loved one. In addition, if you will be caring for your family member, make sure you have all the information you need. Confusion about diet, sleep patterns, activity levels, treatment of side effects, and so on, may be avoided when all who are involved with the patient are aware of medical advice and suggestions. Furthermore, your own fears may be alleviated by taking an active role in your loved one's treatment.

2

Side Effects of Radiation
and Chemotherapy

Patients often ask, "If radiation treatment and chemotherapy are so sophisticated today, why do we still have to cope with so many side effects?" It
is true that medical science has made enormous strides in improving the delivery of radiation and chemotherapy. Certainly, the areas of the body being
treated with radiation are far more precisely targeted than ever before. In medical oncology, considerable attention is being focused on "supportive care."
Focused research is being encouraged not only to cure the disease, but also
to minimize side effects of treatment and better support patients as they go
through it.

Radiation: Some Things Haven't Changed

Although the radiation beam travels directly to the target area requiring treatment, it also affects organ tissues in its path. For example, if someone's uterus
is being treated, the x-ray beams will need to pass through the large intestine,
the small intestine, and bladder to get to the uterus. There is simply no way
to move these tissues aside to prevent the radiation from passing through
them. So, it is the tissue that is "in the way," so to speak, that is likely to react
to the irritating effects of radiation.

It is logical to wonder if normal tissues affected by radiation may be permanently damaged. If you understand the reason radiation therapy is so often
successful, then you will understand why it is unlikely. There is a fundamen-

tal difference in the way tumor cells and normal cells react to radiation. In those patients whose cancers are considered treatable with radiation, tumor cells are much more sensitive to radiation than are the surrounding normal cells. Thus, the side effects are caused by the generally reversible damage to the normal surrounding cells. This is true whether the cells are located on the same organ being treated or on other tissues in front or behind the tumor. So, in essence, when we talk about *radiation side effects*, we mean the effect of the radiation on tissues surrounding the organ affected by cancer.

Most patients experience side effects for only a short time, generally restricted to the course of radiation treatment. These are called *acute* side effects. They should disappear within two to three weeks following the completion of radiation treatment. However, particularly when there are underlying pre- or coexisting conditions, especially involving the intestines or the bladder, the symptoms may never completely go away. Then they are called *chronic* side effects. Fortunately, only a small number of patients experience long-term side effects, which can range from mildly annoying to severe.

Likewise, with chemotherapy, both acute and chronic side effects occur because of effects of the drugs on normal tissue. Most side effects are acute and occur during the period of time during which an individual is receiving chemotherapy. However, chronic side effects are also possible. Rarely, side effects develop later on, appearing some time after the completion of chemotherapy. Side effects vary depending on which drug is being used and at what dose. They also vary from individual to individual.

The information in this chapter provides an overview of the side effects a patient might experience, providing some general background information for the more detailed information that appears in later chapters focusing on specific kinds of cancer. This overview will give you enough background to make the chapters in Part 2 beneficial. Remedies to combat the side effects mentioned here also are discussed in later chapters. Therefore, don't be alarmed if you don't completely understand the information about particular symptoms, particularly those associated with radiation treatment, or the ways to alleviate them described here. There will be more information in later chapters that we hope will clarify things for you.

When it comes to side effects, great variation exists among individuals. For example, one person may experience severe diarrhea or cramping with a particular dose of radiation, while another person receiving the same dose reports only mild symptoms. Some patients mention that the lack of side effects caused them to question whether the radiation treatments were working. Likewise, one individual receiving medication to prevent nausea during chemotherapy may still experience prolonged nausea and vomiting, while another receiving the same drugs may have no symptoms at all. However, there is no relationship between the severity of the side effects and the effectiveness of the treatment. Some people are simply more fortunate than others, and their bodies are able to tolerate the radiation treatment and chemotherapy without significant discomfort.

The following sections describe typical side effects of radiation treatment, beginning with the brain and continuing with other major parts of the body.

Treatment to the Head and Chest

When radiation is administered to the brain, there is often a temporary swelling of brain tissue, due to water retention. The water retention may enlarge the brain tissue just enough to expand slightly against the rigid bones making up the skull. A cortisone-type medication will usually alleviate this swelling, so most patients do not report any symptoms. A few people, however, may begin to experience severe headache, visual changes, or projectile vomiting. When these symptoms occur, the medication is immediately increased and the radiation dose is modified.

Many patients will complain of sleepiness along with confusion or disorientation for an hour or two after radiation treatment to the brain. A short nap is usually beneficial, and the disorientation will likely disappear shortly after waking. The next day, treatment can continue without difficulty.

When radiation is administered to the brain for longer than three or four weeks, most people will begin to notice hair loss. If a small area is being treated, hair loss is confined to that spot. If the entire brain is being treated, hair loss occurs over the whole head. However, in part because there is individual difference in the strength of hair roots, the degree of loss varies from one patient to another. The length of the treatment course and the dose of radiation will also affect the probability of hair growing back.

Tumors in the face and neck usually require high doses of radiation for about five to seven weeks. Radiation to the face and neck usually results in the gradual thickening of saliva within two to three weeks after treatment begins. The amount of saliva is frequently reduced as well, and the patient's sense of taste is often diminished and altered. Patients often complain of having a very dry mouth, difficult and painful swallowing, and a general loss of appetite. In general, salivary changes tend to be progressive, and so worsen over time. These side effects often precede a marked loss of appetite and therefore, inadequate nutrition, so it is crucial that the symptoms be treated. Artificial salivary products are now available and usually help, and liquid diets are often a good way to get needed nutrition and avoid the irritation of eating solids. Drinking fluids frequently and sucking on lemon drops—or a similar kind of hard, sour candy—often helps. Anesthetic gels are available to soothe membranes in the mouth and throat if they become irritated.

Because the skin may redden somewhat, cortisone creams and skin balms are generally helpful. We also recommend using sunblock during the summer months to protect the skin from ultraviolet rays, which accentuate the effects of radiation on the skin.

Radiation to the chest area will also cause some swelling in the esophagus, the tube through which food passes when we swallow. Radiation irritates this area, and a patient may experience it as heartburn or the sensation of having a lump in the throat or chest. This can be controlled by avoiding extremes in temperature of food and liquids and ingesting only lukewarm food and beverages. It's also helpful to chew food extremely well, thereby enabling it to travel through the esophagus easily. Patients are generally told to avoid alcohol and spicy foods, both of which can irritate the esophagus. Judicious use of liquid antacids also helps this condition.

Increased coughing and mucus production in the chest and throat are the result of irritation to the trachea and bronchi. Both home remedies and medicines are available to alleviate these symptoms. In some cases, an over-the-counter (OTC) cough medicine that contains an expectorant, which thins the mucus, is adequate to alleviate this irritation. You can also ask your doctor or others on your treatment team about using a tea made from slippery elm. (Slippery elm has many purported uses, but this specific application is the *only* one we're including here.) In addition, talk with your team about using a home vaporizer. Many of our patients have found them helpful. More severe irritation to the bronchi and trachea may need prescription cough remedies, usually containing an opium derivative such as codeine. Skin creams containing aloe vera are also used on the skin of the chest if mild reddening occurs.

Treatment to the Upper Abdomen

Patients experience nausea and indigestion when receiving radiation to the upper abdomen (i.e., above the navel). These symptoms begin one to two weeks into treatment and may cause loss of appetite, so it is important to treat them. The nausea can be controlled with various medications (see section below on chemotherapy-induced nausea), some of which are similar to preparations used for motion sickness. Indigestion can be treated with both medication and diet. If not controlled, these symptoms lead to loss of appetite. Because a patient's nutrition is important to recovery, these concerns must be addressed. (Food choices and amounts are discussed in Chapter 3.)

Treatment to the Lower Abdomen

When we administer radiation to the pelvic area, the small and large bowels are always in the path of the targeted organ, no matter what the angle of the beam. The bowels may also be in the treatment field in cases of rectosigmoid cancer. Therefore, most patients will begin to experience diarrhea by the second or third week of treatment. Because radiation to organs in the lower body usually requires five to six weeks of treatment, controlling the diarrhea becomes important for maintaining good nutritional status and comfort. Fortunately, a variety of medications are available, all of which are discussed in subsequent chapters.

Radiation to the rectal area often results in additional side effects, irritation to the anal opening being one. Cortisone creams often provide relief for this. Sometimes the rectum will spasm, and cortisone suppositories usually relieve this.

The bladder will often undergo spasm because of radiation. A patient will feel the need to urinate frequently, even when there is almost no urine in the bladder. Thus, even a small amount of urine in the bladder creates a need to empty the bladder, and the patient experiences what is known as *urinary urgency* and *frequency*. Medications are available to alleviate these symptoms and make the patient more comfortable.

How Radiation Affects the Skin

Many years ago, radiation therapy often caused significant damage to the skin. Sometimes the skin would ulcerate; sometimes these open sores didn't heal and other times, when it did heal, a scar formed. However, the radiation equipment used today delivers x-rays that don't cause major damage to the skin.

Some people, particularly those with fair skin, may see some reddening of the skin, especially when higher doses are used. The skin on the neck, for example, will often become inflamed. A small raw area may be produced, particularly in places where the skin rubs together—under the arms, in the folds between the thighs, the buttocks, and beneath the breasts.

Creams that contain lanolin will soften and moisturize the skin. If a small area of skin actually peels and looks raw, a 1 percent cortisone cream is effective; it reduces irritation while it also promotes healing. When the skin becomes itchy, the old standby home remedy of cornstarch seems to work best. It can be used in a bath or applied topically with a towel or a bandage. You may ask your physicians to recommend products as well.

Side Effects Common to Both Radiation and Chemotherapy

Discussed below are two side effects, fatigue and low blood counts, that are not specific to either chemotherapy or radiation therapy. However, if they occur during treatment, approaches to dealing with them are often similar.

Fatigue

One nearly universal side effect of radiation treatment is an overall feeling of fatigue or malaise, and most people experience fatigue during chemotherapy. Exactly when this fatigue begins and how severe it becomes during radiation varies from patient to patient. However, it does not correspond with the severity of the disease. The fatigue is probably caused by the passage of cellular debris out of the body; this debris is the product of the breakdown of both the tumor and normal tissues that results from the radiation treatment. Therefore, this fatigue is *not* related to the activity of the disease, but to the radiation treatment itself.

Nevertheless, when patients begin to feel tired, they invariably believe they are getting worse, not better. Even optimistic and cheerful people will worry when fatigue sets in. However, in the vast majority of cases, this fatigue is a side effect of the radiation. For most people, it promptly reverses itself within two to three weeks following completion of radiation therapy. People who have received chemotherapy in addition to radiation may find that it takes a little longer.

Patients receiving chemotherapy alone also commonly complain of fatigue. Sometimes this is due to deconditioning, the loss of stamina and fitness that occurs when patients do not feel well enough to maintain normal activity levels. Sometimes the fatigue is due to anemia (see section below on changes in blood counts) or it may be related to metabolic abnormalities, such as low levels of potassium or high levels of calcium. It may also be related to endocrine abnormalities, such as those related to the thyroid or adrenal glands. Occasionally, the fatigue may be a direct result of the cancer. If you are experiencing fatigue, tell your doctors about it so they can determine if this is an expected symptom, what the cause is, and the best ways to reduce it.

Changes in Blood Counts

If you are undergoing chemotherapy and/or radiation, changes in the bone-marrow cells must be carefully monitored. The bone marrow produces white blood cells, which fight infection; red blood cells, which carry oxygen; and platelets, which help blood to clot. Many chemotherapeutic agents are selected for their ability to destroy rapidly dividing cancer cells; however, these agents can't discriminate between rapidly growing normal cells and cancer cells. The normal blood cells reproduce very rapidly, so they are also extremely sensitive to chemotherapy and radiation; thus these treatments may depress the marrow's ability to function normally. As a result, the white and red blood cells and platelets may not be formed in the marrow in adequate amounts.

Fortunately, with standard-dose radiation and chemotherapy, time is all that is needed for the bone marrow to recover. However, with high-dose chemotherapy and total body radiation (used for bone marrow transplants in leukemia patients, for example), the point of the treatment *is* to wipe out the diseased bone marrow and replace it with new cells.

A complete blood count (CBC) shows if the red and white blood cells and platelets have dropped below normal. In some cases, we need to temporarily discontinue radiation treatment in order to allow the blood count to return to a normal range. This is particularly true when radiation treatment is used in combination with chemotherapy, because chemotherapeutic agents may significantly lower the white blood-cell count, particularly that of the *granulocytes* or *neutrophils*. Patients who have undergone chemotherapy may already have a lower white blood-cell count before they begin radiation treatments. Radiation oncologists are aware of this possibility when they plan treatments for such patients.

With chemotherapy treatments, we expect to see the blood counts, in particular the white blood-cell count, dip down during the middle of the cycle (known as the *nadir*) and then recover by the time a patient is ready for the next treatment. Normal neutrophil counts are 2,500 to 8,000. A state known as *neutropenia* occurs when the neutrophil portion of the count falls below 1,000. In simple terms, this means that bacteria invading the body can freely multiply because there are not enough white blood cells to protect the body. If the white blood-cell count is slow to recover, the options considered by the medical oncologist largely depend on the patient's overall condition. When the chemotherapy is considered palliative, the best choice may be to modify the dose. When the goal of the chemotherapy is cure, then giving growth factors with the next cycle to help speed up the recovery time may be the favored option.

There are two agents now available that stimulate production of granulocytes in the bone marrow. One agent, filgrastim (Neupogen), is a granulocyte-colony stimulating factor that was first produced by genetic engineering.

Neupogen increases the granulocytes in the bloodstream, thereby reducing the nadir, or period of time, that an individual has a very low white blood-cell count and lowering the risk of infection during cancer treatment. It also allows chemotherapy to be given on schedule in situations where this is crucial. Neupogen is given as a daily injection under the skin starting one day after chemotherapy is given and continued for approximately ten to fourteen days until the white blood-cell count has adequately recovered.

A longer-acting agent, pegfilgrastim (Neulasta), is given as a single injection the day after chemotherapy and the effect lasts for fourteen days. A common side effect of both Neupogen and Neulasta is bone pain, which is most noticeable as the blood counts are recovering and the bone marrow gets "revved-up." This may occur within the first treatment cycle, but may not persist throughout the treatment.

Your physician will determine if Neupogen treatment is appropriate for you, based on your clinical situation. Generally, after Neupogen is taken for the recommended period (this varies among patients), blood tests are used to evaluate the neutrophil count in the bloodstream. Although the medication is injected, and often self-administered, it may also be given intravenously by nurses or doctors. Allergic reactions do occur occasionally, and your physician will tell you what symptoms to watch for. Generally speaking, neutrophil counts reaching 10,000 are expected after the last day of a two-week course of the medication.

Except for increased susceptibility to infection, no specific symptoms usually accompany a low white blood-cell count. A lowered red blood-cell count, however, may cause dizziness and fatigue. (Again, the symptoms of fatigue must be evaluated to see if it is the normal fatigue accompanying treatment.) When the red blood-cell count drops significantly, a blood transfusion may be needed. An alternative today is the use of erythropoietin (Procrit), a genetically engineered hormone that stimulates red blood-cell production. It works to correct chemotherapy-induced anemia but does not work if anemia is due to blood loss or iron deficiency. Therefore, it is important for your doctor to rule out other possible causes before prescribing erythropoietin (Procrit). Procrit is given as an injection under the skin, often as frequently as several times a week. Blood counts need to be monitored so that the red blood cells are not too low or too high. Darbepoetin (Aranesp), a longer-lasting version of erythropoietin, is available and may also be used.

Very low platelet counts will cause areas of hemorrhage, usually first noted on the skin. These appear as blotchy bruised spots. Very low platelet counts are not common but do occur with certain chemotherapy drugs. Because radiation and chemotherapy may reduce the number of platelets, a patient is more prone to bleeding if other medication is used that also affects the platelets. Aspirin is the most common offending drug. One aspirin can affect how a platelet works for its entire life span, which is up to two weeks. Vitamin E in high doses and ginkgo can cause easy bruising, especially if the platelet counts are low. Clearly, it is important to tell your doctor about all the prescription drugs, over-the-counter (OTC) medicines, and nutritional or herbal supplements you take so that he or she can advise you about the possible interactions.

Not all bone-marrow elements are necessarily affected in the same way. Some patients may show lowered white blood-cell counts, but the red blood-cell count remains normal. The reverse can also occur. The white blood-cell count is the most sensitive index by which to judge bone-marrow activity. If it seems like you are always having still more blood drawn, it is likely that your blood counts are being monitored so that bone-marrow activity can be assessed.

Reproductive and Sexual Issues

Women and men in their reproductive years must pay special attention to certain side effects unique to this age group. For example, women who undergo radiation treatment to the pelvic region will lose ovarian function two to three weeks into treatment. This early menopause may be permanent. A surgical procedure called *oophoropexy*, which moves the ovaries out of the way of the radiation beam, is often performed if maintaining fertility is an important issue. Fertility is of special concern for young women who have cancer of the reproductive organs, breast cancer, or Hodgkin's disease. (See Chapter 4.) Because surgery, chemotherapy, and radiation therapy may all affect fertility, temporarily or permanently, female patients for whom future childbearing is an issue should have fertility counseling prior to beginning treatment.

Women treated with chemotherapy may continue to have regular periods throughout treatment, or their periods may stop temporarily but return up to a year later. However, in some women, normal menstrual cycles stop altogether. Many women who continue to have periods may still be fertile, while others are not. Chemotherapy-induced early menopause is influenced by such factors as a woman's age at the time of chemotherapy, the specific chemotherapy drugs and doses received, and underlying genetic factors. (See section below on how to deal with early menopause.)

Young men must also deal with fertility concerns, particularly those men with testicular cancer, Hodgkin's disease, or non-Hodgkin's lymphoma. In some cases, for reasons not well understood, sterility occurs as a result of these diseases, but chemotherapy also may cause sterility that cannot be reversed. Radiation to the pelvic area, even when not aimed at the testicles, will result in some radiation "scatter" reaching them. (*Scatter* is the radiation energy that is transmitted outside the field of treatment.) So, even when the testicles are not directly treated, decreased sperm production and motility, and sterility, may result. In addition, there is the potential for genetic damage, which could result in birth defects in future offspring. In these situations, storing sperm in a sperm bank prior to the onset of radiation treatment is a reasonable option for a patient who may desire a family in the future.

In addition to fertility issues, sexual functioning is an important issue for cancer patients. Women with cervical or uterine cancer may experience sexual difficulties if radiation treatments have caused scarring of the vaginal tissues. Men with prostate cancer may become impotent as a result of surgery (although this occurs less frequently than in the past) or radiation. Because these side effects are limited to particular cancers, we have included more detailed information in the appropriate sections.

Before you begin treatment, discuss any questions you have about potential fertility and sexual dysfunction with your doctor. In many cases, you will have options, so take the time to explore them before making treatment decisions.

Side Effects of Chemotherapy

In between cycles of chemotherapy, your medical oncologist will evaluate you to see how you are doing. Side effects occurring after chemotherapy may be similar from cycle to cycle, so it is important to talk about the way you feel after each treatment so that your medical oncologist can make recommendations that will help minimize your symptoms. The goal is to add medications to take care of the side effects, thus making the next cycle easier to tolerate.

Some side effects may tend to build from cycle to cycle, so it is particularly important to discuss them. For example, some chemotherapy-induced side effects may require lowering the treatment dose. This depends on the goals of treatment. Some treatment is expected to be curative, but chemotherapy is also used to control advanced disease and address symptoms caused by the cancer. In these cases, lowering of the dose makes sense for the simple reason that the primary goal of the treatment is to help the patient to feel better. However, if the goal is cure, everything possible is done to try to treat the side effects without compromising the dose.

Irritation of the Veins

Although some chemotherapy drugs are in pill form, most chemotherapy drugs are given intravenously. This means that an intravenous (IV) line needs to be started so that the chemotherapy drug can be administrated. Some people have veins that are difficult to access. If this is the case with you, make sure you are well hydrated before having the IV placed. The nurse may also suggest wrapping a warm towel over the hand or arm to help the veins to relax and enlarge.

When chemotherapy is given through an indwelling catheter placed in a larger vein, the patient doesn't experience any discomfort. Sometimes, chemotherapy going through a small vein may sting, but generally once the IV is properly placed, there is no pain. If you do feel pain, notice any leakage around the IV, or if your hand becomes swollen, notify the nurse immediately. If necessary, a new IV will be started.

Some drugs are given over a period of just a few minutes, while other drugs are given over several hours; a few drugs are given by a continuous infusion over several days. Most chemotherapy drugs are given through the veins in the hand or lower arm, but drugs given by continuous infusion require a semipermanent intravenous catheter, generally placed in a larger vein in the chest. These catheters may be *tunneled catheters* inserted into large veins and tunneled under the skin until the catheter tubing exits from the skin. (A Hickman catheter is an example of a tunneled catheter.) Or they may be *implanted ports*, which are inserted into large veins in the chest through a small port that stays below the skin. (A Portacath is an example of an implanted port). These indwelling catheters allow for ease of administration of chemotherapy and also provide easy access when blood tests are needed. Surgeons place these catheters during an outpatient surgical procedure. These catheters require minimal care and are generally removed after chemotherapy has been completed. However, they can stay in place for more than a year if needed. As with any other foreign body, there is a slight risk of infection or blood clot formation.

Drugs that may be very irritating or uncomfortable if given through small veins cause no discomfort when given through a Portacath or Hickman. If a breast cancer patient has had surgery that included an axillary dissection (removal of lymph nodes under the arm), the medical oncologist will avoid administering chemotherapy into the arm on that side of her body to minimize the risk of infection. Having to use the same arm and possibly the same vein for each treatment can sometimes be challenging, so women who need chemotherapy over a longer period of time often consider an indwelling catheter.

Hair Loss

Alopecia, or hair loss, is one of the most difficult aspects of chemotherapy. Certain drugs will always cause complete hair loss. These include drugs like doxorubicin (Adriamycin) and epirubicin (Ellence). Other drugs, including cyclophosphamide (Cytoxan), cause hair thinning at lower doses and hair loss at higher doses. Still other drugs, such as vinorelbine (Navelbine), gemcitabine (Gemzar), and capecitabine (Xeloda) do not cause hair loss. Your doctor will let you know what to expect with the recommended single drug or combination of drugs used in your case. When hair loss is associated with chemotherapy, the hair loss is not restricted to the head but may also affect other body hair as well.

If hair loss is anticipated, then you should ask for a prescription for a wig prior to starting treatment. This enables you to select a wig that will match your hair style and color if that's what you would like. Some women prefer to cut their hair short prior to starting chemotherapy so that the hair loss is less dramatic. Others use it as an opportunity to try a new style or color. Hair starts to grow back within three to four weeks after chemotherapy is complete, although the rate of growth is different from individual to individual.

Chemotherapy-Induced Nausea and Vomiting

Patients often dread chemotherapy because of the bad reputation it has for causing nausea and vomiting. Most people have heard chemotherapy horror stories, but these are often based on people's experiences in the distant past. Fortunately, thanks to the availability of better drugs to prevent nausea, and our increased focus on research for even better means of controlling it, these unpleasant symptoms are far less problematic than they once were.

In the past, individuals were often admitted to the hospital, where they could receive intravenous fluids and medications when they were scheduled to receive any chemotherapy drugs with a high propensity to cause vomiting. But today it is not uncommon to see someone enjoying a meal right after receiving a treatment. For most types of chemotherapy, it is recommended that you eat lightly just before treatment and avoid spicy foods or fatty foods right after. Some people find cold foods to be the easiest to tolerate.

Nausea and vomiting seen with chemotherapy can be divided up into three types. The most recognized is the *acute* nausea and vomiting that occurs immediately after the treatment. Some people may experience *delayed* nausea and vomiting two to five days later. More rarely, individuals may experience nausea or even vomiting before treatment starts, brought on by the smells in the office or hospital. This is known as *anticipatory* nausea.

Some people are more prone to nausea than others, and, as a result, they may have a harder time with chemotherapy. For example, those with a tendency to develop motion sickness may need additional medication such as meclizine (Antevert). Although the reasons are unclear, younger patients seem to have more severe nausea than older patients, and women appear to have more severe symptoms than men. We are not sure why, but individuals with a history of heavy alcohol use are less prone to nausea.

Not surprisingly, prevention of nausea is the most effective strategy, so all patients receive medication to prevent nausea. The specific medications and their dosage are partly determined by the chemotherapy drug being used. Sometimes it is hard to predict who will need additional medication and who may be fine with less. You will see your oncologist before your second treatment, so that he or she can make modifications reducing the nausea even more the next time.

To minimize anticipatory nausea, drugs like lorazepam (Ativan) may be used because they address anxiety. Other potentially effective strategies include desensitization, hypnosis, and relaxation therapy.

Acute nausea is best prevented using drugs such as Zofran (ondansetron), Kytril (granisetron), or Anzemet (dolasetron)—a category of drugs known as *5-HT3 antagonists*—along with the steroid dexamethasone (Decadron). Prochlorperazine (Compazine) may be used for chemotherapy drugs that cause mild nausea.

Delayed nausea is best prevented by taking Decadron for three to four days. Metoclopromide (Reglan) is also used.

Additional drugs to treat nausea include a newer class of drugs known as *nk-1 antagonists*, which includes aprepitant (Emend). However, delayed vomiting may be the biggest challenge to treat. We know that, in general, being well hydrated, especially before receiving chemotherapy, helps minimize nausea. So even if you don't feel like eating in the days following treatment, be sure to at least keep taking in fluids.

Not all vomiting is necessarily due to chemotherapy or radiation. Occasionally, complications of cancer such as bowel obstruction, chemical imbalances (such as high calcium levels), or brain metastasis may lead to nausea or vomiting. For this reason it is important to investigate other possible causes of vomiting if it is severe or if the usual treatments are not effective.

Digestive Tract Symptoms

The entire digestive tract, or gut, is lined with rapidly dividing cells that may be very sensitive to the effects of some chemotherapy drugs. Mucositis, or irritation of the mucous membranes of the mouth, starts out as tingling gums. Individual mouth sores may develop, too. For mildly irritated gums, we recommend baking soda and warm water rinses. When discrete sores occur, then a combination of ingredients (sometimes called "magic mouthwash") may include analgesics (such as viscous lidocaine), Kaopectate, and antibiotic or antifungal ingredients. Some people are prone to develop canker sores, which are viral infections (similar to herpes). Occasionally, fungal infections, particularly yeast infections such as thrush, can occur in the mouth or esophagus. Your doctor can look at your mouth and decide on the best treatment, depending on the type of condition you have developed.

Diarrhea

Diarrhea is particularly common with drugs like 5-fluorouracil. Sometimes, the diarrhea that occurs during chemotherapy is caused by an infection, and antibiotics are needed in this situation. However, your doctor may not want to prescribe medicines to stop diarrhea without being sure about its exact cause. In any case, it is important to take in enough fluids. When there is no evidence of infection, diphenoxylate/atropine (Imodium A-D), loperamide (Lomotil), or tincture-of-opium-related drugs may be helpful.

We generally recommend avoiding dairy products, spicy foods, alcohol, high-acid foods such as citrus juices and fruits, high-fiber or high-fat foods, or beverages containing caffeine. On occasion, hospitalization is necessary in order to administer a drug called octreotide (Sandostatin). Talk with your doctor about this symptom, especially if the diarrhea occurs during the period of neutropenia, or low white blood-cell counts.

Symptoms of Menopause

Certain antiestrogen drugs like tamoxifen may cause symptoms usually associated with menopause. Similarly, these symptoms can occur in men who are given androgen deprivation treatments for prostate cancer. Women undergoing chemotherapy for cancers other than breast cancer may find estrogen drugs helpful.

The likelihood of going into menopause after chemotherapy depends on a woman's age, the drugs being given, and the doses used. For example, high-dose chemotherapy and stem-cell rescue (bone marrow transplant) almost always result in the onset of menopause.

Rather than taking estrogen replacement drugs, many women combat the symptoms of menopause by making lifestyle changes. For example, they may dress in layers and remove a layer or two during a hot flash. Drinking more water and curbing consumption of foods and beverages that bring on hot flashes can be very effective. Increasing exercise and quitting smoking may also help reduce symptoms.

Some women have found the herb black cohosh and soy derivatives help reduce hot flashes. These plants contain *phytoestrogens*, that is, plant-based estrogens. However, their potency, especially from dietary sources, is low compared to that of pharmacologic doses of estrogen. Certainly, it is not unreasonable to try these remedies, as long as you understand that they may or may not be effective. We do not recommend that you take high amounts of soy-based supplements or powders because we do not yet know how to quantify their long-term effects.

Based on what we've seen, taking high doses of vitamin E (400–800 IU per day is a safe dose) is generally not effective. However, some women find it somewhat helpful, and it may "take the edge off." It is inexpensive and has minimal side effects (most notably a tendency for bruising or bleeding), so unless your doctor sees a reason that you should not take it, it may be worth a try.

Clonidine (Catapres), a blood pressure medication, appears to help reduce hot flashes in some women. However, if the patient's blood pressure is too low, then fatigue or dizziness could occur. This medicine is available in two forms—pills taken twice a day and a patch, which is applied daily.

Bellergal, a medication once used for migraine headaches, also appears to help some women.

Another drug, megesterol (Megace), a progestin, can bring relief, but many women prefer not to try it because its side effects include weight gain and fluid retention.

In addition, some of the newer antidepressants, such as venlafaxine (Effexor), fluoxetine (Prozac), paroxetine (Paxil), and sertraline (Zoloft) may reduce hot flashes by about half. These drugs have few side effects, but patients may experience grogginess.

Gabapentin (Neurontin), an antiseizure medication, has recently been studied and found to be helpful in reducing hot flashes.

Approaches similar to those described above are all used in treating hot flashes in men with prostate cancer. Both Megace and another progestin, medroxyprogesterone acetate (Lupron), have been effective. For men, we do not see a downside to taking soy supplements.

Other Menopausal Symptoms

Along with hot flashes, women experiencing chemotherapy-induced menopause describe vaginal dryness. Topical lubricants, such as Replens, can be used as a daily vaginal moisturizer, and a lubricant, such as Astroglide, provides additional lubrication and is recommended for use during intercourse. Thinning vaginal tissues may be due to estrogen deficiency, and low-level amounts of estrogen can be given in the form of vaginal estrogen cream (Vagifem suppository) or Estring (an inserted ring), which release small amounts of estrogen into the vagina. It's believed that they are probably safe for women who have been treated for breast cancer because there is too little estrogen to be absorbed into the circulation.

Women who experience early menopause or who are on a class of drugs known as *aromatase inhibitors* need to have their bone density monitored because they are at risk for developing osteoporosis. Calcium intake is important, as is getting enough vitamin D. Osteoporosis may also be treated with nonhormonal medications such as alendronate (Fosamax) and risedronate (Actonel).

Changes in the Skin and Nails

Some people may notice lines in their nails that correspond to each cycle of chemotherapy, and in some, the nails crack. We recommend avoiding artificial nails, and even nail polish can irritate the nails.

Dry skin can result from chemotherapy, radiation, dehydration, or even from some of the medications used to treat nausea. We recommend using a nonscented moisturizer after bathing or showering.

Long-Term Side Effects of Chemotherapy and Radiation

Obviously the goal of radiation and chemotherapy treatment is to control or cure cancer existing in a particular site. Both the daily dose and the total dose of radiation have an impact on the ultimate outcome. Over the past decades, guidelines have been established for maximizing the benefits while attempting to minimize the long-term effects of radiation on the body's tissues and organs.

Long-term side effects of abdominal radiation include injuries to the small intestine, including narrowing, ulceration, and abnormal connections between small bowel loops (fistulae). The resulting symptoms may not show up for several months to many years after radiation treatment, but when they occur, surgery may be required. Fortunately, the incidence is fairly low—approximately 5 percent of all patients undergoing radiation treatment to the abdominal area. The large intestine may be similarly affected.

A slightly larger group of patients, about 10 percent (particularly patients with bladder or prostate cancer), will eventually suffer some side effects related to the bladder from radiation. These patients experience urgency and frequency of urination because the bladder does not distend appropriately. No cure is currently available. More rarely, a patient will experience some bleeding in the bladder, which may require cauterization.

Some scarring of the lung during radiation treatment to the breast and chest may result in persistent respiratory symptoms. The breast tissue may also scar, causing changes in the way the breast feels when touched. Radiation delivered to this part of the body may, depending on the dosage, result in damage to the heart and its blood vessels.

Long-term side effects of chemotherapy on the heart and lungs vary with the drugs, the doses, other medical problems that the patient might have, and also whether or not chemotherapy and radiation are combined. Drugs that fall into the category of anthracyclines (Adriamycin, for example) may affect the way the heart pumps. If doses are given beyond what is considered a lower limit, then heart function tests such as ECHO or the gated heart pool scan, MUGA, are done during treatment. Certain drugs have a higher likelihood of causing damage to the heart when combined with other drugs. The monoclonal antibody trastuzumab (Herceptin) is associated with increased heart damage when used in combination with Adriamycin; thus, these drugs are no longer combined.

Drugs that can cause damage to the lungs include bleomycin (Blenoxane) and high-dose cyclophosphamide (a drug associated with bone marrow transplant). Bleomycin is less commonly used today, but when it is, certain precautions are taken to minimize toxicity.

Neurologic toxicities may be acute or chronic. Drugs like the taxanes (Taxol and Taxotere), the platinums (Cisplatinum), and vinca alkaloids (vincristine, velban, and vinorelbine) can cause neurological side effects. Most occur more commonly with higher doses. For example, when given at a higher dose every three weeks, Taxol may result in more neurotoxicity than when the same dose is divided up and given as lower weekly doses.

Most neurological side effects are reversible early on, which is why it is important to make your doctor aware of any numbness, tingling, or discomfort you may be experiencing. These symptoms must be carefully monitored. In a few individuals, these symptoms may persist for months following treatment, and occasionally they become chronic.

Radiation treatment to the head and neck may leave saliva production deficient and taste sensations chronically altered. In addition, persistent tooth decay and gum and bone infections may be long-term problems. While rare, damage to the temporomandibular joint may, in some patients, result in decreased range of motion, which affects opening and closing the mouth.

At one time, scarring of the skin tissues was a more common long-term side effect of radiation. However, this is becoming less frequent because of the advances in radiation technology.

One particular long-term complication of radiation that is not currently well understood is immunosuppression. What this means is that radiation may significantly alter the body's ability to defend itself against infection and subsequent cancers. This is usually seen when treatment areas are large. For example, patients who have been cured of lymph-node cancers (lymphomas) may, many years later, be more susceptible to the onset of new cancers.

Unfortunately, the first great successes of curing cancers like Hodgkin's disease have been followed years later by the disappointments of seeing second cancers develop in the survivors. There are higher risks of sarcomas (cancers of muscle or bones) in areas of the body that were in the radiation fields. Girls or young women who have received radiation to the chest wall ("mantle" irradiation) as part of their treatment for Hodgkin's disease, have an increased risk of breast cancer twenty to thirty years later. In addition, we know that survivors of Hodgkin's disease are at risk of developing non-Hodgkin's lymphoma. Patients who have received prior chemotherapy may develop secondary leukemias, although this is quite rare.

The good news is that the strategies for treating cancer today emphasize use of the minimal treatment needed to achieve the maximal cure. Radiation fields are more targeted, chemotherapy drugs are being chosen with long-term side effects in mind, and the treatments are being combined more judiciously.

At this point in cancer treatment, we are continually trying to balance the potential for cure with the risks of treatment. It isn't always easy to do, especially in this era when we sometimes combine radiation and chemotherapy with the hope of enhancing the potential for a complete cure. Yet, we must be cautious because we want to minimize the possibility of long-term side effects.

3

Diet, Lifestyle, and Emotional Concerns

The disease of cancer and its treatments often alter patients' ability to meet nutritional needs and to continue their normal lifestyles. Therefore, your treatment team will work with you and provide advice and help so that you can feel as well as possible during treatment and also take advantage of the body's own natural mechanisms to fight the disease.

Because family members and other loved ones may be involved in the day-to-day care of individuals with cancer, the information below is directed to them as well as to patients. We hope it will help all concerned understand the reasons that modifying the diet and being aware of lifestyle and emotional concerns are so important.

Diet and Cancer

The physical and emotional stress created by cancer treatments lowers the body's natural defenses. In addition, the cancer cells compete with the normal cells for survival, further lowering these defenses. The body's ability to handle this stress is known as *immunocompetence*.

Proper nutrition will enable your body to better handle the stress brought on by surgery, chemotherapy, or radiation. In practical terms, a good diet helps you feel better throughout the treatment. Laboratory research with animals has demonstrated that adequate intake of vitamins and minerals, particularly zinc, has an effect on the immune system's response to cancer.

Loss of appetite is a symptom of cancer itself, although we are not sure why. We do know that within the brain there is a central regulatory system for hunger and satiety. (The exact way this system is activated is still unknown.) Cancer alters metabolic functions, thereby interfering with the body's system for regulating appetite. This creates a vicious cycle. The patient has little appetite, but nutrition is essential to help combat the cancer and the effects of treatment.

As discussed in the previous chapter, nausea, diarrhea, and loss of appetite are common side effects of radiation (particularly for that given to the abdomen and pelvis) and also occur with certain chemotherapy drugs. Furthermore, some patients undergoing radiation therapy and chemotherapy may become anxious or depressed, which can also cause their appetite to diminish. As you can see, loss of appetite is a constant risk for a number of reasons, so cancer patients must be diligent about getting adequate nourishment.

Eating When It's Difficult

If you're undergoing radiation treatment, the degree to which you'll experience loss of appetite depends on the area of your body being treated, the size of the treatment field, and the overall treatment dose. For example, a patient receiving radiation to the mouth will often experience drying of the mouth and loss of taste, but will not be nauseated. When the abdominal region is receiving radiation, patients will complain more about nausea than loss of taste or dry mouth. When radiation is given in the pelvic area, diarrhea, cramping, and bladder symptoms are more troublesome than nausea.

Because so many side effects of treatment diminish appetite or make it difficult to eat, many patients will feel like eating only small amounts of food, supplemented with liquid drinks. Pharmacies and supermarkets carry commercial liquid nutritional preparations (Sustical, Ensure, Carnation, Vivonex) designed for patients who, for whatever reason, have difficulty with solid food. They are also available as high-calorie puddings.

Most people are able to continue eating food by mouth during radiation therapy. Otherwise, intravenous feeding, called hyperalimentation, is required. High-calorie solutions are administered through a tube inserted in a vein. This form of feeding may be needed for a period of several weeks, during which the patient is hospitalized or remains at home with visiting-nurse support.

Loss of appetite during chemotherapy depends on the type of cancer as well as the type of treatment. Certain chemotherapy drugs may alter taste buds and leave a metallic taste in the mouth. Sometimes loss of appetite is related to remote effects of certain cancers, lymphoma, for example. Sometimes it is due to direct effects of cancer. For example, a cancer that causes the liver to be enlarged, which then presses on the intestines, may influence appetite. Ask your doctor to recommend medications to help stimulate your appetite if the cancer itself is the reason for your weight loss.

The act of eating, as opposed to the issue of appetite, may become difficult for patients undergoing radiation and chemotherapy. Radiation to the head and neck region may cause the mouth to be sore and make it uncomfortable to eat. Similarly, some chemotherapy drugs like adriamycin and fluorouracil may cause mouth sores. Most patients prefer soft foods or pureed foods during this time and they avoid hard, crunchy foods or high-acid foods, like tomatoes and citrus fruit.

Dry mouth occurring as a result of the radiation therapy and chemotherapy can also make it hard to eat. Commercially available artificial saliva to combat dryness in the mouth resulting from radiation treatment allows food to be swallowed and pass through the esophagus more smoothly.

Eating If You're Nauseous

During radiation therapy (beginning after the first or second week), some patients experience nausea and occasional vomiting, but this side effect is usually not severe and can be easily controlled with medications. When you alter your diet, the dosage of antinausea medication can often be decreased, but it generally isn't effective to simply treat the nausea and then expect to eat normally, meaning three full meals a day. A combination of dietary changes and medication works best.

Patients being treated with chemotherapy will want to eat a light meal on the day of treatment and make sure they drink plenty of fluids. Nausea associated with chemotherapy tends to appear immediately after treatment, although it may occur a few days later. Most important, don't worry if you don't feel like eating; staying well hydrated by taking in fluids is more important. Drink water, ginger ale (the ginger can combat nausea), soft drinks without the fizz, fruit juices that are not too acidic (like apple juice), tea, and broth.

Some individuals find they experience more nausea on an *empty* stomach. Just as many women combat morning sickness during pregnancy with crackers and snacks, chemotherapy patients often try a similar approach.

Chemotherapy patients often prefer cold foods over hot. Strong odors may bring on nausea. Not surprisingly, hot or spicy foods may cause heartburn and worsen nausea, and overly sweet, fried, or rich foods also may lose their appeal. You may find yourself preferring foods like Jell-O, sherbet, Popsicles, fruit smoothies, cold melon, or applesauce.

It helps to chew slowly, take your time eating and drinking, and stay upright after eating to avoid aggravating heartburn. Drink fluids before and after the meal but not necessarily while eating.

Eating If You Have Diarrhea

Radiation therapy may also cause some gastrointestinal enzyme (lactase) deficiencies resulting in intolerance to lactose, the sugar in milk. When lactose is no longer properly digested, water is attracted to the intestine, ultimately causing intestinal irritability that results in watery diarrhea.

Under normal conditions, the cells in the intestinal tract lining slough off very rapidly, and radiation therapy only aggravates this process. The turnover of the cell lining may be so great that small ulcers occur and an inflammation of the intestine, called enteritis, takes place. This condition also leads to lactose intolerance, which means that some patients can't consume milk and other dairy products without risk of irritation and diarrhea. Because lactose is used as a sweetener in many prepared foods and as a filler in many drugs, it's important to become a careful label reader. Lactose intolerance varies so much from individual to individual that trial and error is the only way to tell if dairy products can be comfortably eaten.

Some chemotherapy drugs, such as 5 fluorouracil may result in sores in the mouth, the esophagus, the intestines, or anyplace else in the gastrointestinal tract. Sometimes diarrhea is due to the effects of the chemotherapy, but at other times an associated infection may exist and cause this symptom. While nausea tends to occur immediately or within the first few days after a chemotherapy treatment, diarrhea tends to occur a week or more later.

Diarrhea can also be a problem for some patients receiving radiation therapy and especially with certain chemotherapy drugs such as those used to treat colon cancer.

To control diarrhea, limit the amount of fat in the diet because it appears that fat is poorly absorbed by cancer patients and delays the emptying of the stomach. Some patients are able to eat yogurt because the process of making yogurt transforms milk into a more digestible form. Other foods to avoid if you have diarrhea include milk or milk products (other than yogurt), and raw fruits or vegetables. You can also try a low-fiber diet. The well-known recommendation for children with diarrhea is called the BRAT (bananas, rice, applesauce, and toast) diet, and it also works to control diarrhea for patients undergoing cancer treatment too. In addition, some patients can tolerate soups and pasta.

General Tips

It's crucial that cancer patients and their families adjust to new eating patterns and this usually means breaking away from the notion of "three square meals a day." In fact, patients undergoing cancer treatments are better off eating "like a bird," which essentially means eating a little bit here, and a little bit there. Many patients feel much better if they eat when they feel like it, often six to eight small meals a day, or some variation on constant nibbling. Likewise, we emphasize again the importance of staying well hydrated; be especially careful to take in plenty of fluids the day before a chemotherapy treatment. Dehydration may worsen nausea. For the first few days after chemotherapy, you may not feel like eating. This is expected, so just eat when you feel like it.

Sometimes well-intentioned family members and friends urge their loved one to eat. In fact, they may literally try to force food on the person, only causing further worry and strain. The "food is love" connection is strong for many of us, and family members may think that fixing elaborate meals is the one tangible thing they can do to help their loved one's physical recovery. But exhortations such as "You have to eat to get your strength back" are rarely compelling to a person who has no appetite.

Some patients prefer making their own liquid drinks, such as fruit or vegetable smoothies or milk shakes. However, commercial liquid meal replacements are fine; they add calories and can be consumed a sip at a time.

For the most part, people receiving radiation therapy feel better if they avoid animal protein and eat vegetable proteins such as beans and legumes, peas, corn, and soy products. Some cancer patients do tolerate fish protein as well as poultry, as long as the skin (fat) is removed.

Pasta, rice, and potatoes are excellent sources of calories, although fatty or spicy sauces should be avoided. Some pasta is fortified with protein, making it even more beneficial. Fresh vegetables should be cooked rather than eaten raw. Raw foods tend to create too much bulk in the diet and aggravate the irritation of the small and large bowels created by the radiation therapy and chemotherapy.

It's usually best to avoid caffeine-containing beverages such as coffee, tea, hot chocolate, cola drinks, and so forth because caffeine is an intestinal stimulant. Substitute herbal teas and decaffeinated coffee, tea, and caffeine-free soft drinks (regular or diet).

Most radiation therapy patients can use alcohol in moderation, meaning one glass of wine or serving of beer a day. Exceptions include those with a preexisting problem with alcohol or other medical reasons to avoid it (i.e., acute bladder, prostate, and throat problems). Beer provides extra calories, and a glass of wine in the evening may actually relax a person for restful sleep.

We recommend that you take a standard dose multivitamin-mineral supplement containing folate, the B-complex vitamins, and vitamins C and E. These vitamins assist the body's own defenses in fighting the cancer and the stress of radiation and other therapies. Liquid vitamin supplements are available for patients receiving treatment to the neck or chest, which may make swallowing capsules difficult.

Your Posttreatment Diet

Much has been written about different diets designed to build health and avoid disease. For example, the American Cancer Society recommends at least five servings of fresh fruits or vegetables per day, and some dietary information suggests striving for up to 8 to 10 servings a day. We recommend emphasizing whole grains and low-fat proteins. We also recommend using healthful fats, such as olive oil, in cooking. Drink water—six to eight glasses a day—and limit alcohol intake to an occasional beer or glass of wine.

Try to maintain close to ideal body weight, and ask your doctors about the weight that is right for you. Obesity itself is a risk factor for many cancers, and it may influence cancer recurrence. Women being treated for early-stage breast cancer need to watch for weight gain that may occur during chemotherapy.

You've heard it before and we will say it again—*don't smoke*. Individuals who have survived one cancer are unfortunately at a higher risk of developing a second cancer. This is particularly true of smokers, who may develop second cancers in the head and neck area, lung, and bladder. Nothing is more disheartening than getting through treatment for one cancer only to subsequently be diagnosed with a second cancer. Work with your doctor on strategies for smoking cessation. Today, smokers do not have to go it alone or quit "cold turkey." Ask your doctor about medications to counteract the physical dependence on nicotine, combined with a support program that can help you deal with the emotional dependence. As an aside, cancer can serve as a catalyst to encourage any family members to quit smoking along with you. Make it a family crusade.

Can High Dosages of Vitamins Cure Cancer?

Vitamins are under the auspices of the FDA, so the standard dosage contained in commercial products can be considered safe under most conditions. Vitamin supplements have been produced and sold for many years, so potential toxicity that can occur with certain nutrients is well-known and quality control measures are standardized. Because diet may be compromised during cancer treatment, standard supplementation may help strengthen the body's immunity.

You may have seen reports that "mega" doses of certain vitamins may "cure" cancer and other diseases. By megadoses we mean vitamins taken in amounts well above the Recommended Daily Allowance (RDA). For example, some patients have read that vitamins C and E have properties that may protect against cancer. These two vitamins are among a group of nutrients known as antioxidants, which means that they protect cells from damage caused by *free radicals*, which are unstable molecules that form through a process known as oxidation. Antioxidants are nutrients that neutralize the harmful effects of free radicals. It is true that both nutrients are essential for a healthful diet. Vitamin E is found in green leafy vegetables, whole grains, nuts, eggs, and plant oils. Vitamin C is found in citrus fruits, melons, berries, tomatoes, potatoes, and many other vegetables.

Several studies initiated in the 1970s and 1980s have shown that high (upward of 1,000–2,000 mg) doses of vitamin C are of no benefit to cancer patients. In addition, no evidence exists that *high* doses are needed to enhance the effects of the immune system. Vitamin E has been studied in male smokers and, like vitamin C, it showed no effect on reducing lung cancer risk.

Some oncologists have concerns that high doses of vitamins E or C may lessen the effects of radiation or chemotherapy by protecting the cancer cells along with the normal cells. This is probably unlikely given the relative potency of their antioxidant effect. However, it is important to let your doctor know about any supplements you are taking.

Vitamin E in doses of 400–800 IU may cause easy bruising because of its effect on platelet (the clot-forming element in the blood) function. In addition, be especially careful if you are taking blood thinners such as coumadin, or anti-inflammatory drugs, because of the possibility of increased bleeding tendencies. Vitamin E in doses higher than 800 IU may have side effects such as fatigue, dizziness, headache, blurred vision, or rash.

Do not take vitamin C if you have a history of kidney stones; other possible side effects of higher doses of vitamin C include nausea, diarrhea, stomach cramps, and low blood sugar. The daily recommended dose is 75–125 mg a day. The upper limit on tolerable doses is 2,000 mg. In addition, vitamin C given intravenously or in high doses (more than 2,000 mg) may be dangerous.

Some studies suggest that folate (a B vitamin) and calcium may have a possible protective effect against colon cancer. These nutrients have other health benefits, too. For example, calcium is especially important in maintaining bone density and preventing osteoporosis, which is why more of the mineral is recommended for women after menopause. However, these nutrients are known to be safe only in standard doses, those in line with the RDA established for each.

A diet rich in fruits and vegetables is considered health-building because overall, these foods contain several essential nutrients, including the B-vitamin complex. So, without singling out any particular nutrient, the general advice to eat fruits and vegetables remains sound. In general, while there is no evidence that vitamins can cure cancer, a multivitamin with folate and enough daily calcium to maintain healthy bones is important for a healthful lifestyle. Consult a nutritionist or dietician if you have questions about nutritional supplements and diet.

Herbal Supplements

Many people are curious about reports that certain herbal therapies may prevent or even cure cancer. Hundreds of books, newsletters, and websites offer information about botanical treatments, but much of the material is misinformation. To date, no herbal supplement has been shown to prevent or cure cancer. In fact, data are accumulating that some herbal formulations may be harmful.

Of course, many drugs in use today are derived from plants, but before a drug derived from a plant source can be released, the active compound—the chemical—in the plant is isolated and purified. Extensive testing is done to prove the effectiveness of the chemical, as well as to document any side effects or interactions with other drugs. These studies are expensive and extensive, but they must be done before drugs are released. All drugs, from all sources, are subjected to this process.

Etoposide and Taxol are two examples of plant-based drugs used to treat cancer. Their active chemical has been isolated and tested and the production of these drugs includes rigid quality-control measures. In this controlled situation, the drug is reevaluated for the balance of risk versus possible benefit derived, remembering that not every drug is appropriate for every person.

Under the Dietary Supplement and Health Education Act (DSHEA), manufacturers are not required to prove that dietary supplements, including herbal formulations, are safe or effective, nor are quality control requirements in place for such products. Under this act, the onus is on the Food and Drug Administration (FDA) to prove that the herb or other substance in question is harmful. However, manufacturers may *not* make promises about specific cures on the product label. In March 2003, the FDA proposed new regulations of dietary supplements in an effort to ensure that supplements contain exactly what the manufacturer claims they contain. This would place the responsibility on the manufacturer to prove that the product is not contaminated and contains the specified amount of active ingredient.

Botanical products bring with them special problems. One involves standardization. By this we mean that the active compounds in plants may vary both in amount and degree of concentration. Soil, weather conditions, and handling and storage are not standard across the industry. In the November

1995 issue, *Consumer Reports* magazine compared ten ginseng products and found that, while the amount of ginseng per tablet was the same in all ten products, the active ingredient, ginsenosides, varied from brand to brand. This means that these products did not act on the body in an identical way, because they were not identical products. In addition, ginseng contains an estrogen-like chemical that may cause breast enlargement (gynecomastia) in men and vaginal bleeding in women. It may also cause hypoglycemia (low blood sugar).

For the most part, herbal remedies have not been subjected to scientific study, so toxicity and drug interactions remain unknown. However, there have been reports of cerebral hemorrhage, which means bleeding in the brain, and retinal hemorrhage, which means bleeding behind the eye, caused by the popular and heavily advertised herbal, ginkgo biloba. Ginkgo biloba has an effect on platelets, which as we've said, is the clot-forming element in the blood. In addition, there have been reports about the presence of toxic heavy metals such as lead, arsenic, mercury, and copper in imported herbal supplements.

The situation with ginkgo is especially serious because aspirin also affects blood platelets, and combining the two blood-thinning agents may be responsible for this potentially serious side effect. Many elderly people are told by their doctors to take aspirin in order to keep their blood thin, thereby reducing the risk of stroke and cardiovascular events. Many of these same health-conscious men and women are also concerned about memory and mental alertness, so they take ginkgo to improve memory. However, they may not inform their physicians that they are taking the ginkgo, and therefore, a high-risk situation may develop when the two substances are combined.

You have probably heard about supplements used by bodybuilders and other sports enthusiasts. One such androgen (the hormones associated with masculine physical traits) supplement has anabolic steroidal action in the body and can cause such side effects as liver toxicity and testicular atrophy.

From time to time you will hear about a "breakthrough" study, and you may think that some simple element in food has been found to prevent or cure cancer. For example, you may have heard about lycopene, a chemical in tomatoes responsible for their red color. Based on a small study, it was believed that lycopene was protective against prostate cancer because the group receiving the lycopene showed tumor regression prior to prostate surgery. The problem with this study is that it included only twenty men, ten in the treatment group and ten in the control group (those who were given placebo, not the active lycopene product). In addition, long-term follow-up was absent. Androgen blockers—drugs that block male hormone production—show the same results as lycopene. What we may learn is that lycopene may be helpful in the treatment of prostate cancer, but like androgen-blocking drugs, it may not be a *curative* substance. *It is important to understand the distinction between a substance that may have health benefits and one that may cure a disease.*

Saw palmetto is another plant that receives considerable attention in the popular media. Studies have shown that it is effective in reducing symptoms of benign prostate enlargement, a condition many men develop as they age. Urinary frequency and burning are frequent symptoms, and some older men report that for the first time in adult life, they must get up at night to urinate. Saw palmetto has anti-androgenic effects, and in some men, these symptoms may be reduced in varying degrees. However, it is unfortunate that claims for saw palmetto have suggested that it may reduce the incidence of prostate cancer. This simply is not true. Current studies that evaluate the effectiveness of anti-androgenic substances have thus far failed to demonstrate ability to protect against prostate cancer.

Researchers are encouraging testing of these botanical substances using the same strict criteria required for pharmaceutical drugs. Clearly, there are potential benefits of some herbs and supplements. However, some have potentially serious side effects, while others may have significant interactions with prescription medications. Most importantly, let your doctor know about any herbs or supplements you currently take or wish to consider and have an honest discussion with him or her about the pros and the cons—and the unknown factors—that could affect your treatment.

Lifestyle Changes

We can loosely define lifestyle as the amount and kind of activity cancer patients will feel like taking on, balanced by the amount of rest they need. As mentioned earlier, cancer patients often experience an overall sense of fatigue. Although we aren't sure why this dragged-out feeling occurs, we know that it isn't related to the severity of the cancer—it does not mean that the disease is getting worse.

When fatigue appears a week or two into radiation treatment, or after the first or second cycle of chemotherapy, we generally advise listening to what your body tells you, and therefore, rest as much as possible. However, this doesn't necessarily mean actually sleeping during the day. When possible, it is better to move about during the day, perhaps even taking a walk, unless you've been told not to for other reasons.

For some patients, a short daytime nap may be beneficial, but they usually notice that sleep in itself doesn't relieve the kind of fatigue the radiation therapy and sometimes chemotherapy may induce. (The exception is radiation to the brain. In that case, sleepiness is natural and a nap is usually refreshing.) If you give in to the fatigue and sleep during the day, you may have trouble sleeping at night. This sleep pattern will then make you out of step with the rest of the family and the outside world. If family members are helping with your care and also carrying on their normal activities during the day, then trying to stay up during the night, too, may soon prove overwhelming.

Cancer patients (and their loved ones) often dread the night hours because we all feel more vulnerable to our emotions at night. If a person is already anxious and somewhat depressed, these feelings will be amplified when the house is quiet and others are sleeping. Suffering from physical symptoms combined with fear can turn the night into a very bleak time.

If you have trouble falling asleep or staying asleep, altering the time of the evening doses of medication for pain, nausea, diarrhea, or bladder irritation can help. We recommend taking the medication approximately an hour before going to bed for the night. You will get the maximum benefit from the medication, allowing you to fall asleep while you are comfortable.

Home remedies recommended for insomnia are worth trying. These include a warm bath before retiring, a glass of wine, a cup of herbal tea, or a glass of warm milk (if milk is well tolerated), listening to a relaxation tape or to soothing music, and so on. It is very important that sleep disturbances be dealt with, because studies have shown that sleep disorders are detrimental to the body's ability to fight disease and infection. Sleeping pills are sometimes useful, and are best prescribed by your medical oncologist or family physician, the doctors most familiar with your overall physical condition.

Physical Activity

By using a combination of diet and medication, most patients undergoing chemotherapy and/or radiation treatment should be able to remain alert during the day and enjoy mild physical activity. However, as with diet, well-intentioned relatives and friends may actually try to push you too far. You are the best judge of just how much activity you can tolerate and there is nothing to be gained from excessive, high-intensity exercise.

Walking is an excellent overall exercise, and we encourage our patients to walk as much as they believe they can. Walking (and other exercise) gets you out of the house and out into the world. It may stimulate your appetite, and increased food intake can lead to a greater sense of well-being.

Exercise has significant benefits for most cancer patients, although there's a natural tendency to stop usual workouts or trips to the gym after a cancer diagnosis. Obviously, this is necessary when recovering from surgery. Always check with your surgeon about specific restrictions and the amount of recovery time necessary before you can again engage in certain kinds of exercise. For example, women who have had underarm lymph nodes removed (axillary dissection) after breast cancer surgery need to be careful with heavy lifting and overexertion of that arm.

The initial emotional stress of a new diagnosis, frequent doctor appointments, and the necessary trips for diagnostic tests add to the tendency to exercise less. However, reducing physical activity leads to de-conditioning (loss of strength and endurance you already have), which in turn leads to muscle loss, and that contributes to weakness and fatigue. The fatigue sets up a vicious cycle, whereby patients say they don't have the energy to exercise and that leads to more de-conditioning.

After checking with your doctor, try to start a low- to moderate-intensity exercise program as soon as possible. Considering what you are going through at this point in your life, it's most important that you enjoy your exercise program. Clearly, people who were very fit prior to their diagnosis will have different capacities than people who have not done much exercise before they became ill.

Exercise, especially a weight-resistance program, can help to rebuild muscle mass, which adds endurance and strength. Women treated with chemotherapy for breast cancer may find they have gained a few pounds, so increasing muscle mass and reducing the body fat percentage helps them to maintain ideal body weight.

In addition, exercise can help enhance lung function and reduce the resting heart rate, while possibly improving mood and reducing depression. This is especially true of programs that include other cancer survivors. A study of women following treatment for breast cancer showed that exercise increased energy, reduced fatigue, and also improved mood and reduced anxiety. Although studies have not yet demonstrated that exercise helps cancer survivors live longer or avoid recurrences, exercise enhances certain aspects of immune function, such as natural killer cells and cytokines. (See Additional Resources for a website that offers additional exercise tips.)

Your Work Life

Many employed persons continue their normal work schedules throughout cancer treatment. Some ask to have chemotherapy treatments on a Friday; they take that day off, recover over the weekend, and then go back to work on Monday. Some at-home mothers may prefer to have their treatment early in the week so that they are feeling better by the weekend, when everyone is at home. On the other hand, patients don't want to be pressured to work if they don't feel up to it.

Most patients are able to work during radiation, because most side effects of radiation treatment are not debilitating, although they may be annoying and require medication and adjustments in diet. Some chemotherapy patients are unable to work full-time, but find that a part-time work schedule is fine. Some patients find that taking a temporary leave of absence helps them concentrate on getting through their treatment without carrying the extra burden of a demanding work schedule. Of course, if the disease itself is severe, patients may need to consider altering their work schedules on a longer-term basis.

Hobbies and creative activities, such as art and music, may bring pleasure and joy and are part of a healthful lifestyle. Studies have shown that these kinds of activities may stimulate areas of the brain to secrete chemicals beneficial to the healing process. Basically, the goal is for you to feel as much a part of normal life as possible.

Sexuality

Although few people admit it, the fear that cancer is contagious still lurks. Nowhere does this fear have greater impact than in sexual relationships. All too often, the sex act is viewed as a possible vehicle for transmitting the disease or toxicity from the treatments. Women will ask if their husbands' prostate cancer could infect them through sexual intercourse. Husbands will worry that their wives' uterine cancer could infect them in the same way. However, there is no evidence to date that cancer is in any way contagious. In other words, it can't be sexually transmitted.

As with exercise and diet, patients are the best judges of how much sexual activity they feel like engaging in. When recovering from surgery or immediately after chemotherapy, some cancer patients will not find sexual activity appealing or even possible. On the other hand, some people will feel relatively well, at least some of the time, and they may desire this kind of intimacy. Remember, however, that sexual intimacy need not involve intercourse. Touching, hugging, and so forth, are also part of intimacy.

We know that self-image has an enormous impact on sexuality. Cancer patients are no different, and self-image can be quite fragile in these circumstances. Those around them must be sensitive to this. Loss of a breast, loss of hair, and other visible damage to the body can cause anxiety, not to mention the fear that these changes will mar sexual attractiveness. These fears are understandable, but they are often blown out of proportion. In many cases, support groups or individual counseling can help. Reconstructive surgery is an option for some. Time also helps with these adjustments, especially as the effects of chemotherapy wear off and hair grows back.

Physical limitations may affect sexual function. For some there may be altered sensation after surgery, although increasing efforts such as nerve-sparing prostate surgery are designed to reduce this. Vaginal dryness may result from hormonal and other treatments for breast cancer. Ask your doctor about appropriate creams or vaginal lubricants that may be helpful. Because the treatments for breast and prostate cancers affect sex hormones, such as estrogen and testosterone, sex drive—libido—is affected.

Help for Appearance Issues

Even with improved surgical techniques and radiation technology, many patients must cope with changes in their bodies. Nowadays, there are many resources available to help cancer patients adjust to these physical changes. Support groups and the American Cancer Society can help you. For example, the American Cancer Society sponsors a "Look Good, Feel Good" program, which provides tips for women undergoing cancer treatment. Breast cancer support groups offer advice about the emotional adjustment to losing a breast and the pros and cons of reconstructive surgery. Local resource guides can provide information on specially designed clothing, and wigs and alternatives to wigs such as turbans, hats, and scarves.

Both men and women have to make practical adjustments to such treatment side effects as hair loss, and your local chapter of the American Cancer Society can help you locate centers that specialize in advising cancer patients about appearance and cosmetic issues. While these are never easy issues, seeking help can make them easier to cope with.

Emotional Concerns

The diagnosis of cancer is usually followed by initial disbelief, followed by shock and sometimes anger. Some patients may feel anxious or depressed. For many patients, having cancer also means experiencing an intense sense of isolation and loneliness, along with feelings of dread. It is natural to fear cancer and its possible recurrence, along with fear of the treatments offered. However, gaining an understanding of the recommended treatments will help lessen the fear.

Overcoming Fear of Treatment

Most doctors who treat cancer hear a variety of fears, often expressed in vastly different ways. For example, some patients may blame any symptom that comes up on cancer treatment. A bruise resulting from a minor fall might be blamed on radiation treatment or a tension headache will be linked to chemotherapy.

Some fears involve feeling different because of treatment. For example, patients might have a hidden fear that undergoing radiation therapy transforms their tissues and makes them "radioactive," thus causing the fear that they might somehow "contaminate" those around them. However, radiation delivered to the body is instantaneously changed to a biochemical state and patients undergoing the treatment will never pose a danger to anyone around them. Other individuals have fears about the painless and silent nature of radiation treatment. They believe because they can't see it, feel it, or hear it, that perhaps it isn't working. Some people see the chemotherapy drugs as poisons and fear that their body fluids are contaminated. If an issue is troubling to you, then it's important to ask your doctors or the nurses who work with you and get the answers you need.

Keeping Up Your Emotional Strength

Like many cancer patients, you may experience some depression or anxiety. However, it may be difficult to get the attention you need when you report depression to physicians and even to mental-health-care professionals. You might be told that it's "normal" to feel depressed when you are fighting cancer. This is true. If you take any well-adjusted, emotionally stable individuals and put them face-to-face with a potentially life-threatening illness, they may feel depressed. This type of depression is called a reactive depression, meaning that it's a natural response, given the situation you are in, but just because it's normal or expected, it isn't any less valid.

Depression can be treated with medication, counseling, or both. Antidepressants can be helpful and usually are needed only temporarily, and talking with a psychotherapist may help you through this difficult period. You may be trying to accept the reality of your disease, and anger and denial might surface. Taken together, these issues form an important emotional component of cancer and it cannot be ignored.

Many men and women don't seek help from a social worker, therapist, or counselor because they say they have tremendous support from family and friends. While that may be true, it helps to talk to someone who is *not* a family member or friend. When you confide in a professional, you can speak without concern about adding another burden to a loved one's already heavy load.

Emotional issues may greatly affect the way a patient feels physically during the course of treatment. Patients who are depressed may have poor appetite, weight loss, sleep disturbances, and difficulty concentrating. Patients who are anxious may have palpitations, rapid breathing, or stomach problems. Social workers, nurses, chaplains, and counselors at your cancer treatment facility are there because cancer patients need extensive support. If these services are not available in your treatment facility, ask for a referral from your doctor or through community-based counseling services.

The American Cancer Society sponsors numerous programs and services for cancer patients, family members, and others. This well-known organization has extensive referral services linking those in need of help with the appropriate agencies. Some of the programs are based on the assumption that others who have had cancer can offer the best kind of support and understanding.

Choose programs that meet your individual needs, whether they involve support groups, individual counseling, or working with a spiritual advisor. This support should be considered part of a total treatment plan. The goal is for you and those close to you to be able to deal with the facts of your illness in the most positive way possible. As we've said, family members and friends may need their own support systems. Cancer can put great stress on families, and while some seem to pull closer together, other families are torn apart. If you are able to discuss this additional family stress with your doctors, they may be able to guide you to appropriate help.

Relaxing

You may feel uncertain about either the disease prognosis or your response to treatment. This uncertainty may contribute to anxiety, but techniques to reduce stress appear to help many patients. Relaxation therapy includes learning breathing techniques to help relieve stress and feel calm and centered. For example, some individuals find music and nature sounds to be soothing, while others feel better with guided relaxation exercises. Self-hypnosis techniques also may be helpful when coping with stressful moments and hours. Some patients find these to be beneficial prior to receiving chemotherapy treatments. Over the years, we've seen patients benefit from yoga, which includes stretches and breathing techniques that reduce stress. You may wish to explore other techniques to help you relax, including guided imagery, healing touch, therapeutic touch, Reiki, and massage. In addition to its many other benefits, exercise improves mood and reduces anxiety.

Coping Strategies

Maintaining a positive attitude is sometimes easier said than done. Obviously, attitudes toward having cancer and about cancer treatment will vary greatly from person to person. Some people are more naturally optimistic than others, but all cancer patients will need extra attention and support no matter how cheerful and positive they might seem. In addition, some patients are afraid that the normal periods of fear about their disease and the expected feelings of helplessness or panic will interfere with recovery. However, attempts at false cheerfulness aren't beneficial either.

Patients who understand their illness and their treatments become more active participants, which may reduce the sense of helplessness and panic that accompanies a diagnosis of cancer. Informed patients tend to have more rapid recovery from the side effects of treatment, and they also may better comply with treatment and have an improved health outcome.

Ask questions; don't sit at home and worry about whether a particular symptom is an expected part of your treatment. Call and speak with your doctor or nurse. Even common everyday aches and pains may worry you, and good communication with your physician can help you differentiate what's expected from what needs further evaluation. Often, a few words of reassurance can help put your mind at ease.

Expressing Your Feelings

Many patients have discovered journal writing is an effective coping strategy during any illness. A journal can be a practical tool to help you keep track of appointments, your healthcare team's recommendations, and your list of questions. Journals are good places to note symptoms you may experience after a cycle of chemotherapy or radiation treatments and this record may help you and your doctor figure out what medicine and strategies work best to alleviate symptoms and, just as important, what strategies aren't helpful.

Beyond the practical benefits, journal writing may be a valuable vehicle for self-expression. Even those who may initially hesitate to record their feelings on paper may come to find that this is healing in surprising ways. Some individuals may prefer the self-expression found in writing or reading poetry, painting or sketching, or playing music. For others, comedy and expressing feelings through humor may be a healing path.

Sometimes a patient will confuse the idea of maintaining hope and gaining a sense of control over the illness with denying reality. This book certainly doesn't mean to encourage false cheerfulness or the pretense that the disease doesn't exist. In fact, a crucial step in coping with cancer is addressing anger and depression as they arise. This is the reason we recommend seeking the help and support of family, friends, self-help and support groups, or professional counseling. The people who experience the fewest debilitating side effects are often those who have confronted their fear and the reality of the disease. Furthermore, no cancer patient can be expected to be cheerful all the time. It's simply not possible. Those close to the patient will experience their own shifts in attitude, too, and they cannot be expected to be ever brave and cheerful, never expressing their personal fears and anxieties.

Motivation for Change

A diagnosis of cancer can prompt individuals to look inward and the motivation to make lifestyle changes often rests in the desire to reduce fear of recurrence or to alleviate the anxiety about developing a second cancer. Patients may quit smoking, change their diets, and begin exercise programs. They may often ask themselves important questions: Am I really fulfilled in my current job or profession? Am I hanging on to struggling relationships because of fear of change, or do I have old friendships that need renewal? Do I have hobbies or interests that I've let sit on the back burner for too long?

Men and women may use the strength they gained while fighting cancer to give them the courage to tackle other challenges in their lives. In other words, they try to make something good come out of something bad. Look critically at your life. Do what you can to reduce the stress in your day-to-day routine, and determine what's really important to you. Honestly ask yourself about your goals and then move ahead.

The Truth Is Essential

We believe it's virtually impossible for a patient to cope without knowing the facts. Therefore, we thoroughly describe the cancer to the patient—its origin, location, and stage of aggressiveness. We also explain any test results and, when possible, show the patient the x-ray and other imaging tests. This goes a long way toward alleviating the fear of the unknown. Furthermore, patients can then begin to have a sense of control over their own condition. If cancer patients don't have a sense of participation, the only alternative is feeling like helpless observers or even victims.

Discussions about the cancer, treatment, and outlook can be frank, but they need not be brutal. Beating the odds, no matter how grim, is always a possibility. Some patients considered incurable have outlived their prognosis, and even have gone on to be cured. Today, there are growing numbers of cancer survivors, some that are cured from cancer and some that are living *with* cancer. For those living with cancer, there continues to be the hope that each day brings new discoveries that may be helpful to them.

Spirituality

A spiritual path (defined in individual ways) can help cancer patients and their families cope with the burden of disease, treatment, and uncertain prognosis. Although faith is important to the everyday lives of many Americans, it is surprising how little we know about the effects of spirituality on an illness. Some studies have suggested that seeking spiritual support helps patients cope to a greater extent than psychological support. Spiritual well-being appears to be correlated with hope in cancer patients. Meditation, prayer, or reading of meaningful spiritual material can reduce stress and help patients cope with cancer.

When Treatment Ends

Some patients see the end of a course of radiation treatment or chemotherapy as a kind of "graduation day." They are glad to be finished with the daily obligation of treatment. However, a few patients become anxious as they near the end of therapy. They had a sense that as long as treatment continued, something was being done to combat the cancer. When treatment is over, they may feel a letdown. If this happens to you, don't think you are abnormal; your feelings are understandable. Talk about them with your physicians, family members, friends, or others who are part of your support network.

Likewise, after completing the rigors of adjuvant chemotherapy, patients often feel a surge of anxiety. Many have focused so hard on getting themselves through initial surgery, chemotherapy, and radiation, that they don't let themselves feel the anxiety; instead, they muster up all their emotional strength to get through it all. Then, after coming in for chemotherapy every three weeks for several months, and radiation daily for several weeks, they suddenly have this fear that they are no longer actively doing anything to fight the cancer. Many patients feel more worried and anxious after finishing treatment rather than earlier in the process. If you haven't already done so, post-treatment is a good time to look into support groups or counseling. With time, the worry and fear will lessen.

Because of individual differences and reactions to cancer, it is difficult to do more than generalize about lifestyle and emotional issues. In addition, how a person feels has much to do with age, other medical conditions, and the severity of the disease. The goal of emotional support is to come to an acceptance of the reality of the disease without letting it thoroughly defeat you. We recommend that you find tools that will help you and your family members openly talk about how you are feeling and come to terms with the illness.

PART 2

CANCER TREATMENT: RADIATION THERAPY AND CHEMOTHERAPY

PART 2 OF THIS book is designed to give you information about specific cancer sites. However, we recommend that you read through Part 1 first so that you have a general understanding of the purpose and process of radiation therapy and chemotherapy.

Chapter 4 explains treatment for the most commonly occurring cancers and the control of side effects that may result from treatment. Subsequent chapters discuss treatment for sites to which cancer has spread and ways in which pain can be managed or alleviated.

The cancers discussed in the pages that follow are those for which radiation therapy and/or chemotherapy are often recommended. Childhood cancers are not discussed because the types of cancers that affect children are not often found in adults. Furthermore, most children are treated in special centers that are equipped to handle the unique medical and emotional concerns associated with childhood cancers.

4

Cancers Most Commonly Treated with Radiation and Chemotherapy

The following sections, each of which focuses on a particular cancer site, are designed to provide a foundation of knowledge that you can use when discussing your specific case with your team of physicians. Radiation and chemotherapy dosages and treatment times will vary among treatment centers and according to the patient's clinical picture. Your medical and radiation oncologists may, for example, recommend a different dosage of radiation, delivered over a different period of time, or they may suggest different drugs or a combination of chemotherapeutic agents. They may prescribe medications to combat side effects other than those we have cited, and they also may offer different suggestions to alter your lifestyle during treatment. Your own team of physicians will have good reasons for the advice they offer, and the information provided here is intended to serve as guidelines to treatment but is not a substitute for the individualized care you will receive.

Bladder Cancer

Bladder cancer originates in the cells that line the urinary tract and is the fourth most common cancer in men and the tenth most common cancer in women. Most men and women are diagnosed at older ages, and the disease is considered rare in those under age forty.

Cigarette smoking is the number one environmental risk factor for the development of bladder cancer, and certain industrial chemicals increase one's risk, particularly among dye workers. The parasitic worm schistosomiasis also represents a major cause of bladder cancer in countries where it is prevalent. Genetic abnormalities account for a small percent of the cases.

The most common presenting symptom is blood in the urine, but patients often report other complaints, such as frequent urination or burning with urination. Diagnosis is made with cystoscopy and biopsy. A *cystoscopy* is a procedure in which growths are detected when the bladder is viewed through a special instrument. Other tests, such as an intravenous pyelogram, CT scan, or MRI, may be helpful in determining whether the disease is invasive or has spread.

Fortunately, most patients are found to have *superficial* bladder cancer, which means the cancerous cells are confined to the lining of the bladder and have not invaded the underlying bladder muscle tissue. In many cases the urologist can estimate if invasion is present during cystoscopy, but the final determination is made when the pathologist examines the biopsy specimen. The pathologist also grades the tumor from low- to high-grade, depending on how abnormal and aggressive the cancer cells look. Prognosis and treatment depend on tumor grade and the presence or absence of invasion or spread.

Treatment

Treatment depends on whether the tumor is superficial or invasive, low- or high-grade, and whether there is local or distant spread. Superficial tumors are treated with *transurethral resection*, a procedure in which a urologist inserts an instrument into the bladder through the urethra that allows him or her to see the tumor, scrape it away, and then cauterize the underlying tissue. In most cases of superficial bladder cancer, this is the only treatment required.

If the tumor is very large, high-grade, and/or multifocal (meaning that more than one tumor exists in more than one location of the bladder), some specialists might recommend an additional treatment. This would consist of six weekly "instillations" of bacille Calmette-Guerin (BCG) delivered through a catheter inserted into the bladder. Interestingly, BCG is also an immunization vaccine against TB. These instillations are usually done once a week for six weeks; however, some physicians believe in repeated doses for three weeks every three months over the course of a year.

Unfortunately, superficial tumors have a high rate of reoccurrence, 40 to 80 percent, depending on the grade. This means that the patient must be cystoscoped every three to six months for three to five years. Once a patient has been diagnosed with a bladder tumor, there is risk of new tumors in the same part of the bladder or different parts. If there are multiple recurrences or grade progression, then it is advisable to have BCG or chemotherapy instillations into the bladder.

Fortunately, only a small percent of superficial cancers progress to an invasive cancer. When this occurs, though, more aggressive treatment is necessary. The gold standard for *invasive bladder cancer* is now considered to be a *cystectomy*, the surgical removal of the bladder. Prior to surgery, a patient will be evaluated to see if there is any evidence of spread. This evaluation is limited, however, and it is often not until after surgery that a more accurate assessment of disease can be made. At the time of surgery for invasive bladder cancers, lymph nodes are also removed and reviewed by the pathologist. Adjuvant chemotherapy may be recommended prior to surgery to shrink the tumor, or after surgery depending on the findings. (See below.)

Ten years ago we believed that a bladder-sparing procedure consisting of chemotherapy concurrent with radiation therapy yielded the same results as surgery, but long-term follow-up revealed a higher rate of recurrences with this approach compared to cystectomy. The good news is that in most cases a patient does not need a ureterostomy bag. A *neobladder* can be reconstructed utilizing a length of colon; thus, most patients remain continent and can urinate in a normal manner.

Radiation and medical oncologists have not given up on developing a bladder-sparing procedure, and research goes on.

Combination Treatment. Combination radiation and chemotherapy (the bladder-sparing option) is generally reserved for patients who are medically unfit for surgery or who refuse surgery for other reasons. Those who undergo this combination procedure may experience side effects from both the chemotherapy and the radiation.

The usual course of radiation is approximately forty daily treatments delivered over eight weeks. Patients can miss an occasional day, but prolonged interruptions should be avoided because it reduces the effectiveness of the radiation.

A dose of 5,000 units are delivered over a five- to six-week period. The patient is then cystoscoped again by the urologist. If there is a total, or almost total, response, the patient will receive an additional 2,000 units of radiation over a two- to three-week period. A total of 7,000 units of radiation may be delivered to the bladder and surrounding lymph nodes on a daily basis over this period. Treatment is directed through the front, back, and sides of the patient; and the treatment field is shaped to treat the bladder and adjacent lymph nodes while avoiding the bowel as much as possible. The patient receives chemotherapy concurrent with the radiation therapy.

If the patient has a poor response to combination treatment, then the patient is advised to have surgery. If the person is unfit for surgery, the options include radiation or chemotherapy alone, with the objective of temporarily reducing growth rate or controlling bleeding or pain. If the patient does not respond to the combination or individual therapies, has significant side effects of treatment, and also is not considered a suitable candidate for surgery, then sometimes the best option is to stop all treatment other than supportive care.

Because of poor physical condition, some patients may not be able to tolerate surgery or combination chemotherapy and radiation, although they may be candidates for radiation therapy alone. In these cases we deliver 6,000 to 7,000 units over a seven- to eight-week period. Radiation alone can cure as much as 30 to 40 percent of invasive bladder cancer if it is confined to the bladder and has not spread. Even in cases in which the tumor has spread and cure is unlikely, radiation may be offered to reduce bleeding or relieve pain.

Multidisciplinary Approach for Invasive or Metastatic Bladder Cancer. When bladder cancer is invasive and has extended outside of the bladder (*nonorgan-confined bladder cancer*)—to lymph nodes, for example—multidisciplinary approaches use combinations of surgery, chemotherapy, and radiation. Here, chemotherapy may be given first, followed by surgery. Alternatively, chemotherapy and radiation may be given together, followed by surgery. If a patient is not referred to a medical oncologist until after the surgery, chemotherapy may still be considered, although the benefits are greater when the chemotherapy is given first. This is an example of the ways in which it can be advantageous to begin with a "team" assessment, with consideration of all treatment options, before beginning any treatment.

Chemotherapy is the principle treatment for advanced bladder cancer that is inoperable or bladder cancer that has metastasized. The combination of the drugs methotrexate, vinblastine, doxorubicin (Adriamycin), and cisplatin (MVAC), first used in 1983, has been considered the standard treatment.

While very effective in shrinking bladder cancers and helping patients to live longer, this combination has a number of side effects. These include lowering the white blood-cell counts to critically low levels, which makes individuals susceptible to potentially life-threatening infections. The use of growth factors (drugs like granulocyte-colony stimulating factors Neupogen and Neulasta) helps the white blood cells to recover faster from chemotherapy and reduces the risk of infection. Other side effects include the risk of toxicity to the heart and kidneys.

There has been significant progress in the use of chemotherapy for bladder cancer, as there are now several new agents being used for treatment. These include the taxanes paclitaxel (Taxol) and docetaxel (Taxotere), gemcitabine (Gemzar), ifosfamide (Ifex), and carboplatin (Paraplatin) or cisplatin (Platinol). These drugs are used in two-drug or three-drug combinations. Combinations like the triplet of paclitaxel, cisplatin, and ifosfamide or the doublets gemcitabine and carboplatin or carboplatin and paclitaxel have shown encouraging results and have manageable side effects.

These less-toxic drug combinations are preferred for patients with bladder cancer who have other significant medical problems, such as frailty or heart or kidney problems, or whose cancer has spread to organs such as the lung, liver, or bones. Your medical oncologist will carefully weigh the advantages and disadvantages of these different combinations to help you decide on the best options. These two- and three-drug combinations have a number of clinical benefits and are rapidly changing the approach to the use of chemotherapy in bladder cancer. The hope is that we will continue to see improved outcomes with fewer side effects in the future.

Side Effects of Radiation

The side effects directly attributed to the radiation are frequency of urination, nocturnal urination (being awakened from sleep to urinate), urgency of urination, rectal irritation, and diarrhea. These side effects are caused by the radiation dose to the bladder and rectum. By using modern treatment planning systems, we can minimize the dose to the rectum.

Allowing a month to pass between the bladder biopsy and the first treatment can minimize radiation side effects. Obstruction of the ureters caused by the cancer is treated by inserting tubes (stents) to bypass the obstruction.

Antibiotics are given to patients with bladder infections, which, while not common, can occur.

In general, side effects during the seven or eight weeks of radiation therapy are moderate. It is common for the bladder to become irritated, thus producing urinary frequency, some burning, and urgency. These symptoms are well controlled with appropriate medications—phenazopydine (Pyridium) or oxybutynin chloride (Ditropan), for example. Warm baths, especially prior to going to bed at night, are also helpful in reducing urinary urgency.

The side effects must be distinguished from symptoms of urinary-tract infection (UTI), because bladder irritation caused by the radiation can mimic an infection or coexist. Therefore, a urinalysis may be done to determine if the patient has an infection; both antibiotics and medications to relieve bladder irritation are typically prescribed in such cases.

Bowel symptoms may also be present, because radiation affects the rectum and the lower intestine. Patients will experience diarrhea, cramping, and an urge to evacuate even when no fecal material is present. (The latter is called *tenesmus*.) Lomotil or Imodium A-D are medications used to relieve diarrhea and cramping.

Irritation in the rectal area may require a medication such as Anusol HC suppositories or Proctofoam enemas to relieve symptoms. Moderate reddening of the skin over the area receiving radiation, particularly between the folds of the buttocks, can be treated with soothing skin creams or cortisone ointments. These and other symptoms can be controlled, and most patients are able to continue radiation treatments without major difficulty.

A minority of patients may have long-term side effects following radiation treatment. These include occasional bleeding from the bladder, known as *hemorrhagic cystitis*, and bladder contraction with decreased ability to retain urine. A few patients may develop an obstruction or bleeding from the small intestine.

Side Effects of Chemotherapy

The most common side effects from chemotherapy include fatigue and malaise. Nausea is not as big a problem as it was before the routine use of antiemetics. There may be hair loss, but the hair will ultimately return. The patient's blood count must be monitored closely, as the combination approach may cause significant suppression, particularly of the white blood cells and platelets. If the counts become too low, the patient may require hospitalization and antibiotics, because lowered white blood-cell count leaves the patient at risk for an overwhelming generalized systemic infection.

Follow-Up and Outlook

It is essential that, following treatment, patients undergo periodic urologic examinations. Patients who have not had a cystectomy and have received only radiation therapy will receive follow-up cystoscopies, chest x-rays, intravenous pyelograms (IVPs), and CT scans of the pelvis (see Chapter 8). Those patients who have had cystectomies will undergo CT scans for follow-up evaluation.

Clinical trials are currently being done to evaluate the results of surgery, radiation therapy, and combination treatment plans. Chemotherapy has been shown to enhance the effects of radiation therapy. More trials are needed to better determine the role of chemotherapy in future treatment of this type of cancer.

Brain Cancer

A number of different types of tumors originate in the brain; some are benign and some malignant. Generally, primary malignant tumors do not spread outside of the brain, so the serious nature of these tumors arises from the fact that the brain is enclosed within the skull, without much space to accommodate a growing tumor.

The most common malignant tumors of the brain are generally classified as *gliomas*. They are relatively rare and are *primary* brain tumors, as opposed to those that can occur when cancers originating in other organs metastasize to the brain. This section deals with primary tumors; cancer that has spread to the brain from a distant site is discussed in Chapter 5.

CT scans and MRIs (see Chapter 8) are generally used to detect brain tumors. These tests enable neurosurgeons and radiation oncologists to precisely locate the tumor and its extensions. Although these tests are sensitive, they are not specific, meaning that they also show conditions that mimic cancer. Therefore, if a primary brain cancer is suspected, a biopsy is usually required before a definitive diagnosis is made.

Treatment

Surgery followed by radiation is the most common treatment for these tumors. Surgery is used to confirm the diagnosis of cancer, determine the cell type, and reduce the size of the tumor by removing as much of the diseased tissue as possible. This is a very delicate procedure in which care is taken not to damage the surrounding normal structures. Radiation alone is used to treat those tumors which, because of location, are not accessible surgically without causing serious impairment to the patient. After surgery is completed, if it is determined that the cell type is sensitive to radiation, radiation therapy may begin. Both CT scans and MRIs are used to design an appropriate treatment field. If the tumor is the type that is invasive, larger areas of the brain are treated. However, in many patients, the treatment portal includes only the area of known disease and some of the surrounding tissue. (This is different from treatment for metastatic disease, which generally involves the whole brain.)

Depending on the location of the disease and its particular characteristics, radiation treatment may involve multiple portals through the front, back, or the sides of the head. A multiple-portal treatment plan maximizes the dose of radiation to the tumor, while minimizing the radiation that reaches normal tissue. Using IMRT (see Chapter 1) we are better able to define the treatment area and spare as much normal brain tissue as possible.

Treatments are generally given daily over a five- to seven-week period. The dose and length of the treatment course depends on the clinical situation, the patient's overall health, the particular cell type of the tumor, and its location. A typical dose is approximately 6,000 to 6,500 units delivered over seven weeks.

Although external beam radiation therapy is usually administered, other forms of radiation treatment may be used. One form that has shown particular promise is radiosurgery (see Introduction), a noninvasive method of delivering a localized, high dose of radiation in an outpatient session. This unit directs beams of radiation to the tumor, which is localized by special neurosurgical techniques known as a *stereotactic system*. Radiosurgery is limited to tumors less than two inches in size, but it enables us to deliver a very high dose to a small area. Treatment dosage is individualized, based on the amount of previous radiation, if any, to the brain and the radiosensitivity of the cancer cells. The average dosage is approximately 2,500 units of radiation delivered in a single treatment, although this may sometimes be increased to 3,500 units. The gamma knife treatment may also be used for tumors that have spread to the brain from a distant primary cancer (see Chapter 5).

Evidence exists that radiosurgery is of some benefit for benign tumors, such as those that may occur in the pituitary gland (pituitary adenoma) or in the nerves that control sound (acoustic neuroma). *Arterial venous malformation,* an abnormal collection of blood vessels, may also benefit from radiosurgery.

Another method of delivering radiation to the brain involves implanting a radioactive source into the tumor. Although this treatment is used only occasionally, it can be sometimes associated with serious complications such as destruction of surrounding normal brain tissue or destruction of skull bone tissue.

Chemotherapy may be considered after initial treatment with surgery and radiation, and studies are looking at the simultaneous use of chemotherapy and radiation. Chemotherapy is most often given to treat recurrent disease. The specific type of tumor helps determine the specific chemotherapy drugs recommended. Chemotherapy can be given orally, intravenously, or through a catheter a neurosurgeon inserts into the tumor or the spinal fluid.

One particular drug, the Gliadel Wafer, is a biodegradable wafer inserted into the tumor at the time of surgery and it slowly releases the chemotherapy drug carmustine (BCNU) directly into the tumor area. However, carmustine is more often used intravenously. Oral chemotherapy agents include lomustine (CCNU), procarbazine, and temozolomide (Temodar). Temozolomide is usually used for recurrent brain tumors, but is sometimes given with radiation as part of initial treatment. When treating these brain tumors, we've found that, at present, using a single chemotherapy drug is just as good as drug combinations.

Side Effects of Radiation

To combat the immediate side effects of radiation therapy, patients are usually given two types of medication during the period when they are receiving radiation treatments. The first, a cortisone medication (Decadron or prednisone), reduces swelling, or edema, in the brain tissues. This swelling may be caused by the tumor itself, or it may occur as a side effect of treatment. The second type of medication (Dilantin) is given to prevent convulsions.

Hair loss is one of the most psychologically troubling side effects of radiation therapy, and most people do lose the hair over the treated area, beginning two to three weeks into treatment. Some patients do not experience significant hair loss because of strong hair follicles, a genetic characteristic. However, because we know that hair loss is likely, we recommend arranging for a hairpiece when treatment begins, thus avoiding a period of noticeable baldness. Hair loss will continue throughout treatment and for several weeks after the radiation therapy course is completed. Occasionally, the hair grows back, but the texture is altered and the growth is sparse.

On rare occasions, a patient may become drowsy and possibly slightly disoriented after receiving a radiation treatment to the brain. Because this side effect may occur, we advise patients to rest or sleep following treatment. Patients sometimes become alarmed by these symptoms, but there is no cause for concern. Both the drowsiness and the disorientation disappear within a few hours. A more generalized fatigue may begin at some time during the course of treatment as well.

Nausea is an infrequent side effect, but if it occurs, it can be well controlled with medication, such as Compazine. Following treatment, some patients experience mild headaches that can be treated with over-the-counter medications. The skin over the area of treatment also reddens because of the radiation irritation, and a soothing skin cream is effective in relieving this symptom. These side effects may be annoying, but they are not serious.

Severe headaches, projectile vomiting (forceful vomiting), and visual changes occur infrequently, but they must be reported immediately. These symptoms may signal an increase in pressure, caused by swelling within the brain. In some cases, it is necessary to temporarily interrupt treatments and increase the dosage of cortisone medication to reduce swelling.

Patients are understandably concerned about receiving radiation treatment to the brain. Any disease process going on in the brain is especially worrisome. After all, the brain is the organ that directs all human activity. Our thoughts and emotions originate in the brain, and it is considered the center of the self. Therefore, we urge patients to seek emotional support from family, friends, and also from health-care professionals if possible. It is essential to call on all available support systems during this stressful time.

Unfortunately, delayed side effects of radiation to the brain include long-term changes in intellectual functioning and memory. However, some adults with brain tumors do not survive long enough to experience these effects, because many primary brain cancers are very aggressive and long-term survival rates are low.

Side Effects of Chemotherapy

Similar side effects occur with carmustine (BCNU) and lomustine (CCNU), and both can cause significantly lowered blood counts. This side effect is delayed in that it occurs three to six weeks after treatment. (With most other chemotherapy drugs, the lowest counts are noted two weeks into treatment.) In addition, the drugs may cause nausea, vomiting, and fatigue. Carmustine may irritate the vein into which it is injected. The drug procarbazine, administered in pill form, may cause low blood counts, nausea, vomiting, headache, numbness or tingling, and mood changes. Temozolomide, a more recently developed oral agent, is relatively well tolerated; side effects are usually mild but may include nausea, vomiting, headache, fatigue, drowsiness (somnolence), constipation, and lowered blood counts.

Follow-Up and Outlook

Current research on brain tumor treatment focuses on better strategies to get through the blood-brain barrier. For example, the potential exists that new drugs may temporarily open up the blood-brain barrier. Because of the rarity of these tumors and because standard treatments have been somewhat disappointing, this is a disease in which clinical trials should be strongly considered. Surgical techniques are becoming more refined; and radiation methods are focusing more directly on the tumors, with less radiation reaching the rest of the brain. The goal for future treatment is helping patients to live longer while preserving as much neurological function as possible.

Breast Cancer

Breast cancer usually arises from ducts in the breast. At first, it may be confined within the ducts, in which case it is known as *ductal carcinoma in situ*

(DCIS). At this stage, it does not have the potential to spread outside the breast. However, at some point, the cancer can become invasive, meaning that it spreads outside the breast ducts and replaces normal breast tissue with a tumor mass. This progression describes the most common breast cancers.

The first theory about the way breast cancer spreads held that it starts in the breast and spreads in an orderly fashion to the surrounding region that includes the chest wall muscles and lymph nodes, eventually invading blood vessels and distant organs. This theory led to the first breast cancer treatment, radical mastectomy, a surgery in which chest muscle is removed along with the breast and all the lymph nodes under the arm. It was thought that radical surgery was necessary to cure the cancer because it removed the areas of potential invasion.

A more recent theory holds that, from the start, breast cancer is a *systemic* disease, meaning that cells have likely escaped the breast very early, often bypassing the lymph nodes. This is why systemic treatments, those that travel throughout the bloodstream, came into use. In reality, no ultimate theory for the progression of breast cancer exists, and the truth is likely a combination of these two theories. Some cancers may be cured with surgery alone, but most benefit from a combination of treatment strategies.

Risk Factors and Genetic Testing

Risk factors for developing breast cancer include age, hormonal factors, certain benign breast conditions, family history, and, of course, being female (ninety-nine out of one hundred breast cancers occur in women). Because breast cancer is a common disease, it is not uncommon to have a relative that has breast cancer. However, this does not imply that an abnormal gene is being passed down from generation to generation. In fact, less than 10 percent of all breast cancers are caused by a known inherited genetic defect, or mutation. The most common of these mutations occur in two genes, BRCA-1 or BRCA-2. Both genes normally play a role as a tumor suppressor and in DNA repair, so mutations in these genes allow damaged cells to grow out of control.

Mutations have been found less commonly in other genes, but we're sure we'll find more. People who have an inherited mutation in BRCA-1 or BRCA-2 genes are at increased risk for breast and ovarian cancer. Based on current estimates, female carriers of BRCA-1 or BRCA-2 have a 50 to 80 percent chance of developing breast cancer and a 15 to 45 percent chance of developing ovarian cancer in their lifetime, usually at younger ages. Males who carry the gene also are at an increased risk of developing breast cancer.

Individuals with suspicious family histories of cancer may want to consider genetic testing. A computerized risk assessment may help better define the likelihood of being a gene carrier. Although it is just a simple blood test, the process is anything *but* simple because of the many psychological, ethical, and societal issues. Because of all these possible factors, we recommend pre- and posttest counseling with a qualified genetic counselor. We generally discuss testing when a patient has two or more other family members (such as a mother, sister, aunt, and/or grandmother) from the same bloodline with a history of premenopausal breast cancer and/or ovarian cancer or male breast cancer. We are also more concerned if we hear that family members have had breast cancer in both breasts.

A woman with a personal history of breast cancer and who is found to have inherited a mutation in BRCA-1 or BRCA-2 does not appear to be at higher risk of recurrence in that breast. However, she is at higher risk of developing a new, unrelated *second* cancer in the same or opposite breast. Some women may approach treatment decisions differently because of this knowledge, thus they may consider genetic testing soon after being diagnosed with breast cancer. This may change what she and her doctors decide to do to prevent second cancers. Stage for stage, though, these women have the same chances for a cure as those patients who don't carry a susceptibility gene.

Women who have inherited mutations in BRCA-1 or BRCA-2 but have not been diagnosed with cancer may want to consider strategies for prevention. These strategies include preventative surgery (prophylactic mastectomy or oophorectomy) or use of medications such as tamoxifen. They may also seek high-risk screening programs, available at many breast centers or cancer centers, for close surveillance and to help them access new strategies for prevention and early detection.

Diagnosis

Mammography is still the gold standard and complements clinical breast exam (the physical exam of the breast done yearly by your doctor), because some breast cancers are felt as a change or abnormality in the breast, while others are diagnosed by mammography alone. Although mammography can pick up better than 90 percent of breast cancers, it has limitations. In women with dense breast tissue, or young or pregnant woman with a prominent glandular pattern, even large, palpable masses can be obscured. In these cases ultrasound can be helpful in detecting tumors that may be cancerous and distinguishing cysts from solid masses. MRI has gradually seen increased use for diagnosing breast cancer. No current criteria have been established for its use, but early reports suggest it may be beneficial in woman with dense breasts or for those who are diagnosed with certain types of breast cancers that tend to involve multiple sites in the same breast.

Biopsy. When a lump can be felt, fine-needle aspiration (FNA) is a simple way of obtaining a tissue specimen because it is a relatively quick outpatient procedure. Usually under x-ray or ultrasound guidance and with local anesthesia, a 22- to 25-gauge needle (approximately 1/32 of an inch) is inserted into the abnormal area and tissue is aspirated into the syringe. A pathologist may be present to examine the aspirated tissue on the spot, and more often than not multiple aspirations are necessary. The disadvantage of this method involves the small amount of tissue obtained, resulting in a higher rate of false negatives then other methods.

A *core* biopsy uses a similar approach and also is an outpatient procedure. However, instead of a 22-gauge needle, it requires a specialized needle that has a spring-loaded device that extracts a core of tissue. The needle is larger than that used in FNA, approximately 1/16 of an inch, but it yields more tissue and overall, is more accurate than FNA. Core biopsies may be used to diagnose palpable or felt lumps and, under mammographic guidance (stereotactic) or ultrasound guidance, may also be used for abnormalities seen on mammography or ultrasound but that are too small to be felt.

Surgery. Over the past twenty years, there has been a shift from radical breast surgery to *minimally invasive approaches* to breast cancer treatment. Today, many breast cancers are found through routine yearly screening mammograms and may be too small to feel. In the case of a tumor too small to detect during physical exam, the breast surgeon may use a technique known as *needle localization* to remove it. In this procedure, a radiologist places guidewires into the breast, guided by mammography images, in order to "localize" the tumor. The patient is then brought to the operating room, where the surgeon follows the guidewire to the exact location of the tumor in order to cut it out (excise it). This insures that the abnormal area is removed, and it has the advantage of allowing the surgeon to go right to the lesion. The abnormal tissue just removed is then x-rayed while the patient is still in the operating room, which is called a *specimen mammogram*, to verify that the abnormality seen on the original mammogram is actually *in* the tissue that was surgically removed. If a tumor is large enough to be felt, the surgeon can remove it without using the needle localization technique.

The pathologist carefully examines the tumor specimen under the microscope, a process that usually takes a few days and includes examining the edges, or *margins*, of the specimen for the presence of cancer cells. Ideally, we would like to see a rim of normal tissue removed along with cancer, so that we can be sure it is all out. Most surgeons try to balance the removal of enough tissue to achieve negative margins, while leaving as much of the breast intact as possible.

It is difficult to estimate margins at the time of the initial surgery, so it is not uncommon to need additional surgery to achieve wider margins. In addition, the optimal margin size remains controversial. However, if there are cancer cells reaching to the edge of the specimen, this is associated with higher rates of local recurrence, meaning the cancer comes back in the breast. A *post-excision* mammogram of the breast is another way to check the adequacy of the surgery. We generally do this in cancers that are associated with calcium deposits on the mammogram so that the doctors can see that no abnormal calcifications remain.

Breast surgery for *invasive* breast cancer includes examination of the lymph nodes under the arm (axilla). Knowing whether or not there is any cancer in the lymph nodes and how many lymph nodes contain cancer are factors in the patient's prognosis. Higher numbers of involved lymph nodes are associated with a higher risk of cancer having spread. One way to get this information is to do a *complete axillary dissection*, meaning that we remove all the nodes located under the arm and examine them. Approximately 20 to 30 percent of women who have had a complete axillary dissection may be susceptible to a condition of chronic swelling of the arm known as *lymphedema*. This may occur shortly after the surgery or even up to ten years later. (Radiation to the underarm area may also increase the risk.) For many women, especially those with small breast cancers, all the lymph nodes will be free of tumor. These women could be spared from having a complete axillary dissection with a more recent procedure known as *sentinel node biopsy*.

Sentinel node procedure is another component of the minimally invasive approach to breast cancer surgery. In the sentinel node procedure, the "leader," or sentinel lymph node, is examined first. This axillary node is identified after a radioactive material and/or a blue dye are injected into the breast. Studies have shown that if the sentinel lymph node is free of tumor cells, it is unlikely that other lymph nodes are involved; and when this is the case, it is not necessary to remove the rest of the underarm lymph nodes. However, if cancer cells are found in the sentinel lymph node, then the rest of the lymph nodes should be removed and examined for tumor cells. In general, the sentinel lymph node biopsy is not needed in *noninvasive* breast cancer (ductal carcinoma in situ, or DCIS), although certain circumstances exist in which the treatment team may believe it is appropriate.

A number of unresolved questions remain about sentinel node procedure. For example, diagnostic methods are now so sophisticated that it is now possible to identify just one single cancer cell in a lymph node. But what does this mean? Do these patients have as high a risk of relapse as patients with a lymph node that is entirely replaced by tumor? How important is it to remove additional lymph nodes if the sentinel lymph node *is* involved but no treatment decisions will change based on the results? For example, if the same chemotherapy is recommended if there is one lymph node involved as opposed to several, then why do the additional surgery? We hope that several large, ongoing clinical research trials will answer these questions in the future.

The Pathology Report. The pathology report is important in determining both the treatment plan and prognosis. It is helpful when the breast surgeon, the radiation oncologist, and the medical oncologist can review the slides under the microscope with the pathologist, while simultaneously checking the mammography films with the radiologist. We ask questions, such as: Do the abnormalities on the mammogram appear to correspond with what was removed? Are the margins adequate, or is additional surgery needed, and how will this affect other treatment decisions? No matter how detailed a pathology report is, seeing the actual slides is still better, so ask your doctor if all the specialists involved have had a chance to review your case in this fashion.

The pathology report also contains information on whether the cancer is invasive (infiltrating) or noninvasive (in situ), the type of breast cancer (the vast majority are *ductal* as opposed to *lobular*), the grade (low, intermediate, or high), the size, the margin information, and lymph node information. Additional tests may be selected that will reveal features of the cancer that may be important in determining response to treatment. The presence of estrogen and/or progesterone receptors on a tumor means that the tumor growth may be blocked by hormone treatments that interfere with estrogen's ability to stimulate tumor growth. (It does not imply that estrogen caused the cancer.) Another specific test looks at whether or not the tumor has excess amounts of a protein known as *Her-2 neu*. This is only found in excess amounts on the surface of about 20 to 30 percent of all breast cancers but is associated with more aggressive cancers.

Treatment of Ductal Carcinoma in Situ (DCIS)

DCIS is a noninvasive type of breast cancer, meaning that it does not have the potential to spread outside of the breast. However, it requires appropriate treatment because if not adequately treated it may recur as an invasive breast cancer that does have the potential to spread and metastasize.

DCIS may be treated with mastectomy or breast-conserving therapy, similar to invasive breast cancer. In select situations, radiation therapy may not be used. For example, if the area of DCIS is very small or low-grade and is removed with substantial margins of surrounding normal tissue, then the surgery may be sufficient. Clinical trials are currently investigating if radiation can be safely omitted in highly select individuals.

For some women, the hormone medication tamoxifen may be considered for additional treatment. Tamoxifen can reduce the risk of DCIS recurring by 50 percent and the development of a new cancer in the opposite breast by 50 percent. Currently, the hormone treatment anastrazole is also being studied in postmenopausal women with DCIS. Chemotherapy is never indicated in the treatment of DCIS.

The remaining information on treatment of breast cancer pertains to invasive breast cancer at early stages, locally advanced breast cancer, and metastatic disease.

Treatment Decisions: Mastectomy or Breast-Conserving Therapy?

In the past, radical or modified mastectomy was the treatment of choice for breast cancer. Because these procedures removed the breast, underlying superficial muscle, and underarm lymph nodes, they were physically deforming surgeries with possible psychological effects. Every time they look in the mirror, these patients are reminded of their bout with cancer. However, a radical mastectomy is rarely needed today, and most newly diagnosed women are candidates for breast-conserving therapy. For those who are not, reconstructive surgery is now an option in most cases. Reconstructive surgery mitigates the physical and psychological effects of extensive surgery, especially when immediate reconstruction is done.

Women who are not candidates for breast-conservation treatment include those who have had prior radiation to the breast, who are pregnant, or who have a connective tissue disease such as lupus. Certain situations, such as two or more tumors in separate quadrants of the breast or failure to obtain margins free of tumor cells despite additional surgery, may also indicate the need for more extensive surgery. Breast size alone is not a reason that breast-conserving treatment cannot be done, but if the tumor is large and the breast is small, then, for cosmetic reasons, a mastectomy with reconstruction may be more desirable to some women. Your doctor will let you know if you are a good candidate for breast-conserving therapy. If you are, then you have a choice between breast-conserving therapy and mastectomy. (Insurance coverage is not a factor here; breast reconstruction is always covered when mastectomy is done to treat cancer.)

With early detection almost all early breast cancers can be treated with breast-conserving surgery and postoperative radiation. Only a lumpectomy and axillary node sampling are performed. Briefly, this means the tumor is removed, along with just enough surrounding breast tissue to insure clear margins, plus either a sentinel node procedure or complete axillary dissection.

Stage for stage, treatment results with breast-conservation surgery and radiation are similar to those for mastectomy alone. We now have sufficient long-term follow-up to make this claim. Most women who are able to have breast-conserving therapy prefer this option for treatment because the surgery is less involved and the breast is spared. In some women the cosmetic results are so good that years later it is hard to tell which breast was treated.

Today, most women who are candidates for breast-conserving treatment choose breast conservation, while a smaller number may choose mastectomy. Personal preferences and lifestyle issues are important. Some women live in remote areas and, therefore, would need to travel long distances to a radiation facility, which may be a factor in their decision. Overall, it appears that in the United States, the rates at which women choose breast-sparing surgery vary greatly from region to region around the country. In other words, in some geographic areas breast-conserving therapy is underused. This underuse contrasts with some areas of Europe, such as England, where breast-conserving therapy rates are higher than found in many places in the United States. We hope you will use the information in this book to ask that all options be presented to you before you make definitive decisions.

Radiation. If you choose to have breast-conserving surgery for treatment of invasive breast cancer, then it is understood that you will have radiation to the breast. On the other hand, if you choose mastectomy, then radiation is recommended only in select cases.

Four to six weeks after the surgical wound has healed, or three to four weeks after completing all chemotherapy (if it is part of the treatment plan), then patients can begin a seven- to eight-week course of radiation. For the first five to six weeks, the entire breast is treated, and remaining treatments are delivered to boost the dose to the lumpectomy site because this is the location where any remaining cancer cells are most likely to reside.

We're often asked if the postoperative radiation is necessary following lumpectomy. The answer is emphatically *yes*. Many studies have demonstrated recurrence rates of 50 percent or higher without it.

Currently, we are looking at a new procedure called *mammocyte therapy*. This entails inserting a catheter-like device at the lumpectomy site during surgery. In the following thirty-six to forty-eight hours, a high-intensity radioactive source is inserted, usually in three sessions. The major advantage of this treatment is that the patient does not have to go for an eight-week course of external treatment. At this time, this procedure is not appropriate for all patients, and many questions remain unanswered. For example, which patients do not require irradiation of the entire breast? Will the cosmetic results be satisfactory, because we are delivering a very high dose in a short time? Nonetheless, we do recommend this procedure to those patients with very small tumors or to those who are not overly concerned about cosmetic results. We would not advise it for younger patients because we do not have long-term follow-up results. With breast cancer, it is standard to have a ten-year follow-up period, which we do not yet have for this treatment.

Most patients who have a mastectomy do not need radiation. However, it is given in some situations following mastectomy. These include: cells found on the margins of the removed breast, large tumors, and involvement of many lymph nodes. These recommendations are always evolving, so it is worthwhile to review options with a radiation oncologist.

The treatment is usually twenty-five to thirty treatments to the chest wall and axilla, plus an additional five or more booster doses to the scar, for a total of approximately 6,000 units. During treatment, the patient is in a supine position, with her arm out of the path of the beam. As much as possible, the beam passes through the breast while avoiding the lung and heart.

Treatment: Chemotherapy and Hormonal Therapy

The majority of breast cancers today are diagnosed at early stages, meaning that the cancer may or may not have spread to lymph nodes, but does not involve skin or muscle. Even in early-stage breast cancer, with small tumors and no involvement of lymph nodes, adjuvant treatments may prolong life and reduce risk of recurrence. These extra treatments include hormone medications, chemotherapy, or both. You will also need to sit down with a medical oncologist to ask about the likelihood of cancer coming back *outside* of the breast area and about what treatments you can consider. In addition, you should ask to what extent each of these treatments may help to lower the risk of the cancer coming back, thereby helping you live longer.

Anyone who has a tumor that is estrogen or progesterone receptor-positive should strongly consider taking a hormone treatment, regardless of whether they are old or young, or pre- or postmenopausal. If a breast cancer is hormone-receptor positive (estrogen or progesterone receptors are present), then a strategy that reduces the effect of estrogen on cancer cells is recommended.

Tamoxifen is the most common agent in current use, and because we have over thirty years' experience with tamoxifen, the benefits as well as the possible side effects are well understood. Tamoxifen interferes with the binding of estrogen to its receptor; therefore, it has what is called an *antiestrogenic effect* on breast tissue and the tumor cells, but may have estrogen-like effects on the bone, lipids, and the uterus. Because of this, tamoxifen is sometimes referred to as a *selective estrogen receptor modulator*, or a *designer estrogen*. Tamoxifen can reduce the risk of cancer recurring in the treated breast, reduce the risk of cancer coming back outside of the breast in distant organs, and reduce the risk of a new cancer in the opposite breast by 50 percent.

Tamoxifen is taken orally in the form of a pill and is usually prescribed for five years. It is generally started after completion of chemotherapy and may be given at the same time as radiation.

For postmenopausal women, a new class of hormonal agents can be considered. These are aromatase inhibitors and include medications such as anastrozole (Arimidex), letrozole (Femara), and exemestane (Aromasin). In premenopausal woman, estrogen is produced primarily by the ovaries. In postmenopausal women, once the ovaries have stopped producing estrogen, estrogen is produced by the conversion of androgens from fatty tissue using an enzyme called aromatase. Aromatase inhibitors work in postmenopausal women to reduce estrogen production so that the hormone does not have a chance to stimulate cancer growth.

Studies have compared anastrozole to tamoxifen and it appears that anastrozole is as good, if not better, than tamoxifen, but long-term follow-up of women on these newer medications is not yet available. Side effects noted in early studies include hot flashes and joint and muscle pain. There is a slightly higher risk of osteoporosis and bone fracture with anastrozole, in contrast with the slight protective effect of tamoxifen. In addition, anastrozole is associated with a lower risk of blood clots than tamoxifen and does not appear to increase the risk of cancer of the uterus.

As previously stated, tamoxifen is generally recommended for five years. This is because studies have shown that two years are better than one, five years are better than two, but ten years are not better than five. In fact, we see a tendency for slight worsening of prognosis after five years, possibly due to the cancer becoming resistant to tamoxifen. In addition, more years of tamoxifen is more time during which serious side effects like blood clots and endometrial cancer may develop. These two side effects in particular are seen more frequently in women over sixty.

The aromatase inhibitor letrozole has been studied in women who have completed five years of tamoxifen and then take letrozole. This strategy is associated with a 43 percent further reduction in the risk of cancer recurring or new cancer developing in the opposite breast. Side effects of letrozole are similar to anastrozole and include hot flashes, joint and muscle pain, and increased risk of osteoporosis.

Studies have recently been reported using aromatase inhibitors such as exemestane, following two to three years of tamoxifen use. This strategy was associated with fewer recurrences compared to five years of tamoxifen, although at this early stage no difference in overall survival has yet been reported.

Many questions remain unanswered. Is it better for a woman to take tamoxifen for five years and then take an aromatase inhibitor? Is it better to use tamoxifen for two to three years and then follow with the aromatase inhibitor? Is it better to start with an aromatase inhibitor in the first place? What is the optimal duration for using the aromatase inhibitors and what are the long-term side effects? Several large studies are underway that we hope will help answer these questions.

A new era of options has emerged, and, where previously we had one standard option for hormonal treatment of early-stage breast cancer, we now have several alternatives and sequences, so it is important to have a detailed discussion with your medical oncologist about what options are best for you.

Chemotherapy for early-stage breast cancer is determined by level of risk based on size of the tumor; the presence or absence of lymph node involvement; and certain features of the cells, seen only under the microscope, associated with more aggressive cancers. The medical oncologist will also take into consideration a woman's age and any medical conditions she may have. In situations in which there is no disease in the lymph nodes, chemotherapy options include four cycles of AC, which is doxorubicin (Adriamycin) and cyclophosphamide (Cytoxan) or six cycles of CMF, which is cyclophosphamide, methetrexate, and 5-fluorouracil (5-FU). The cycles are typically every three weeks.

In situations in which the lymph nodes are involved, we generally recommend longer regimens of chemotherapy. Some treatment plans last six months and include AC followed by paclitaxel (Taxol) or CAF (cyclophosphamide, Adriamycin, and 5-FU).

In 2003, a large study was published that looked at using the same doses of drugs as in AC followed by Taxol but giving them every *two* weeks instead of every *three* weeks, a strategy called *dose-dense treatment*. In order to give the chemotherapy every two weeks, *growth factor* support was necessary. The side effects were not considerably greater but the reduction in risk of relapse and the survival were improved. Other options for women with node-positive cancer include TAC (the docetaxel [Taxotere], Adriamycin, and cyclophosphamide) or combinations substituting epirubicin for Adriamycin.

The ideal chemotherapy combination continues to be an area of active research, so be sure to ask about clinical trials that may be appropriate for you. Even if you choose not to participate, a discussion of active clinical trials can help you gain a better understanding of why certain drugs are recommended and what side effects can be expected.

To summarize, systemic treatment may be: a hormone medication alone for the lowest risk, estrogen receptor-positive women; chemotherapy alone in estrogen receptor-negative patients; or both chemotherapy and hormonal therapy in estrogen receptor-positive patients considered moderate to high risk. Chemotherapy is given first; after chemotherapy is completed, hormonal treatment can start. (Radiation, if it is planned, also follows completion of all chemotherapy but can be given simultaneously with hormonal treatments.)

Some patients at extremely low risk of cancer coming back (less than 10 percent) may choose not to have systemic treatments of any kind. You and your medical oncologist will decide based on your health and age, your risk of cancer coming back, and the degree of benefit you can expect to derive from any given treatment. These are difficult decisions, but the ultimate decision is yours.

Locally advanced breast cancers involve skin or muscle and are approached differently than early-stage breast cancers. For example, it is necessary to shrink the tumor before surgery can be done, usually by using preoperative or *neoadjuvant* chemotherapy or hormonal therapy. This means that chemotherapy is given first to reduce the tumor as much as possible, and then a mastectomy is done. When the wound heals, radiation to the chest wall follows. The same chemotherapy medications and combinations are used in these cases as are used for early-stage breast cancer.

Although in most cases chemotherapy is given as the initial treatment, in elderly women or women with significant medical problems hormonal agents, such as tamoxifen or an aromatase inhibitor, may be given first. If these treatments are not successful in shrinking the tumor, then radiation may be used prior to surgery. In these locally advanced cancers, it is important that surgery is *not* done first because the risk of recurrence and treatment failure is extremely high if surgery is done first. Here, the multidisciplinary approach to treatment and planning is especially important. Because all three modalities will be used (surgery, radiation, and systemic treatments), all three specialties should be consulted prior to starting any treatment.

Metastatic breast cancers have spread outside of the breast, chest wall, and lymph nodes to involve distant sites, most commonly bone, liver, or lung. At this stage, the cancer is not curable but is still *treatable*, much like a chronic illness. For a few women, the cancer is found to have spread at the time that the breast tumor is found, but for most women this news comes months to years later. Often, women feel more devastated with this news than they did when they were first diagnosed.

When cancer has metastasized, many patients ask for the most aggressive treatment possible. However, the goals of treatment are different and approach to decision making is very individualized. Each treatment needs to be considered in its totality, including how likely it is to work, but also what side effects can be expected and how the treatment affects day-to-day quality of life. Each patient should think about what is most important to her.

Patients must weigh the pros and cons of, for example, oral medications they can take at home versus intravenous medications that are given in the clinic. Some patients may want to avoid medications that cause nausea or lead to hair loss. By thinking about priorities, you and your family, together with your medical oncologist, can choose an effective treatment that maximizes your quality of life.

Hormone agents are highly effective in women with metastatic breast cancer that is estrogen or progesterone receptor-positive. These hormone agents are generally considered first, because they work well while having few side effects. In addition to tamoxifen and aromatase inhibitors (see above), another strategy involves using a drug that destroys the estrogen receptor. This drug is called fulvestrant (Faslodex) and is administered as a monthly injection.

Chemotherapy for metastatic breast cancer is considered for women whose tumors are estrogen receptor-negative; women whose tumors are estrogen receptor-positive but who have been resistant to hormonal therapy; or women whose tumors are estrogen receptor-positive and whose disease is rapidly progressing in critical organs such as the liver. Chemotherapy can be given as single agents, tried one at a time and continued as long as they are working and side effects are tolerable. Alternatively, combinations of drugs may be given, often similar to the combinations used for early-stage disease. Active drugs include: Taxol, Taxotere, capecetabine (Xeloda), vinorelbine (Navelbine), gemcitabine (Gemzar), or liposome forms of doxorubicin, such as Doxil.

In women who have metastatic disease, it is crucial to know whether or not the tumor over-expresses the *Her-2 neu* oncogene. In those 23 to 30 percent for which this is the case, it is important to add the monoclonal antibody *Herceptin* to the treatment regimen. Herceptin is most effective when used in combination with a chemotherapeutic drug or combination, although it can be used alone. Active combinations include Herceptin and either Taxol or Taxotere; Herceptin and Navelbine; or Herceptin, Carboplatinum, and Taxol.

Once again, ask about clinical trials. This may be an opportunity to get a new biologic agent, a targeted treatment, or a new drug that is not yet commercially available. You can get more information about clinical trials by logging on to the website for the National Cancer Institute: cancer.gov/search/clinical_trials.

Side Effects of Radiation

Side effects of radiation therapy to the breast include some moderate skin reddening over the breast, often extending to the surface of the breast where it rubs against the chest wall. This rubbing makes the skin especially vulnerable to irritation. Fair-skinned women generally experience greater skin irritation than those with darker skin.

We usually initially advise patients to use a hypoallergenic or aloe moisturizing cream because the radiation will cause skin dryness. When the skin develops redness, we then prescribe a hydrocortisone preparation or other commercial preparations such as Biafine or Aquaphor. If skin breakdown occurs, we then advise a sulfadiazine cream.

Skin creams, along with deodorants, should be removed before each radiation treatment because they can add to the irritating effect of the radiation beam. Improved equipment means that skin irritations are generally not very troublesome and can be compared to a mild sunburnlike reddening. The darkened area will gradually peel and return to its normal shade in a few months. Talcum powder and cornstarch products can relieve the itching that results from the skin peeling. When skin reactions occur, they generally begin in the second or third week of treatment, and skin-care ointments can be applied at that time.

Some women complain of some mild soreness, tenderness, and pain in the breast. This discomfort is generally relieved by mild over-the-counter pain medication, such as aspirin or Tylenol. Occasionally, women complain about mild fatigue toward the end of the treatment course—the fifth through seventh weeks. However, this, as well as the other symptoms mentioned above, disappear within two or three weeks following completion of the radiation-treatment course. Some patients (about 10 percent) who have had surgery in the underarm area to evaluate lymph nodes will develop some swelling in the affected arm. This can be minimized with exercises, such as squeezing a ball or "walking" that arm up a wall.

Many women do not experience any significant side effects while under treatment, and most symptoms are reported as annoying rather than serious. For the most part, these patients are able to carry on normal schedules and lead their usual lifestyles.

In addition to the immediate side effects described above, there may be some long-term changes. In some women, the skin of the treated breast may permanently thicken; in others it may become thin. There may also be some depigmentation of the nipple and adjacent tissue. There will be some internal scarring of the breast, which may cause firmness in the tissue and a slight reduction in breast size.

Side Effects of Chemotherapy and Hormonal Therapy

Some side effects are associated with hormonal therapy using *tamoxifen*. Hot flashes are the most commonly reported side effect and occur in approximately 40 percent of women on the drug. In younger women, tamoxifen may be associated with irregular menstrual periods; however, pregnancy may still be possible, so young women need to use nonhormonal contraception to avoid pregnancy during the years they take tamoxifen. Some women notice mild nausea during the first few days on tamoxifen, but this generally disappears after a few days. Some women may find it helpful to take the medication with food or to experiment with taking it at different times of the day.

Less common side effects include abdominal bloating, leg cramps, headache, and ankle swelling. Weight gain is generally not associated with tamoxifen alone but is common in women who have received chemotherapy for breast cancer and is also seen in women after menopause. It is possible that the tendency to gain weight may also be affected by such additional factors as hormonal influence and age. Studies have shown that healthy women who took tamoxifen for five years for prevention did not show a significant difference in weight gain than seen in women who took a placebo.

Fortunately, serious side effects from tamoxifen are rare. They include a slight increased risk of developing blood clots, but this risk is less than 1 percent and is similar to the risk reported with estrogen therapy. If a woman has a history of prior blood clots or her doctor believes she is at particularly high risk for developing blood clots, then alternative hormonal agents such as Arimidex (see below) should be considered. Because of its estrogenlike effects on the uterus, tamoxifen can be associated with ovarian cysts and, very rarely, uterine cancer.

The risk of developing cancer of the uterus for a fifty-year-old woman is 1 in 1,000; the risk of developing endometrial (uterine) cancer for a fifty-year-old woman who takes tamoxifen is 2 in 1,000. So, although the risk is double, it remains an uncommon event. Generally, endometrial cancer makes itself known by irregular vaginal bleeding, or bleeding that you don't expect and that occurs outside of normal periods. Thus, women on tamoxifen who have not previously had hysterectomies need close gynecological follow-up, and we recommend routine yearly exams. If a woman has symptoms such as abnormal bleeding, prompt evaluation is needed. At that time, the gynecologist may choose to do an endometrial ultrasound or biopsy. However, studies have shown that women who are not having symptoms such as abnormal bleeding do not need these tests just because they are on tamoxifen. Finally, tamoxifen can be associated with a high risk of cataracts, so we recommend eye exams every one to two years.

Side effects of *anastrozole* include hot flashes and joint and muscle pain. There is a slightly higher risk of osteoporosis and bone fracture with anastrozole, in contrast with the slight protective effect of tamoxifen. In addition, anastrozole is associated with a lower risk of blood clots than tamoxifen and does not appear to increase the risk of uterine cancer.

Side effects of *letrozole* are similar to those associated with anastrozole and include hot flashes, joint and muscle pain, and increased risk of osteoporosis.

Side effects of adjuvant chemotherapy are generally temporary. Some women may experience vein irritation, prompting them to consider an indwelling catheter, which eases the administration of the chemotherapy drug. With Adriamycin, hair loss occurs by the second to fourth week of treatment; in some individuals this may include loss of body hair, eyebrows, and eyelashes.

Nausea, vomiting, mouth sores, and fatigue may also occur. Blood counts need to be watched carefully; low white blood-cell counts are common and may increase risk of infection. Anemia is not a common side effect of chemotherapy for breast cancer.

Combinations that include taxanes (either Taxol or Taxotere) may have mild and generally reversible neurologic side effects, such as numbness or tingling in the fingers or toes. These drugs are also associated with a slight risk of allergic reaction, so medications (including the steroid Decadron) are given just prior to treatment to avoid this. Some people experience muscle and joint pains two to five days after the treatment is given.

Chemotherapy may cause changes in the nails, including discoloration of the nails and infection in the nail beds. Excessive tearing and blockage of the tear ducts also may occur.

Although most people assume that chemotherapy leads to weight loss, some women receiving chemotherapy for early-stage breast cancer actually gain weight. For some women, the nausea is similar to what they experienced while pregnant and they assume they should eat something to help control it. The important point is to try to maintain your weight during treatment. It is certainly not the time to diet, but gaining a lot of weight is not beneficial either.

Early menopause is the most common long-term side effect of adjuvant chemotherapy. Young women may become infertile and experience menopause earlier than usual (premature menopause). Women under age forty may continue to have regular menstrual periods; women over forty may experience abrupt cessation of menses during chemotherapy, which means that they may need to deal with the side effects of menopause at the same time as they cope with the side effects of chemotherapy. Symptoms of menopause include hot flashes, sleep disturbances, vaginal dryness, and mood swings.

Other long-term side effects of adjuvant chemotherapy are uncommon. However, the drug Adriamycin may affect the ability of the heart to pump. Fortunately, the risk of this occurring is low with the doses generally used for adjuvant treatment for breast cancer. This is particularly true in women who have normal heart function to begin with. Chemotherapy can very rarely be associated with blood diseases and *extremely* rarely with leukemia.

Chemotherapy used in the treatment of metastatic disease may be associated with similar side effects described above. In addition, the drug Xeloda can cause "hand-foot syndrome," which is characterized by redness, drying, and cracking of the skin and nails. Products known as "bag balm," skin moisturizers, and pyridoxine can sometimes help.

Some drugs used to treat metastatic breast cancer, such as Navelbine and Gemzar, may actually have minimal side effects and are usually well tolerated.

Follow-Up and Outlook

What happens after all the treatment is done? Most women ask how they will know if their cancer comes back and how they will be monitored during the years ahead. To begin with, many possible tests can be performed. While some are important, such as mammography, others, such as CAT scans and bone scans, do not contribute to longer survival rates and may lead to unnecessary anxiety, additional tests, and biopsies. The American Society of Clinical Oncology (ASCO) has published guidelines, "A Patient's Guide to Follow-Up Care for Breast Cancer." You can view this document on their website. (See asco.org, the "People Living with Cancer" section.)

It is important to see your cancer specialist for regular checkups. Medical oncologists and surgeons often do these checkups, while radiation oncologists may see the patients only for the first one to two years. Sometimes the checkups can be rotated among your team of cancer specialists. Although your family doctor should continue to see you for routine physical exams, it is still important to see a cancer specialist, who will be particularly aware of issues important to breast cancer survivors.

During the first three years after finishing treatment, you should have a checkup no less than every three to six months. During these visits it is important for you to share with your doctor any new symptoms you may be experiencing. For example, do you have any breast lumps or changes in your breast or chest region? Are you experiencing any persistent bone pain? Any problems breathing? Any abdominal pain or bloating that does not go away? Unexplained weight loss? In addition to carefully examining the breasts, your doctor will do a full physical exam.

After the first three years, these visits can be less frequent, perhaps every six to twelve months for the next two years. After five years, an annual checkup is sufficient for a routine exam. However, if you are experiencing any new symptoms, you should let your doctor know and arrange to be seen for evaluation. Although most recurrences happen in the first two to three years, they can happen much later on, even up to ten or more years after initial diagnosis and treatment.

Mammography is an important part of your follow-up. If you are treated with breast-conserving therapy, then you will have a mammogram of the treated breast six months after completing radiation. After that, mammograms are generally done yearly, although your doctor may recommend them at additional times if any questions arise during your clinical breast examination. If you have had a mastectomy, then every year you will need a mammogram of the opposite breast.

Routine gynecological examinations are also important, and women taking tamoxifen need to be especially careful about telling their doctors about any abnormal bleeding.

If you have any symptoms, or if your doctor finds any abnormalities on your physical exam, then appropriate tests will be ordered. These may include blood tests, x-rays, bone scans, MRIs, or CT scans. However, if you are feeling fine and your exam is normal then these tests are not recommended.

The work of identifying a blood test that is sensitive and specific enough to be helpful in follow-up is an active area of current research but, unfortunately, at this time no such test exists. Blood tests called tumor markers CA 27-29, CA 15-3, and CEA are not recommended for routine follow-up because they are often normal when cancer has already spread, and they may be abnormal when there are no clinical signs of cancer. In other words, frequent false positive and false negative results make them unreliable.

Cancer of the Cervix

The cervix is the lower portion of the uterus, and it connects that organ with the vagina. Cervical cancer is biologically different from that occurring in the rest of the uterus and is, therefore, discussed separately. Cancer of the cervix can often be detected in its early stages because we have the Pap smear available as a diagnostic tool. This test allows cells that are shed by the cervix to be analyzed for the presence of cancer. A sexually transmitted virus known as human papillomavirus (HPV) is now thought to cause many cervical cancers. HPV is also associated with genital warts.

Treatment

Fortunately, most cervical cancers are found early and have an excellent outlook. They may be treated with surgery alone, or with combination chemotherapy and radiation. The specific treatment that is recommended takes into consideration not just the cancer, but also a woman's desire to retain her ability to bear children in the future.

Treatment for this condition is very individualized, because many treatment options are available depending on the total clinical situation. In its early stage, the treatment of cervical cancer is not complex. Localized surgery to remove the area affected by the cancer is usually all that is necessary. (Fertility is not affected.) When more of the cervix is involved, the uterus, the fallopian tubes, and sometimes the ovaries are removed.

If there is concern about a higher risk of recurrence, then surgery, chemotherapy, and radiation are all used. In more advanced cervical cancers, chemotherapy and radiation are given together prior to surgery to shrink the tumor first, thus allowing for less extensive surgery.

When cancer spreads beyond the cervix, the lymph nodes in the pelvis and upper vagina are frequently affected, and radiation and chemotherapy are the usual treatments. (The human body has thousands of lymph nodes whose function is to filter elements that are foreign to the body—infection and cancer, for example. Because they are so widely distributed throughout the body, lymph nodes are often affected when cancer spreads beyond its original site.)

Radiation. Radiation treatments may be both external and internal. External radiation is delivered to the outside of the body in the conventional manner. Internal radiation, or brachytherapy, consists of placing radioactive material, commonly referred to as "sources," in the vagina. The decision to use one or the other method of radiation is based on each patient's clinical situation. Patients who are not considered candidates for surgery, or who have more advanced disease, are treated with a combination of external and internal radiation. Sometimes a patient may have surgery but require postoperative radiation because of findings on the specimen. There are also cases in which both radiation and chemotherapy are required.

A total dose of 5,000 to 6,000 units of external radiation may be delivered in a five- to seven-week period. Treatment is delivered through portals to the front, the back, and the sides of the pelvis.

By placing radioactive sources into the vagina, very high doses can be delivered to the tumor. This procedure may be performed by placing specialized applicators into the cervix and vagina and then placing radioactive cesium into this applicator. The sources are left in for twenty-four to forty-eight hours. This procedure requires anesthesia and hospitalization.

The radioactive material is very powerful and lethal to the cancer cells. However, some of the radioactive energy escapes beyond the body and is considered a potential hazard to others if exposure is prolonged. Therefore, hospitals take precautions to minimize this risk and to insure the safety of visitors and hospital staff. As a result, patients stay in isolation except for necessary visits by health-care providers.

Quite recently, an alternate method of administering internal radiation has been introduced in the United States, although it has already gained wide popularity in Europe and Asia. The method involves inserting the radioactive sources but the treatment is delivered on an outpatient basis, thus avoiding the complications and cost associated with general anesthetic and a hospital stay. Satisfactory results have been achieved with five treatments, which are combined with external radiation therapy. It has been demonstrated that this rapid, high-dose method is as effective as the traditional low-dose treatment previously described. However, it involves extensive technical and nursing support staff.

Chemotherapy. Chemotherapy in combination with radiation is superior to radiation alone for patients with all but the earliest cervical cancers. Cisplatin is used alone or in combination with other chemotherapy drugs, including 5-FU, hydroxyurea, and combinations of vincristine and bleomycin.

In advanced cervical cancer, cisplatin is often used alone, although newer combinations have been very promising. Cisplatin may be combined with topotecan (Hycamtin) and has been shown to lead to similar side effects but is more likely to improve survival with recurrent disease.

Side Effects of Radiation

Diarrhea and urinary frequency usually occur two to three weeks into treatment. The diarrhea can be treated with medications such as Lomotil and Imodium A-D; urinary frequency is treated with medications such as Pyridium and Ditropan. Irritation of the skin over the area receiving radiation can be treated with skin creams and cortisone ointments.

When radiation is the only treatment, high doses are required, and chronic side effects may result. Intestinal side effects include rectal irritation and ulcers, and sometimes a narrowing of the bowel with some accompanying obstruction. Chronic bladder inflammation and narrowing of the outlet to the bladder are also possible, and there will be a narrowing of the vagina because of scarring of the tissues. When radiation and surgery are used in combination, the severity of side effects is decreased.

The highest incidence of cervical cancer occurs among women forty-five to fifty-five years old. There is often a considerable emotional component in treatment decisions because it is possible that radiation treatment will affect sexual functioning. If cervical cancer has spread to the uterus, necessitating its removal, the loss of the uterus may be perceived as a loss of sexuality. This perception is more pronounced in women of childbearing age if pregnancy is desired in the future. In addition, some of the delayed side effects of radiation may include vaginal scarring with accompanying sexual dysfunction because the vaginal tissues may lose elasticity. Most women seek psychological counseling to cope with this problem, and some women may need surgical procedures to counteract the effects of the scarring. In order to minimize the effects of lost elasticity, the vaginal tissues may need periodic stretching.

Side Effects of Chemotherapy

Chemotherapy drugs used in the treatment of cervical cancer may cause fatigue, hair loss, and loss of appetite. Chemotherapy also affects the white blood-cell counts, which is associated with increased risk of infection. The red blood-cell count may also be affected and result in mild anemia. These effects on the blood counts may be more pronounced when cisplatin is given in combination with other drugs such as topotecan, in which case, side effects may include nausea, vomiting, diarrhea, nail darkening, or mouth sores. In addition, numbness or tingling in the fingers or toes may appear. Cisplatin may affect kidney function, so it is important to stay well hydrated before and after treatment. Sometimes, additional intravenous fluids may be given to protect the kidneys. These chemotherapy drugs also may be associated with infertility and early menopause.

Follow-Up and Outlook

Regular follow-up with a gynecologist is essential. To date, the best hope for curing cervical cancer lies in its early detection through routine gynecological exams, including Pap smears.

Colorectal Cancer

Cancer of the colon usually develops in the tissues that line the inner surfaces of the intestines. Undetected, it extends outward into the local intestinal muscle walls and then to surrounding tissues, lymph nodes, lymph vessels, and blood vessels.

All patients with colon cancer should be made aware of the importance of family history. This is another cancer for which a number of abnormal genes have been isolated and carriers have a 50 to 80 percent risk of developing colorectal cancer. Because genetic testing is expensive and may have social and psychological implications, strict criteria are established in determining who should be tested. Currently the criteria called for in the *Amsterdam Criteria* that cover testing requirements, are three relatives in two generations with at least one being a first-degree relative of the other two and one having colorectal cancer prior to the age of fifty. First-degree relatives are parents and siblings.

People with a family history of *polyposis* (multiple polyps in the colon) are known carriers of genes that predispose them to colon cancer. Another inherited syndrome is *hereditary nonpolyposis colorectal cancer* (HNPCC). These syndromes account for only about 10 percent of all colorectal cancers. Individuals with ulcerative colitis or Crohn's disease also are known to have a high risk of developing colorectal cancer.

Much has been said about the role that fat and fiber play in the occurrence of this cancer, but the jury is still out on this issue. (However, a low-fat diet is still recommended for other known health benefits, including in the prevention of cardiovascular disease.) Likewise, despite many unfounded claims, no herb or dietary supplement has been proven to prevent or cure colorectal cancer. What has been demonstrated is that aspirin use is associated with a reduction in the number and size of recurrent polyps in those who have previously had polyps removed. Therefore, because polyps are thought to be precursors to cancer, aspirin may be a chemopreventative agent.

Rectal bleeding, a change in bowel habits, a narrowing of stools, or change in consistency *may* be signs of colorectal cancer. Some patients may only experience anemia; this is not uncommon with tumors on the right side of the colon. Unfortunately, in too many cases, no symptoms appear until the tumor has progressed to an advanced stage.

Colorectal cancer is the second-leading cause of cancer deaths in the U.S. However, if discovered early, it is very curable. Several screening tools are available. For example, testing stools for occult (not visible) blood is painless and has been shown to pick up cancers in their early phase.

Flexible sigmoidoscopy is a procedure in which a relatively thin fiber-optic tube is inserted into the rectum and can be passed up the left side of the colon. Because 50 to 75 percent of colon cancers occur on the left colon, it's thought that this test will pick up most cancers. A safe test that does not require anesthesia, it does have drawbacks, including the slight risk of bowel perforation. It is also an uncomfortable test and can miss right-sided tumors.

Colonoscopy is considered the gold standard among screening tools for this cancer. In this test, a much longer fiber-optic scope is inserted, allowing visualization of the entire colon. If a small polyp is seen, it can be removed; a large polyp can be biopsied. This procedure requires sedation, and there is a risk of a bowel tear or perforation.

A *barium enema* also shows the entire colon, with much less risk, but it can miss smaller lesions. The combination of a barium enema and a CT scan, called a *virtual colonoscopy*, is a more recent development. It has the advantage of not requiring sedation and it can pick up lesions as small as 1 cm.

Discussions about screening intervals are ongoing. Most experts agree that screening should start at age fifty with colonoscopy. If the colonoscopy is negative, a sigmoidoscopy should be done in five years, and then a repeat colonoscopy in ten years. Those with inflammatory disease or family history should start younger and be examined every three years. As we gain experience, we may see the CT or virtual colonoscopy replacing a colonoscopy.

Treatment

Surgery to remove the tumor and the lymph nodes is the treatment of choice for cancer of the colon proper. For early-stage colon cancer, surgery alone is often curative. After surgery, it is helpful to consult with both a radiation oncologist and a medical oncologist to review the need for extra treatments.

If, following surgical resection, there is no involvement of lymph nodes, then observation may be recommended. However, recommendations for some patients may include chemotherapy or the possibility of participating in a clinical trial that looks at the use of new targeted agents along with chemotherapy. Chemotherapy may be recommended if the tumor is larger, and if viewed under the microscope its features suggest a more aggressive cancer (high-grade, lymphatic, or blood-vessel invasion), or if the cancer has caused blockage of the bowel.

Chemotherapy and radiation may be recommended for large tumors that have broken through the bowel wall (perforation), even in the absence of lymph node involvement. If these tumors are found to be close to the edge of the resected tissue (the tissue surgically removed), then chemotherapy and radiation may also be appropriate.

If lymph nodes were found to be involved at the time of surgery, chemotherapy is routinely recommended. Radiation is added in those cases of larger tumors or tumors that have spread to nearby areas.

In cancers that arise in the rectum or lower sigmoid colon, multiple studies have now confirmed that preoperative radiation and chemotherapy improves survival and local control. Very low-lying tumors that previously required a colostomy can now be treated with chemoradiation prior to surgery; frequently, the chemoradiation treatment gives a sufficient reduction in the mass, thereby allowing the patient to avoid a colostomy. We have also demonstrated that the cure rates for many tumors of the rectum are the same for chemotherapy and radiation combination and for surgery. So, if the cure rates are the same, then patients have the advantage of avoiding a colostomy.

Sometimes it's thought that a patient has a very early lesion and, therefore, he or she does not receive preoperative chemoradiation. If, however, at the time of surgery, the tumor is found to be more advanced, then the patient may receive postoperative treatment.

Radiation. The course of radiation usually consists of a dose of 4,500 to 5,000 units delivered over twenty-five to thirty daily treatments. The patient lies prone on the treatment table and is treated from three to four different angles; the beam shaped in such a way that it spares as much normal tissue as possible from unnecessary radiation. We usually obtain a CT scan and incorporate the images into our treatment planning system and outline the areas to be treated. The computer does the rest. The information is then transmitted to our linear accelerator and the beam is automatically shaped by a device on the unit called a *collimator*.

Chemotherapy. For years, the standard (and in fact the only) chemotherapy for colon cancer was 5-FU, given along with leucovorin (also known as folinic acid) to maximize its effect. This drug combination is given intravenously in the office or may be given by continuous infusion.

In studies focused on drugs to reduce the risk of colon cancer recurrence, promising drug combinations include irinotecan (Camptosar), oxaliplatin (Eloxatin), and a pill form of 5-FU known as *capecitabine* (Xeloda). One combination known as *FOLFIRI* (continuous infusion 5-FU, leucovorin, and irinotecan) may be more effective with, possibly, fewer side effects. Preliminary results of another combination known as *FOLFOX* (5-FU, leucovorin, and oxaliplatin) suggest possible improvements over standard 5-FU and leucovorin for advanced colon cancer.

The drug bevacizumab (Avastin) is a new targeted treatment approved for use in colon cancer and helps prevent the cancer from developing a blood supply from which it can feed. It targets a blood vessel growth factor, so it is more specific than chemotherapy, which affects both normal and cancer cells. Avastin is most effective, however, when given in combination with chemotherapy.

Cetuximab (Erbitux) is another new targeted agent used to treat colon cancer. This agent stops cancer growth by blocking the epidermal growth-factor receptor (see Chapter 6). Cetuximab is used in combination with chemotherapy drugs.

Be sure you review all options and ask your doctor about clinical trials. Even if you do not choose to participate, reviewing clinical trial options will help you understand the status of new treatments. The last decade has brought with it very promising new treatments for colon cancer, and recommendations continue to evolve.

Side Effects of Radiation

The most common side effects of radiation to the colon are cramping and diarrhea, usually appearing toward the end of the second week and early in the third week of treatment. As with other side effects, there is great variation in severity among individual patients. Fortunately, in most cases these symptoms are easily relieved with various antidiarrheal medications. If patients experience rectal irritation, hydrocortisone suppositories or foam may be helpful.

Although dosages of medications are gradually reduced during treatment as symptoms subside, patients should stay on some medication throughout the entire course of radiation treatment once the diarrhea and cramping begin. If symptoms are present when the treatment is complete, then patients can continue the medication for another week or two.

Persistent symptoms warrant barium tests (see Chapter 8) or colonoscopy, because underlying medical conditions such as colitis or diverticulosis may be causing the symptoms. Medications that relieve the gastrointestinal (GI) side effects work best when combined with dietary modifications. In addition, changes in diet may allow the dosages of medications to be reduced. Generally, patients feel best on a low-fat diet that also excludes raw fruits and vegetables. All foods and beverages must be caffeine-free (see Chapter 3).

At about the same time, or shortly after the GI symptoms begin, most patients experience urinary frequency and urgency. They may feel the need to urinate but pass only small amounts of urine. Again, good results are usually achieved with available medications such as Pyridium or Ditropan. Before the medication is given, however, a urinary-tract infection (UTI) must be ruled out, because the symptoms are the same. If an infection is present, antibiotics are administered. (Patients with a prior history of UTIs have an increased chance of developing a UTI during treatment.) Immersing in a warm bath once or twice a day, particularly before going to bed, also helps alleviate urinary urgency and frequency.

Toward the end of treatment (four to five weeks), patients may complain of irritation between the folds of the buttocks and in the rectal area. Cortisone creams are effective in eliminating discomfort, usually within a few days.

Fatigue is another side effect frequently encountered, and unfortunately we have no medications to counteract fatigue. Patients may also experience side effects of the chemotherapy, although nausea is readily controlled. The local GI and GU (genitourinary) effects may be intensified, which then amplifies fatigue. However, in our experience, most patients tolerate this period quite well and many continue working. We generally advise patients to continue as much of their normal routine as possible. In other words, to the extent they can, patients should fit the treatments into their life rather than letting them dominate it.

During treatment, we almost always see lowered blood counts, primarily of the white blood cells and platelets. In a minority of cases, the drop may be severe and require hospitalization and antibiotic coverage to protect against infection.

Side Effects of Chemotherapy

Side effects of standard 5-FU treatment include diarrhea, nausea, mouth sores, or low white blood-cell count, which can lead to risk of infection. Hair loss is uncommon. A rash may sometimes appear on the hands or feet.

Side effects of the drug combinations are similar to those associated with 5-FU and leucovorin (diarrhea, mouth sores, and lowered white blood-cell count), with the additional side effect of sensory neuropathy (numbness and tingling). Oxaliplatin may cause numbness and tingling in the fingers and toes, but this is usually reversible and decreases with time after treatment ends. In some cases, the chemotherapy dose may need to be reduced because of side effects.

Side effects of Avastin include flu-like symptoms (fever, chills, and headache), rash, possible elevated blood pressure (hypertension), and increased tendency to bruise.

Side effects of cetuximab treatments include weakness, breathing difficulties, and abdominal pain.

Follow-Up and Outlook

After completing treatment, you should see your doctor every three months for the first two years, and then every six months for five years. The visit includes taking your history (discussing any symptoms that may be present) and performing a complete physical exam. Blood tests include the CEA, a marker that helps monitor for cancer recurrence. Colonoscopy is done one year following treatment and is repeated the next year if there are any abnormalities such as polyps; if no abnormalities appear, the colonoscopy is repeated every two to three years.

Metastatic Colon Cancer

The multidisciplinary team also is important when colon cancer has metastasized outside the lymph nodes to other organs, including the liver and/or other abdominal tissue and the lungs. Sometimes liver metastases may be resected, or surgically removed; chemotherapy drugs used include combinations of 5-FU, leucovorin, irinotecan, capecitabine, and oxaliplatin. Occasionally, chemotherapy agent may be infused directly into the liver; this procedure is called *hepatic artery infusion*. (See also Chapter 5.)

Esophageal Cancer

The esophagus is the narrow tube that allows food to pass from the throat down to the stomach. It begins in the neck, extends down through the chest, and ends in the upper abdomen at the level of the stomach. Cancer of the esophagus usually develops in the cells that line the organ's inner wall. Because the esophagus is narrow and has very thin walls, small cancers may quickly cause symptoms. A person notices that the passage of food and liquids is obstructed and frequently seeks medical advice because of this change.

Cancer of the esophagus used to be relatively uncommon but over the past decade incidence has increased. Although it remains among the less-common cancers (only 1 percent of all new cancers diagnosed each year in the United States), it brings with it the high mortality rate of 90 percent. Cancer of the esophagus is the most rapidly increasing cancer in the United States when looked at in the group of other cancers we have discussed here such as breast, lung, colon, and prostate.

Much speculation exists as to the cause of this increased incidence, but at this time we have no concrete facts. Most cancer of the esophagus occurs in people over the age of sixty, and an aging population may account for some, but certainly not all, of the increased incidence. Use of alcohol and tobacco products are well-established risk factors, and gastroesophageal reflux (GERD) currently is a known risk factor. Many new effective medications are available to treat GERD, and, in severe cases, surgical procedures can be considered. In addition, a condition known as Barrett's esophagus is definitely a precursor to esophageal cancer. In this condition, the cells of the lower esophagus change to cells that normally line the stomach. This happens over a period of time because of chronic gastric juice reflux. Surgery may be advised if Barrett's esophagus is discovered.

There are two types of cancer of the esophagus—squamous cell carcinoma, which arises in the upper two-thirds of the esophagus, and adenocarcinoma, which arises in the distal (lower) one-third. Cancers in the lower third of the esophagus are more common in the Western countries.

Unfortunately, cancer in the esophagus generally spreads rapidly and usually has affected lymph nodes by the time it is detected. (The human body has thousands of lymph nodes, whose function is to filter elements that are foreign to the body—infections and cancer, for example. Because lymph nodes are so widely distributed throughout the body, they are often affected when cancer begins to spread from its original site to adjacent tissues.) The majority of patients who are diagnosed with cancer of the esophagus have extensive local disease or metastases to distant sites. Cure is generally not possible in these cases.

Treatment

The treatment of esophageal cancer is complex and may involve combining a number of different treatments. When possible, we recommend that newly diagnosed patients see a surgeon, radiation oncologist, and medical oncologist for a multidisciplinary evaluation and treatment plan. The initial evaluation with a treatment team will determine if surgery is an option, and it may also be important in deciding if an individual can receive chemotherapy. In addition, a nutritional evaluation is beneficial before beginning treatment in order to determine additional needs, such as intravenous feeding prior to surgery.

There are a number of different treatment options. If cancer of the esophagus is found at its earliest stages, surgery alone may be curative. There may be situations in which radiation and/or chemotherapy are recommended following surgery, particularly if local lymph nodes were found to contain tumor.

Chemotherapy and radiation may be combined and given prior to surgery. Although it has uncertain benefits and is less commonly done, chemotherapy alone has been given prior to surgery in an attempt to shrink the tumor. However, the combination of chemotherapy and radiation given at the same time does show benefits for patients with locally advanced disease.

Patients who are not able to have surgery may be treated with combined chemotherapy and radiation. Studies indicate that survival and local control benefit with concurrent radiation and chemotherapy. In fact, the Radiation Therapy Oncology Group (RTOG) established the combination of concurrent chemotherapy and radiation for patients with locally advanced esophageal cancer, but who could not have surgery, as the standard of care. It is thought that this treatment is better than radiation alone. In addition, patients live longer and have fewer recurrences in the area of the original tumor.

This treatment is done by combining certain chemotherapy drugs, such as cisplatin, with a continuous infusion of 5-FU given by pump. Radiation treatment usually consists of 5,000 to 6,000 units delivered in twenty-eight to thirty-five daily treatments over a six- to seven-week period. This treatment may be given as definitive treatment by itself or prior to surgery. In as many as 20 to 25 percent of those who receive concurrent chemoradiation, there is no sign of remaining cancer at the time of surgery, and these patients have a particularly good outlook.

When radiation therapy is recommended following surgery, it is usually administered to control growth and reduce symptoms, and is therefore considered palliative. In these cases, there is usually known disease in lymph nodes that surgery can't remove.

Another group of patients is given only radiation therapy. Some patients in this group have only localized disease, and radiation is given to cure the cancer without surgery. In other patients, the cancer is believed to be inoperable, and therefore the palliative treatment is performed to temporarily stop the growth of the tumor and to relieve symptoms.

Radiation treatments generally extend into normal tissue on either side of the known, or visualized, cancer because this type of cancer commonly extends beyond the identified area. In addition, radiation is directed to the adjacent lymph nodes in the esophagus. Treatment is delivered through multiple portals—the front, the back, and each side. On occasion, there is a rotational treatment plan, meaning that the radiation therapy machine rotates around the patient's body. Approximately 5,000 units of radiation are delivered over a six-week period. If there appears to be a good chance for a cure, a higher dose is delivered in seven or eight weeks.

Side Effects of Radiation and Chemotherapy (Combination and Individual Treatment)

Unfortunately, more side effects occur with the combination strategy. These include nausea, mouth sores, and significant irritation of the esophagus. Sometimes this is bad enough to keep a patient from eating or drinking, and it also can cause pain. Some cancer specialists recommend the placement of an enteral feeding tube, or a tube placed into the stomach, so patients are sure to receive adequate fluid and nutrition during the treatment period.

The combination of cisplatin and 5-FU chemotherapy along with radiation can be quite toxic, and many new chemotherapy drugs are being studied in clinical trials to improve upon the results obtained with these two drugs. These clinical trials attempt to find more effective treatments with fewer side effects. Drugs in the taxane family, such as paclitaxel and docetaxel, are used alone or in combination with drugs from the platinum family (cisplatin or carboplatin), with or without using 5-FU, too. Although promising, those combinations may lead to additional side effects. Drugs like the taxanes may cause numbness and tingling and may more severely lower the blood counts.

Other newer drugs being used in the treatment of esophageal cancer include irinotecan, vinorelbine, and oxaliplatin. Irinotecan appears promising in that there is less irritation of the esophagus.

Medical oncologists are also looking at the best ways to combine drugs. The rationale for combining chemotherapy and radiation is to achieve synergy against the cancer—meaning that the combination works more effectively than either treatment by itself. However, we also must be careful that side effects don't increase. Drugs may work differently depending if they are given weekly, daily, or by continuous twenty-four-hour infusion. For example, some drugs are given weekly along with the radiation, and this may help to reduce the possible toxicity.

Radiation therapy to this area of the body may cause acute symptoms of nausea and vomiting, and irritation of the esophagus makes swallowing painful. Patients with this type of cancer generally have poor nutritional status to begin with because the nature of the illness makes normal eating difficult. The onset of these side effects can be the start of a cycle of deterioration that must be managed. It is essential that the radiation oncologist directs dietary changes and prescribes medication to reduce side effects.

Pain medication is used for the esophageal irritation. (Xylocaine Viscous, an anesthetic gel, and common over-the-counter pain tablets are used.) Because of blockage caused by edema (swelling) at the tumor site, patients may have to resort to pureed foods. Sometimes a *percutaneous endoscopic gastrostomy* (PEG), or tube inserted through the abdominal wall into the stomach, is needed so nutrition and hydration can be maintained. In fact, some physicians recommend inserting a PEG prior to beginning treatment because it is easier to insert at that time. Commercially prepared, nutritionally balanced liquid preparations (Ensure, for example), available in pharmacies and food markets, are particularly helpful in maintaining sound nutritional status. Liquid multivitamin and mineral preparations may also be advisable.

Nausea and vomiting may be controlled with an antinausea medication such as Compazine. When these strategies are followed, symptoms usually improve and are tolerable. In most cases, patients are able to complete radiation therapy. When an x-ray test called an *esophagram* is performed halfway through the treatment course, it often reveals significant improvement in the appearance of the esophagus, signaling that the patient is then able to increase intake of solid food.

Delayed complications of radiation therapy may occur many months or years after the treatment is completed. These side effects generally include narrowing or stricture of the esophagus or radiation scarring of the adjacent lung. These long-term side effects are seen infrequently.

If a patient's cancer is advanced at the time of initial diagnosis and it is believed that they are unable to tolerate chemotherapy, a palliative course of radiation may help the patient continue to eat and drink fluids for a period of time. If a patient has a short life expectancy, then a stent, or short tube, is passed through the cancerous areas into the stomach to allow the patient to maintain hydration and nutrition. Sometimes a PEG is performed.

In some cases repeated laser treatments may be used to keep the esophageal lumen, or cavity, open. A procedure known as *photodynamic therapy* can also be used to maintain esophageal function. The patient is given a drug that makes cells sensitive to light and then a laserlike light is focused on the cancerous tissue, thus killing the cancer cells. Another way to sometimes improve swallowing is by expanding, or dilating, the esophagus. This can be done repeatedly if needed.

Follow-Up and Outlook

Best treatment results are obtained when cancer of the esophagus is found early and has not spread to distant sites. Unfortunately, this cancer often is advanced when detected, in which case the outlook is poor. The majority of patients do achieve a relatively good quality of life after their treatment course, especially when they have not had radical surgery.

When radiation is not successful in achieving a satisfactory result, surgery and chemotherapy are still treatment options. Although chemotherapy has been shown to be useful in shrinking tumors, to date, survival rates have not improved. Although we can sometimes control the disease locally, distant metastases are usually responsible for the cause of death. Currently, the only hope for curing this cancer lies in early detection. X-ray esophagrams, endoscopy (examining the esophagus through an inserted tube), and CT scans are used to evaluate the patient's progress.

Head and Neck Cancer

Head and neck cancers are a complex group of tumors, and each site of origin has its own individual biological characteristics. Cancers of the head include tumors of the tongue, gums, the lining of the mouth, tonsils, sinuses, and lymph tissues above the soft palate. Cancers of the neck include those that originate in the larynx, or vocal cords, or in the pharynx, the adjacent soft tissues.

Treating cancers of the head and neck often involves multiple specialties. For example, treatment may include surgery, radiation, and chemotherapy, making a multidisciplinary approach especially important. Because of this, your treatment team may include an ear, nose, and, throat surgeon, and/or a cancer surgeon, and sometimes a plastic surgeon, a radiation oncologist, a medical oncologist, a dentist or an oral surgeon, a dietician, as well as speech and physical therapists.

Before starting treatment, in particular radiation therapy, it is important to be evaluated by a dentist who is familiar with effects of cancer treatments and can help reduce risk of tooth decay and help you maintain optimal oral hygiene. As with all cancers, we treat with cure as the goal; however, with this group of cancers, maintaining function is extremely important, too. Patients are understandably concerned about how they will look after surgery, how treatment will affect the quality of their voice and speech, and whether they will be able to eat normally once treatment is over.

These cancers may be treated with surgery, radiation, and chemotherapy alone or in combination. The specific recommended treatment depends on the type of the cancer and the extent of the cancer, but also takes into consideration the overall health of the individual patient. Surgery may be done first and then followed by radiation, with or without chemotherapy. In some situations, chemotherapy may be given with or without radiation prior to surgery to try to shrink the tumor to allow for a less extensive surgery.

Radiation therapy–treatment plans for each of these cancer groups are in principle quite similar. Therefore, all head cancers will be discussed as one group, and all neck cancers as another. Because tumors and normal tissues are located in a small space near one another, vital structures are either included or excluded from the treatment beam. This depends on the particular clinical situation. Extreme precision is necessary in the treatment of these areas, and therefore the radiation oncologist, the radiation physicist, and the surgeon work closely together and consult with one another often.

Radiation Treatment to the Head

Most primary tumors of the head and neck require doses of 6,000 to 7,000 units delivered in thirty to thirty-five treatments, given on a daily basis for a period of six to seven weeks. They are usually administered through treatment fields on each side of the head, but more complex treatment plans may deliver the radiation through different angles. The locations for the treatment beams are marked with small temporary tattoos, not visible to others.

Radiation may be the only form of treatment, or it may be administered in an attempt to shrink the tumor before surgery, so that less radical tissue need be removed. Radiation may also be used following surgery if cancer remains. The variation in treatment plans depends on many factors, including the original site of the cancer, its size, and the degree to which it has spread to adjacent tissues and lymph nodes. The extent of surgery performed is individualized for each patient. As a general rule, patients with cancers of the head have surgery first, which may include removal of adjacent lymph nodes.

Side Effects of Radiation to the Head

The most common symptom resulting from radiation to the head is dry mouth, caused by decreased production of saliva and drying out the mucous membranes, or the lining of the mouth. The decreased salivary production can lead to rapid deterioration of the person's dental condition. Patients with preexisting dental problems or poor oral hygiene are advised to see a dentist before radiation treatments begin in order to minimize dental side effects. Fluoride treatments, plaque removal, filling cavities, and only necessary tooth extractions should all be done *prior* to treatment. When dental problems exist, infections can result and seriously complicate radiation therapy. Patients who do not need immediate dental work are closely monitored during treatment to insure that decreased saliva does not lead to deterioration of dental health. Routine dental care is recommended, in particular fluoride applications, to insure that dental health status remains satisfactory.

Patients who wear dentures must remove them during treatment, because they interact with the radiation and irritate the mucous membranes in the mouth. Dentures may be replaced after each treatment session. However, the dentures may not fit properly because of the weight loss associated with the disease and its treatment. Once treatment is completed, the dentures may be refitted.

The severity of the dry mouth caused by the radiation can be reduced as much as 30 percent with a relatively new drug, amifostine, which reduces radiation-related injury to salivary glands. The drug is cumbersome to use because it must be given intravenously with each daily radiation treatment; it must also be administered slowly. In addition, it can cause a drop in blood pressure, so the patient must be monitored for that as well.

Sugar-free sour candies, sucking on fruit pits, or using the old remedy of sucking on a button sometimes may make the dry mouth more tolerable. An artificial saliva product such as pilocarpine (Salogen) is helpful, and similar products are constantly being improved. Drugs to stimulate saliva production are being tested and may come on the market shortly. These products act as a lubricant but do not prevent dental problems.

Drinking and eating may aggravate tissues that are already sore because of the radiation. Taste sensations are also altered during radiation treatment to the head, and thus many patients find that the pleasure usually derived from eating is markedly reduced. This side effect, which results both from decreased saliva and from the effects of radiation on the tongue, begins two to three weeks into the course of treatment and lasts throughout the treatment plan. It may be a month or two before taste sensation returns, and the reduced reduction in saliva, as well as the thickened consistency, may persist for months or years after treatment.

Because radiation irritates the tissues lining the mouth, infections may occur that must be treated with antibiotics. If left untreated, local infections may spread to other areas of the body. Oral pain is treated with gels to numb the mouth (Xylocaine Viscous, for example) or other common pain medications. The skin over the treated area often becomes reddened and dry, and, because of the high radiation doses, it may also blister. Skin creams and cortisone ointments are helpful in alleviating these symptoms.

Loss of taste, decreased salivary production, and soreness of the mouth often lead patients to reject food. This sets up a vicious cycle, because the person's nutritional status may have been already compromised by the presence of the painful tumor, which also discouraged eating. Radiation therapy may then aggravate the problem. Family members should attempt to provide nutritional support during this very trying period. Liquid dietary supplements, available at drug stores and food markets, are valuable because they provide nutritional balance but do not require much effort to ingest. We also recommend using an ordinary kitchen blender to make drinks and shakes from cooked or raw vegetables. When tolerated, spices can be added to make these drinks as appealing as possible. Talk with your doctor about the advisability of liquid vitamin and mineral supplements. Your radiation oncologist will monitor your nutritional status and suggest ways to keep calorie intake adequate and balanced.

Radiation oncologists monitor progress by physical examination throughout the course of treatment. The size of the treatment field and the angle of the delivery may be modified, depending on the patient's nutritional status and general health.

Radiation Treatment to the Neck

Radiation therapy to the neck for tumors in the vocal cords and other surrounding structures requires high doses because the tumors may, when large, exhibit some resistance to radiation. Approximately 6,000 to 7,000 units of radiation are usually delivered daily for seven to eight weeks. The treatment beam is directed to each side of the neck, but a more complex approach may be required, depending on the patient's clinical situation.

Radiation may be the only treatment and is usually used for early vocal-cord cancer. It may also be administered in an attempt to shrink the tumor before surgery, thereby allowing less radical removal of the tissues. Radiation may also be used following surgery if cancer remains. The variation in treatment plans depends on many factors, including the original site of the cancer, its size, and the degree to which it has spread to adjacent tissues and lymph nodes. The extent of surgery performed is individualized for each patient. As a general rule, patients with cancer in the neck have surgery first, which may include removal of adjacent lymph nodes.

Side Effects of Radiation to the Neck

About two to three weeks into the treatment course, difficulty in swallowing and hoarseness may begin. Some patients are hoarse before therapy begins, particularly those with vocal-cord cancers. Patients also complain of dryness in the tissues and thickening of the secretions in the throat. They may also experience some pain, particularly when swallowing. This can be partially alleviated by avoiding hot or cold liquids and foods. If necessary, the diet can be further modified by following the guidelines discussed in the previous section that dealt with cancers occurring in the head. However, most patients being treated with radiation for cancers of the neck are able to tolerate foods.

Room humidifiers and drinking plenty of fluids can help control excess phlegm in the throat. Throughout treatment, everything ingested should be room temperature. In addition, alcohol should be avoided, and patients must not smoke.

Some reddening of the skin over the area of treatment may occur because of the high dose of radiation necessary to control the cancer. Soothing skin creams or cortisone creams will alleviate discomfort. A throat infection may develop as well, and may cause cancer-bearing lymph nodes in the neck to become infected, which further exacerbates the patient's discomfort. Pain medication and antibiotics are used to treat these symptoms. Patients are also encouraged not to strain their voice if hoarseness is a problem. These side effects may be troublesome throughout treatment, but they gradually subside once the radiation therapy is complete, and usually disappear in a month or so.

Chemotherapy for Head and Neck Cancers

Chemotherapy may be given before surgery or after. Cisplatin is the most commonly used chemotherapy drug for early-stage head and neck cancers. This drug may be given concurrently with radiation. In head and neck cancers that have metastasized, chemotherapy drugs may be given alone as a single agent or in combinations. Drugs that are commonly given alone include cisplatin, carboplatin, docetaxel, paclitaxel, 5-FU, ifosfamide and methotrexate. Frequently used combinations include cisplatin or carboplatin in combination with 5-FU. Cisplatin or carboplatin are also sometimes combined with paclitaxel or docetaxel.

Side Effects of Chemotherapy to the Head and Neck

Side effects of chemotherapy used to treat head and neck cancers include nausea and vomiting, diarrhea or constipation, mouth sores, and hair loss. As with most chemotherapy drugs, lowered white blood-cell count may occur, thus increasing risk of infection. Sense of taste may be altered, and patients may experience fatigue. Attention to nutrition, mouth hygiene, and infection control is key. Dietary changes may be required, and may involve choosing soft or pureed foods; in some cases, intravenous feeding may be recommended. When chemotherapy is given along with radiation, some of these side effects may be more pronounced.

Follow-Up and Outlook

The surgeon or radiation oncologists examine the mouth and throat to evaluate results of treatment of head and neck cancers. In many instances, it is necessary for an ear, nose, and throat surgeon to insert a tube to look at areas that can't be seen directly by the naked eye, a procedure called *endoscopy*. It is also essential to have periodic follow-up physical examinations.

CT scans and MRIs of the head and neck are valuable because they can image tissues not seen by the naked eye or endoscopy. Lymph nodes are also examined with CT scans and MRIs (see Chapter 8).

People who have had one cancer in the head and neck region are at higher risk of getting a second, new cancer in that region. This means that it is not too late to quit smoking or drinking. Doing so helps reduce side effects during treatment and also helps to reduce risk of new cancers.

Because radiation to the neck may affect the thyroid gland, individuals who have received radiation to the neck should have blood tests done to monitor their thyroid function. If the thyroid is found to be underactive, thyroid replacement hormone is usually prescribed.

Hodgkin's Disease

Hodgkin's disease is believed to originate from abnormal cells in the lymph nodes. The human body has thousands of lymph nodes, which filter elements that are foreign to the body—common infections and cancer, for example. Virtually everyone has had a throat infection that caused lumpy swellings on the sides of the neck. The lymph nodes have filtered the draining infection and have swollen in response to this invasion of a foreign element.

When Hodgkin's disease originates in lymph nodes, these normally small structures grow, but the swellings are often painless. More than 80 percent of patients with Hodgkin's disease will have lymph node swelling in the neck; 50 percent of patients will have lymph node swelling in the mediastinum, or middle portion of the chest.

Hodgkin's disease has a marked tendency to affect lymph nodes in adjacent body tissues. For example, if lymph nodes in the upper neck are involved first, the next affected areas will likely be the lower neck and the upper shoulder area, the chest, and the underarm region. This physiological fact is of great importance when planning treatment.

In most patients, Hodgkin's disease does not cause symptoms other than the swelling of the lymph nodes. However, approximately one-third of Hodgkin's patients have fevers, weight loss, and anemia. The presence of these symptoms usually indicates a more serious stage of the disease.

Treatment

Prior to treatment, patients undergo a diagnostic workup to evaluate the extent or stage of the disease. At one time, surgery was performed to remove the spleen and to determine the extent of the disease in the abdomen and pelvis. Today, with CT scans and PET scans available, this surgery is not necessary in most cases.

Hodgkin's disease may be treated with chemotherapy alone, radiation alone, or a combination of the two. The treatment of Hodgkin's disease is dependent on the health status of the patient, the stage of the disease, the size of the lymph nodes, the cancer cell type, and symptoms. Some patients report fever, night sweats, or weight loss. Age is also taken into consideration. Children are almost always treated with chemotherapy. Radiation therapy is used sparingly in children because radiation can affect bone development; that is, the growth plates in bone are affected by radiation, resulting in skeletal deformities. By adulthood, the growth plates have fused, and so there is no longer a problem. In those children for whom radiation is advisable, techniques can be used to minimize the developmental deformities.

Once the diagnosis and stage of the disease is established, a team of cancer specialists determines the most appropriate treatment or combination of treatments. The cure rates for Hodgkin's disease are high, and the more recent research focuses on finding ways to reduce the side effects of the treatments without compromising the high cure rates. Some patients may be advised to have chemotherapy alone or radiation therapy alone. Other patients are advised to have both treatments. This means undergoing chemotherapy for a shorter period of time and having radiation therapy directed to a smaller field. In this way, side effects from each may be less. In other situations in which the area of disease is large or "bulky," longer courses of chemotherapy will be recommended, followed by radiation therapy.

The usual dose of radiation is 3,000 to 3,600 units delivered in fifteen to twenty daily treatments depending on the size of the area treated and how well the patient tolerates treatment.

Chemotherapy used to treat Hodgkin's disease is given as a combination of drugs. One of the most commonly used combinations today is called *ABVD* and includes the drugs doxorubicin (Adriamycin), bleomycin, vinblastine, and dacarbazine. Another commonly used combination is called *Stanford V* and includes mechlorethamine, doxorubicin, vinblastine, vincristine, bleomycin, etoposide, and prednisone. With the Stanford V protocol, growth factors are always used to help the white blood cells recover from the effects of chemotherapy. With ABVD, growth factors are used only if needed.

In situations in which Hodgkin's disease has recurred and is resistant to standard treatments, bone marrow transplant may be suggested. The source of the bone marrow cells may be from the patient, collected as stem cells, or from another donor. (See Chapter 6.) High-dose chemotherapy is given that eradicates the patient's bone marrow; then the patient is rescued with the infusion of stem cells or bone marrow.

Acute Side Effects of Radiation

The acute side effects of radiation therapy to the chest and neck include some hair loss on the back of the head, occasionally nausea, sore throat, some dryness in the mouth, and mild reddening of the skin over the areas being treated. Dryness of the mouth can be alleviated by drinking plenty of fluids and by sucking on sour, hard candy. Skin irritation can be relieved with a soothing skin cream, and nausea can be treated with Compazine. Occasionally, diarrhea occurs when treatment is directed to the abdomen; it can be treated with Lomotil.

With the exception of the hair loss, these side effects are easily controlled with medication. They are acute, meaning that they appear during the treatment course but promptly disappear when radiation therapy is completed. These side effects are generally more of an annoyance than a serious problem.

Throughout the course of treatment, the patient's blood count is carefully monitored because the large radiation fields, which include the bones, affect the bone marrow. This can result in lowered white blood-cell count, which then compromises the body's ability to fight infection. Platelets, another type of blood cell manufactured in the marrow, may also be reduced, causing small hemorrhages to occur. Treatment may need to be interrupted until the blood count returns to normal.

Acute Side Effects of Chemotherapy

Chemotherapy used to treat Hodgkin's disease affects the blood counts and in particular may reduce the number of white blood cells, which may lead to increased risk of infection. Growth factors called *granulocyte-colony stimulating factors* (G-CSF), such as Neupogen or Neulasta, may increase the speed of white blood-cell recovery, thereby reducing the risk of infection and helping the patient to continue chemotherapy on schedule. The uses of G-CSF may be associated with achiness in the bones as the blood counts recover. Chemotherapy may also lead to fatigue and anemia, and hair loss is common. Other symptoms may include sores that develop in the mouth or the lining of the intestines, and occasionally, patients experience diarrhea, nausea, or vomiting.

Chronic Effects of Treatment

Some chronic complications may result from the extensive radiation treatment to the lymph nodes. For example, thyroid dysfunction is possible; however, it can be treated should it occur. Persistent dryness of the mouth may result in an increase of dental problems that require regular follow-up care. On occasion, pneumonia may develop as a result of radiation to the lung, and cortisone medication may be required to treat the condition. Similarly, there is a possibility that a radiation-induced heart condition may occur, usually involving fluid formation in the lining of the tissues around the heart. Medication or surgery may be necessary to correct this condition. Although carefully blocking healthy tissues during treatment reduces the incidence of these complications, they are not entirely avoidable.

Chemotherapy combinations containing Adriamycin may be associated with red discoloration of the urine, which is a temporary side effect. However, Adriamycin may affect the heart's ability to pump. For this reason, the total cumulative dose of Adriamycin is monitored because, when given at higher doses, in more numerous cycles, or in individuals with preexisting heart disease, there is a slight increased risk of developing heart disease. Tests that measure the heart's function may be done intermittently during treatment.

After initial treatment, bleomycin may cause allergic reactions characterized by fever, chills, difficulty breathing, or low blood pressure. By giving a test dose and/or medications prior to the chemotherapy, this can usually be avoided. Higher cumulative doses of bleomycin can cause scarring of the lungs, thereby affecting lung function.

Most male patients and half of the female patients become sterile as a result of the combination of radiation and chemotherapy. An operation known as oophoropexy, which moves a woman's ovaries out of the path of the radiation beam, may be an option, depending on the individual's clinical situation. Some male patients may consider placing sperm in a sperm bank before undergoing radiation treatment or chemotherapy. However, for reasons not well understood, some patients (both men and women) with advanced Hodgkin's disease may already be infertile as a result of their disease. Fertility is a complex issue for patients with Hodgkin's disease, and we urge patients to seek fertility counseling before starting treatment.

The most serious potential side effect of treatment of Hodgkin's disease is the possible development of another cancer years later. When chemotherapy and radiation are given together in higher doses, the bone marrow and immune system may be weakened, allowing for the possibility that non-Hodgkin's lymphomas and leukemias may develop later. Leukemia was noted with the use of a drug combination known as MOPP (nitrogen mustard, vincristine, procarbazine, and prednisone). At one time, MOPP was a commonly used chemotherapy combination, but it is now rarely used. New chemotherapy combinations were developed with the goal of minimizing this risk of another cancer.

Sarcomas, or tumors of the bone or soft tissues, may occur within the radiation field years later. Young women and girls who were treated with mantle irradiation (extensive fields to the chest) are at higher risk of developing breast cancer ten to twenty years later. Radiation fields are now more selective, limiting exposure of normal tissues. Today's strategies focus on limiting the radiation field and carefully selecting chemotherapy drugs and duration of treatment to continue to achieve high cure rates but avoid these serious complications.

Follow-Up and Outlook

Follow-up evaluation of the treatment results includes blood tests and physical examination of the lymph nodes and organs such as the spleen and liver. PET scans and CT scans of the chest and abdomen are particularly useful for evaluating the size of chest and abdominal lymph nodes (see Chapter 8).

Radiation therapy and multiagent chemotherapy and aggressive combinations of both treatment methods have resulted in significant improvements in the five-year survival rate for Hodgkin's disease. Over the past several decades, the survival rate has more than doubled, and Hodgkin's disease is now considered curable in early stages as well as when it is moderately advanced. The focus of clinical trials today is to reduce the side effects of treatment while maintaining the high cure rates.

Lung Cancer

Lung cancers most often develop in the cells that line the bronchial tubes and often initially cause few symptoms. Some patients may complain of a chronic cough or unexplained weight loss, while others develop a pneumonia that does not heal in spite of treatment.

A biopsy is necessary to make a definitive diagnosis, and it can be accomplished in one of two ways. In the first, a flexible tube is passed into the bronchial tree of the lung, enabling the physician to obtain a small piece of tissue to examine. In the second, cells that have sloughed off from the tumor into the bronchial tree are collected. A fine needle is passed through the chest under local anesthesia to the suspected tumor with the guidance of a CT scan (see Chapter 8). A CT scan will also be performed to see if the tumor has spread beyond the lung into the adjacent lymph nodes in the center of the chest. (Human beings have thousands of lymph nodes, which act as filters for elements that are foreign to the body—infections and cancer, for example. Because lymph nodes are so widely distributed, they are often affected when cancer begins to spread from its original site to adjacent tissues.) A PET scan is frequently performed to determine if there is regional or distant spread. The abdomen and brain may also be scanned to determine if additional organs are involved. This evaluation is necessary before physicians can design a treatment plan that is appropriate for the particular stage of the disease.

It is rare for patients with lung cancer to feel very ill from the cancer itself at the time they begin radiation therapy. The exception occurs when the cancer has obstructed the bronchial tubes or caused extensive pressure on the major blood vessels. Difficulties arise when the tumor cells compete with the normal cells for nutrition, in which case the patients' fatigue and illness are caused by poor nutritional status and general malaise. In many cases, the tumor is significantly arrested and patients note a marked improvement in the way they feel within a month or two following completion of treatment. The major problems that arise with lung cancer are those that occur when the cancer spreads to distant sites. In these cases, the symptoms may be very debilitating.

Treatment

Lung cancer treatment generally involves more than one treatment modality and may include surgery, radiation, and chemotherapy. Lung cancer is divided into two categories: small cell, or oat cell, lung cancer and non-small-cell lung cancer. Non-small-cell lung cancer (NSCLC) includes the majority of lung cancer. Staging is important in order for you and your team of doctors to determine the best treatment for you.

For early-stage lung cancer (Stages I and IIA), surgery or radiation are used alone or together. For Stage IIB, surgery or radiation is used alone, together, or with chemotherapy. Surgery is used to remove the tumor in these early-stage lung cancers in which there is no evidence that the cancer has spread outside of the chest region. The chest surgeon needs to carefully assess how feasible it is to remove the tumor, carefully reviewing its size and location and any involvement of lymph nodes. In other words, the surgeon must determine if surgical removal is possible. A complete assessment of how well the patient can tolerate surgery is also necessary. Postsurgical issues, such as how breathing will be affected when part or all of one lung is gone, must also be assessed.

In other words, before going ahead with lung surgery, the patient must be able to tolerate surgery and it must be feasible to surgically remove the area affected by the cancer.

Radiation is used against early-stage lung cancer in patients who can not tolerate surgery or in situations where surgery may be too difficult. Chemotherapy may be given before surgery or radiation to shrink the tumor, thereby making it easier to treat. When given beforehand, the chemotherapy is called *neoadjuvant*; when chemotherapy is given after surgery, it is adjuvant, or "extra," meaning that it is given to try to eliminate any leftover cancer cells that are impossible to detect.

Stage III lung cancers are ones that have spread locally and are not initially amenable to surgical removal. These patients are treated with radiation and chemotherapy. Current studies have demonstrated survival benefits with chemotherapy and radiation administered concurrently in certain patients, those who have only adjacent lymph node involvement. Occasionally, depending on response, surgery may be considered after chemotherapy and radiation. Sometimes the chemotherapy is given at the same time as the radiation. The chemotherapy combinations include cisplatin or carboplatin.

Stage IV lung cancers have spread or metastasized outside the chest region. These cancers are treated with chemotherapy alone; however, radiation may be used for palliation. Chemotherapy may help to improve symptoms caused by the cancer itself and in this way improve quality of life. If a patient has distant spread, then chemotherapy is the treatment of choice, with radiation reserved to spot-treat an area that is causing pain or another problem that affects quality of life.

In about 20 percent of lung cancer patients, the cancer cell present is a more aggressive small-cell type. In these cases, the brain, liver, and bone are evaluated because the tumor is so aggressive that the cancer has frequently spread to these sites. Surgery generally is not performed in these cases, and chemotherapy is the primary mode of treatment. Radiation therapy then supplements the chemotherapy, if necessary.

Most patients referred for radiation treatment usually have a six- or seven-week course of treatment. When radiation is the primary treatment, approximately 6,000 units of radiation may be delivered. Less radiation may be used in patients who have had surgery or chemotherapy.

Sometimes the cancer may cause special problems. These involve extensive bleeding from the lung or rapid onset of shortness of breath because the large blood vessels or the bronchi are obstructed. In these cases, the daily and total dosage of radiation will be altered. The daily treatments may then be delivered in high doses in the often successful attempt to reduce these acute symptoms.

Radiation is delivered daily to the front and back of the chest or at different angles, with the portal arrangement tailored to the particular clinical picture. Treatment includes the lung tumor itself, if it has not been surgically removed, plus all the nearby lymph nodes. Radiation treatment can control the local primary tumor much of the time. However, by the time many lung cancers are diagnosed, they are already in an advanced stage and the cancer has spread to other parts of the body. Some of these metastases may not be clinically detectable at the time of the diagnostic work-up.

Unfortunately, many are not detected until after the primary cancer has been treated. Chemotherapy for lung cancer is often administered either prior to surgery or postoperatively. Survival among patients who are treated with surgery, radiation, and multidose chemotherapy is significantly higher than for those patients who have only surgery.

When the patient is not a good candidate for surgery, we prefer to administer radiation prior to chemotherapy. When administered first, chemotherapy significantly lowers the patient's ability to tolerate the radiation therapy. (There is considerable controversy in the medical literature over the sequence of these treatments.) The total radiation dose and the daily dose may be modified if the patient is also receiving chemotherapy, because the tissues may be less able to tolerate radiation while chemotherapy is being administered.

Chemotherapy drugs used to treat lung cancer include combinations of cisplatin, docetaxel, carboplatin, gemcitabine, paclitaxel, vinblastine, etoposide, vinorelbine, and irinotecan. Two-drug combinations, usually including either cisplatin or carboplatin, are commonly used. Three-drug combinations are also being studied, but at this time they do not appear to be significantly better, and they are associated with more side effects. For patients who have more advanced disease, or who have previously been treated with platinum-based chemotherapy, combinations including docetaxel are used. Clinical trials of targeted therapies, such as epidermal growth factor (gefitinib) receptor and antiangiogenesis agents have shown great potential.

Small-cell lung cancer is fast growing, so it is less likely that surgery is an option. Patients may be treated with concurrent chemotherapy and radiation if the disease is limited and the patient is fit. Chemotherapy followed by radiation is another option. When the disease is limited, the chemotherapy drugs used in combination with radiation include cisplatin and etoposide or carboplatin and etoposide. When the disease is more extensive, irinotecan and cisplatin may be combined. Other chemotherapy combinations used in recurrence include gemcitabine, paclitaxel, docetaxel, ifosfamide, vinorelbine, doxorubicin, and cyclophosphamide.

Side Effects of Radiation

The side effects of radiation therapy to the chest are generally moderate, and most patients are able to pursue their normal lifestyles. However, many patients complain of fatigue, which generally disappears approximately one month after radiation therapy is completed. Although we encourage patients to work and carry out their normal daily activities, the fatigue may sometimes make it too difficult, and daily routines must be altered. Underlying and preexisting physical conditions and, of course, mental attitude, will influence a person's lifestyle during this period.

Side effects begin approximately two to three weeks after treatment has started. The primary side effect is moderate irritation of the esophagus, the swallowing tube. However, there is wide variation in the severity of this symptom. Some people may report very little difficulty; others may find this symptom quite annoying. Liquid antacids help to soothe the esophagus, and we advise patients to avoid very hot or very cold liquids and foods, along with spicy foods, because they may cause further irritation. Chewing foods well before swallowing is also advantageous. Some, but by no means all, patients complain of moderate nausea. Compazine usually controls this symptom.

On occasion, a radiation-induced cough appears. This is actually a mild bronchitis brought on by the radiation. Various cough remedies relieve this problem, and it is never a serious side effect. These side effects generally disappear a week or two after completion of treatment. Because of their weakened state, some patients may develop an infection, and antibiotics are needed to control it. More rarely, a patient may develop mild radiation-induced pneumonia one to two months after radiation treatment is finished. Antibiotics and cortisone may be used to treat this condition.

Side Effects of Chemotherapy

Chemotherapy used to treat lung cancer may be associated with nausea or vomiting, fatigue, or low white blood-cell count. Low blood counts may predispose a patient to infection.

In addition, these drugs may lead to mouth sores or diarrhea. Most of the drugs cause hair loss, but the notable exceptions are carboplatin and gemcitabine, which do not. Some of the drugs (especially paclitaxel, docetaxel, carboplatin, and cisplatin) may cause numbness and tingling in the fingers and toes.

Follow-Up and Outlook

Follow-up treatment for lung cancer includes regular chest x-rays to detect recurrent disease and CT scans of the chest and abdomen. Lung cancer most commonly spreads to the bone, liver, and brain. If symptoms appear, diagnostic tests generally ordered include a CT scan of the brain, a CT scan of the abdomen to evaluate the liver, and a nuclear bone scan if bone symptoms are present (see Chapter 8). Blood tests for liver function that can reveal signs of early liver disease are also performed.

Although the cure rate for lung cancer is low because of the high incidence of distant metastases present at the time of diagnosis, we have had personal experience with cures. Therefore, we recommend that an aggressive treatment program be instituted to achieve the maximum benefits. Remember that we have treatments for all stages of lung cancer and these treatments help people to live longer. Research continues to explore better techniques for surgery and radiation, and ongoing clinical trials are looking at the use of new drugs, especially targeted treatments, which may be the key to future advances in lung cancer treatment. Of course, ultimately, the hope is to continue to educate people about the perils of cigarette smoking. If it were not for smoking, lung cancer would be a rare disease.

Myeloma (Multiple Myeloma)

Multiple myeloma originates in plasma cells. Plasma cells are blood cells that produce immunoglobulin, or proteins that make up antibodies. Patients with myeloma often will have evidence of these abnormal proteins in their urine or blood. When plasma cells multiply in an uncontrolled fashion, they cause abnormalities, generally in the skeleton. When plasma cells form one tumor or affect only one bone, the condition is called a *solitary plasmacytoma*. More commonly, plasma cells affect many bones along with the bone marrow, and the condition is considered *multiple myeloma*.

Sometimes, myeloma is diagnosed in the course of a routine evaluation when blood tests show the presence of abnormal proteins. Sometimes myeloma is diagnosed because it has caused kidney problems, anemia, or bone pain.

Other sites in the body, such as the nasal passages, the sinuses, the lungs, and lymph nodes, can be affected, but this occurs less frequently. Myeloma causes pain in the affected bones, and the patient has increased susceptibility to infection. Multiple myeloma is often associated with cycles of remissions and flare-ups. The remissions can occur spontaneously or as a result of treatment.

Treatment

Because myeloma is a systemic disease, the primary treatments are medications that travel throughout the bloodstream; these include chemotherapy, steroids, and biologic agents. Radiation is added, if needed, and is directed to sites where pain is experienced or to shrink plasmacytomas, or masses of plasma cells. For young patients with myeloma, bone marrow transplantation may be considered, as it is the only potential *curative* treatment.

Many patients with myeloma may not need treatment when they are first diagnosed. For example, if they have no symptoms from the disease, they may be watched closely and the disease may remain stable for years. Treatment in the form of chemotherapy is needed when symptoms such as bone pain or anemia appear, or because myeloma has caused complications such as kidney problems or high calcium levels in the blood.

For many years, a combination of two drugs, melphalan and prednisone, has been used as an initial chemotherapy option. They are given orally, intermittently in cycles, and may be continued for months. A more aggressive initial chemotherapy option is known as the *M2 protocol* and includes a combination of oral and intravenous medications, consisting of five drugs: vincristine, carmustine, melphalan, cyclophosphamide, and prednisone.

Another treatment is called *VAD* (vincristine, Adriamycin, and Decadron); this combination is given intravenously and generally requires placement of a Portacath, a semi-permanent device that is placed in the chest into a large vein, which can be used to draw blood for tests and for IV treatments. The vincristine and Adriamycin is given continuously over four days through the IV, and the Decadron (a steroid) is given orally. Sometimes the Decadron is given alone.

Chemotherapy is continued until patients reach a period of stable disease, or plateau phase. Once in this stable phase, patients are closely monitored and treatment may not be needed for a period of time, that is, until the disease becomes more active again.

Interferon, an immune therapy, is sometimes given after completion of chemotherapy and may prolong the duration of remission. Interferon is given as an injection under the skin three times per week. Side effects of interferon treatment may be quite bothersome.

Following most treatments for myeloma, the time eventually comes when the treatment is less effective and a change needs to be made. This situation is known as *refractory myeloma*. The same chemotherapy drugs can be used again if there has been a long interval since treatment. Other chemotherapy drugs can be given, such as cyclophosphamide (Cytoxan), VAD, or the M2 protocol.

Thalidomide is a recent drug option for treating myeloma. You may remember hearing about this drug because it was used in the 1950s to treat nausea in pregnant women. It was later taken off the market because it was found to cause malformations in the fetus. This occurred because the drug inhibits new blood vessel formation, which, when treating myeloma, is useful to slow the growth of abnormal plasma cells. It is taken orally on a daily basis, but *it cannot be used in pregnant women.*

A new strategy for the treatment of myeloma is a drug called bortezomib (Velcade). This new drug belongs to a class of agents known as *proteosome inhibitors*, and is given intravenously to patients who have refractory myeloma.

Patients under age seventy with myeloma may want to consider bone marrow transplantation. Transplants may be allogeneic, that is, from a matched donor who contributes marrow, or autologous, meaning that patients donate their own stem cells. They then receive high-dose chemotherapy, and their own stem cells are reintroduced in order to allow their bone marrow to recover. (See Chapter 6.) Some patients who receive an allogeneic transplant may be cured; however, because of the high risk of complications and death from this procedure, it is only considered in the youngest myeloma patients, where the risks are lower.

Patients with myeloma are at high risk of developing infections because the disease interferes with the body's ability to make antibodies. Immune defenses are further challenged with the use of chemotherapy, broadening the susceptibility to infection. In individuals with myeloma in the bones, the bone-strengthening agents, pamidronate or zoledronic acid, are given monthly to minimize pain and reduce the risk of fracture.

Radiation therapy is used to control bone pain and to shrink masses that may be disfiguring. It is also performed to relieve compression of the spinal cord and nerve roots if the disease has spread to that area of the body.

Most patients receiving radiation therapy for multiple myeloma report prompt relief of the bone pain, and the masses usually shrink rapidly. If treatment has been initiated very soon after the myeloma has begun to affect the spinal cord and nerves, normal nerve function can be restored.

Doses of 2,000 to 4,000 units of radiation may be administered over a two- to four-week period, usually without significant side effects. There is a wide variation of response to the treatment. Some patients obtain prompt relief of symptoms with 2,000 units; others need the higher dose of 4,000 units for the same symptom relief.

Side Effects of Radiation Treatment

When treatment is delivered to the long bones of the arms and legs, no side effects are expected. However, when radiation is directed to the spine, the patient may experience symptoms if enough radiation reaches adjacent soft tissues. For example, treatments to the neck might cause a sore throat; treatments to the lower spine might cause nausea. These symptoms can be alleviated with medication and dietary modifications (see Chapters 2 and 3).

Side Effects of Chemotherapy and Other Systemic Treatments

Side effects of chemotherapy for myeloma include lowered blood counts, which further increases the already-higher risk of infection. Granulocyte-colony stimulating factor (G-CSF) may be given, depending on which chemotherapy agent is used. Erythropoietin stimulates red cell production, improves anemia, and reduces the need for blood transfusion.

Vincristine may be associated with numbness and tingling in the fingertips or toes. Adriamycin may cause nausea, vomiting, hair loss, and diarrhea. With repeated dosing, heart function needs to be followed, because this drug can also affect how well the heart pumps.

The steroid Decadron can irritate the stomach and cause heartburn. Some people may feel restless and have difficulty sleeping while taking Decadron. In addition, weakness in the muscles may occur.

Interferon may cause flu-like symptoms such as fever, chills, fatigue, and muscle aches. Some people may experience depression, drowsiness, headache, nausea, or loss of appetite. Blood counts and liver function need to be followed closely.

Thalidomide may cause drowsiness, numbness in the fingertips or toes, and, rarely, blood clots. Men and women taking this drug *must* take precautions so that no pregnancies occur while on this drug.

Bortezomib may be associated with nausea, vomiting, or diarrhea. In a few patients, blood pressure may drop, resulting in fatigue or dizziness. Numbness, tingling, or a burning sensation may be experienced in the fingers or toes. The platelet count needs to be monitored because it may drop in up to 40 percent of patients; however, reducing the dose or delaying the next treatment generally corrects this problem. Note: Refer to Chapters 2 and 3 for a discussion of ways to relieve the side effects associated with these drugs and combinations.

Follow-Up and Outlook

It is unusual, but not impossible, for the disease to recur in the radiated area. Those patients who have initially received a lower dose of radiation may need to return for additional treatment to the same areas. However, multiple myeloma is usually characterized by new growths, which, over time, appear in other parts of the body. For this reason, many patients are seen over a period of months for additional treatment to different bones in the body.

Chemotherapy may eliminate bone pain and temporarily halt the progression of the disease. Unfortunately, chemotherapy often depresses the bone marrow's ability to manufacture new platelets and red and white blood cells.

Bacterial infections may result from weakened immunity. In addition, long-term consequences of this treatment may include acute leukemia.

Both radiation and chemotherapy are quite effective in temporarily arresting multiple myeloma, and about 90 percent of patients will obtain good pain relief. Those patients whose disease progresses slowly may live for many years. However, in some patients, multiple myeloma is much more aggressive and only short-term survival is possible.

Patients with myeloma are followed on a regular basis and have blood tests and sometimes urine tests done to monitor the level of abnormal protein. X-rays and CT scans are commonly used to evaluate the results of treatment and detect new disease. In addition, bone marrow biopsy may be done as part of follow-up.

New strategies include combining new targeted treatments, such as bortezomib along with chemotherapy. New drugs that are similar to thalidomide, but possibly less toxic, are also promising. New transplant strategies include double transplants and minitransplants (see Chapter 6).

Non-Hodgkin's Lymphoma

Non-Hodgkin's lymphomas are a group of diseases in which abnormal cells develop in lymph nodes; the disease may then spread to other sites throughout the body. Human beings have thousands of lymph nodes distributed throughout the body. They trap elements foreign to the body—infections and cancer, for example. This type of lymphoma differs from Hodgkin's disease in the way in which it spreads. Rather than moving to adjacent lymph-node groups in a step-by-step progression, its spread is much less predictable. Non-Hodgkin's lymphomas also tend to affect an older population than Hodgkin's disease, which usually affects younger people. Non-Hodgkin's lymphomas also frequently involve the bone marrow.

The rise in the number of AIDS patients has resulted in increasing cases of non-Hodgkin's lymphoma. This is probably the result of immunosuppression, the weakening of the body's own defenses.

The classification of non-Hodgkin's lymphomas is very complex. Simply put, these lymphomas can be best understood by dividing them into two groups: *indolent* lymphomas and *aggressive* lymphomas. Indolent lymphomas are slow growing and respond very well to treatment. Patients may live for years with these lymphomas although the disease is not generally considered cured. Aggressive lymphomas grow fast, but respond well to chemotherapy and are potentially curable.

Treatment

Most non-Hodgkin's lymphomas are considered a generalized disease and chemotherapy is the primary treatment. However, depending on the cell type, radiation may be delivered to initial disease sites or to residual disease after chemotherapy.

Because indolent lymphomas are generally not curable, chemotherapy is given only under specific circumstances. For example, if a patient has symptoms related to the lymphoma, such as fevers, sweats, or weight loss, or if they experience discomfort due to enlarging lymph nodes, treatment is recommended. These lymphomas may commonly involve the bone marrow, where they crowd out normal blood cells causing anemia or low platelet counts. Chemotherapy is then recommended to clear the bone marrow out. If lymph nodes enlarged due to lymphoma are located in critical locations—for example, the breathing tube or spine—then treatment is given to shrink the lymph nodes down. Prior to treatment, most patients with indolent lymphomas are observed for a period of time, because the disease can wax and wane on its own.

Unlike indolent lymphomas, aggressive lymphomas are treated immediately after the diagnosis is made. The most common type of aggressive lymphoma is *diffuse large-cell* lymphoma. Treatment may consist of chemotherapy alone or in combination with radiation. In patients with early-stage aggressive lymphomas, a combination of chemotherapy plus radiation to the involved area may be recommended. Alternatively, chemotherapy may be given alone but for a longer duration. For advanced aggressive lymphomas, chemotherapy is given alone; however, after chemotherapy is complete, radiation may be added to bulky areas of disease.

Bone marrow transplantation is used in the treatment of relapsed or refractory aggressive lymphomas. These transplants may be done using the patient's own bone marrow stem cells or by using bone marrow from a donor. (See Chapter 6.)

Chemotherapy drugs used in the treatment of indolent lymphomas include medications that can be given as pills (chlorambucil and prednisone) as well as intravenously. Combinations used include CVP (cyclophosphamide, vincristine, and prednisone) or CHOP, which is the same drug combination as CVP, but with the addition of Adriamycin. The CHOP combination is commonly used in the treatment of the aggressive large-cell lymphoma. Fludarabine and cladribine are agents that have come into use more recently, either alone or in combination with other chemotherapy drugs.

A monoclonal antibody called rituximab (Rituxan) has been extremely effective in the treatment of lymphoma. This antibody is directed against a protein on the surface of most lymphoma cells known as *CD20*. Rituxan is most commonly given in combination with chemotherapy or following the completion of chemotherapy.

New agents used in the treatment of relapsed lymphoma also target specific molecules on the surface of lymphoma cells. Two of these agents target the lymphoma cells using a monoclonal antibody, directed against the CD20 protein. The agent carries a radioactive isotope right to those cells. For example, ibritumomab tiuxetan (Zevelin) is a monoclonal antibody combined with the radioactive isotope yttrium 90. This agent is used along with the drug Rituxan. Side effects include allergic reactions, lowered blood counts that may last three to four weeks, weakness, nausea, vomiting, headache, or rash.

Tositumomab (Bexxar) combines an anti-CD20 monoclonal antibody with the radioactive isotope iodine 131. This is also associated with low blood counts.

Several vaccines are being studied in clinical trials especially for low-grade lymphomas to try to prevent these lymphomas from coming back after treatment.

Radiation therapy is often successful in treating local disease in the advanced stages of non-Hodgkin's lymphoma when chemotherapy is no longer effective. Radiation shrinks the tumors, alleviates pain, and reduces swelling in the tissues. It is particularly beneficial for treating large lymph nodes, the nasal passages, the bones, the spine, the intestinal tract, and the brain. A total of 3,000 to 4,000 units of radiation may be delivered in daily treatments over a four- to five-week period.

Side Effects of Radiation

Expected side effects of radiation therapy depend on the part of the body being treated. For example, dryness of the mouth and painful swallowing are common when treatment is delivered to the head and neck. Nausea and vomiting are likely to occur when treatment is directed to the abdomen. Appropriate medications and dietary modifications will help alleviate these symptoms (see Chapters 2 and 3). When large areas of the chest or abdomen are treated, the considerable irradiation of the bone marrow may lead to a lowered platelet and white and red blood-cell counts. These symptoms may be exacerbated if chemotherapy is given either simultaneously or immediately before the radiation treatment.

Side Effects of Chemotherapy

Chemotherapy used to treat lymphomas commonly affects the blood cells. Lowering the white blood-cell counts may be associated with increased risk of infection. Granulocyte-colony stimulating factors (G-CSF) such as Neupogen or Neulasta may be used to reduce the period of time that the white blood cells are low, may reduce the risk of infection, and may help the patient receive chemotherapy on time. G-CSF may cause discomfort in the bones and joints as the bone marrow cells recover. Chemotherapy also may lower the platelet counts, increasing risk of bruising. However, the platelets are rarely lowered to the extent that spontaneous bleeding occurs. Sometimes the red blood-cell counts are reduced, which can cause fatigue; blood transfusions may be necessary. However, erythropoietin, a hormone that stimulates the production of red blood cells, can be given to reduce the need for transfusion.

Nausea and vomiting may occur; however this is minimal with combinations that do not include Adriamycin. Combinations containing Adriamycin may be associated with red discoloration of the urine (a temporary change), hair loss, and mouth sores. The total cumulative dose of Adriamycin is monitored. When given at higher doses, more numerous cycles, or in individuals with preexisting heart disease, there is a slight increased risk of heart disease, because the Adriamycin may affect the heart's ability to pump. Tests that measure the heart's function may be done intermittently during treatment.

Rituxan, a monoclonal antibody, may be associated with allergic reactions, such as fever, chills, and low blood pressure. This is more common with the first dose, so it is generally given more slowly and with medicines given prior to treatment that reduce risk of reactions.

Follow-Up and Outlook

PET scans, CT scans, and blood tests are used in the follow-up of patients with lymphoma after treatment, and patients are seen on a regular basis by their medical oncologists. New biologic and targeted therapies are contributing to major strides in the treatment of lymphomas.

Ovarian Cancer

The ovaries are the female reproductive organs that contain eggs and produce hormones. Although ovarian cancer can develop in younger women, it occurs more frequently in women between ages forty and sixty-five. Ovarian cancer in its early stage may be difficult to detect, because initially the symptoms may be vague. These symptoms may include nausea, bloating, and pain, but by the time they become noticeable—or put another way, notable—the cancer is often more advanced.

Tests such as CT scans or MRIs are sometimes done as part of the evaluation. A blood test called *CA 125* is a tumor marker that is elevated in the majority of women with ovarian cancer. This blood test may be helpful in diagnosis, but it is most helpful for monitoring women who have completed treatment.

Treatment

Surgery and chemotherapy are the main treatments recommended to patients with ovarian cancer. Radiation is less commonly used.

Patients will generally have initial surgery to make the diagnosis, determine the extent of the disease within the abdomen, and to remove as much of the tumor as possible. (This is called *debulking*.) The surgery usually removes the ovaries, fallopian tubes, and uterus. Women with early-stage disease who wish to maintain fertility can consider having only the affected ovary and fallopian tube removed, thus sparing the uterus and the remaining ovary and tube.

To reduce the risk of recurrence, chemotherapy is recommended to most patients following surgery. Only those women whose disease is diagnosed in the earliest stages are not given chemotherapy recommendations. Because the majority of women are diagnosed with more advanced disease, this means that chemotherapy is recommended for most women with this cancer.

Chemotherapy drugs commonly used to treat ovarian cancer are given intravenously. These drugs include cisplatin, carboplatin, paclitaxel, and docetaxel. A combination of either carboplatin or cisplatin usually is used along with paclitaxel or docetaxel. The carboplatin and paclitaxel combination is effective and has fewer side effects than combinations that include cisplatin.

After completion of initial chemotherapy, some women may undergo second operations, called "second look" surgery. This is to see if the disease that could not be removed surgically is gone as a result of the chemotherapy.

If ovarian cancer recurs, it is sometimes possible to use the same chemotherapy drugs again and see the tumor shrink. Other drugs sometimes used at this stage include topotecan, gemcitabine, liposomal doxorubicin, and vinorelbine. Drugs in pill form include oral etoposide and tamoxifen (the hormone also used for breast cancer treatment). Sometimes chemotherapy drugs may be injected intraperitioneally, or directly into the abdominal cavity. Radiation may sometimes be given to the abdomen to treat recurrences.

Side Effects of Chemotherapy

Side effects of the chemotherapy used to treat ovarian cancer include lowered blood counts, which may increase risk of infection. The chemotherapy can be associated with fatigue, hair loss, diarrhea, and darkening of the nails. Cisplatin and carboplatin may be associated with kidney damage, hearing loss, numbness or tingling in the fingers or toes, or allergic reactions. Extra fluids may be given to reduce the risk of kidney damage. Carboplatin generally has fewer side effects than cisplatin. Paclitaxel and docetaxel may be associated with allergic reactions, numbness and tingling in the fingers or toes, and joint or muscle aches. (See Chapter 2 for a discussion of ways to control side effects.)

Follow-Up and Outlook

Patients who have completed treatment for ovarian cancer will have regular checkups that include history (details about any current symptoms or health concerns); physical examination, including a pelvic exam; and blood tests. Blood tests are done to check the tumor marker CA 125. For the first two years following completion of treatment, patients may be seen every two to four months; for the next three years, they may be seen every six months. If needed, CT scans, MRIs, or PET scans are used to assess symptoms or abnormal blood test results.

Women with ovarian cancer and a family history of breast or ovarian cancer should have their family history reviewed. In particular, patients with a family history of two or more first-degree relatives (mother, sister, or daughter) with ovarian cancer, or other relatives with breast and ovarian cancer, may be at risk of carrying a susceptibility gene. The most common mutations are in the BRCA-1 and BRCA-2 genes. Identification of mutation carriers does not change the approach to treating ovarian cancer, but would be important in determining an appropriate strategy to reduce breast cancer risk.

Currently, high-dose chemotherapy and stem cell transplant are being studied in patients with ovarian cancer, but these treatments remain investigational, and may be considered only if you are participating in a clinical trial.

Pancreatic Cancer

The pancreas, a gland located in the abdomen near the stomach, is responsible for manufacturing digestive juices. In its early stages, pancreatic cancer causes no symptoms. When symptoms appear, they generally include gradual weight loss, pain, and, depending on location, jaundice, or yellowing of the skin.

The cancer is often best detected with a CT scan (see Chapter 8) followed by a biopsy, which is necessary for a definitive diagnosis. Tumor markers that can be found in the blood of patients with pancreatic cancer include CA 19-9 (a marker specific to pancreatic cancer) and carcinoembryonic antigen (CEA). Detecting these substances in the blood is useful in establishing the diagnosis and in evaluating the results of treatment.

Treatment

Treatment may include surgery, radiation, and chemotherapy. Because of its complexities and the high risk of postoperative complications, studies indicate that pancreatic surgery is best done by surgeons in hospitals that handle many cases of this type of cancer.

Unfortunately, in many cases, the disease is locally advanced at the time of diagnosis. Sometimes chemotherapy and radiation may be given in advance to try to shrink the tumor enough to allow for surgery. Patients with more advanced disease may do just as well with the combination of chemotherapy and radiation as with surgery alone. Patients who are not considered likely to be cured will sometimes have some tumor tissue removed in order to relieve obstruction of the bile ducts. (When present, this obstruction may cause jaundice.) In cases where pancreatic cancer has metastasized to distant sites, chemotherapy is the main treatment, although radiation may be considered for treatment of pain.

For years, the only chemotherapy drug used for pancreatic cancer was 5-FU. More recently, the drug gemcitabine (Gemzar) has been shown to be effective in reducing the symptoms of pancreatic cancer, such as pain and weight loss, but also in improving chances of survival. Sometimes, this is used in combination with 5-FU or other agents.

When radiation is used, approximately 4,000 units of radiation are delivered to the pancreas through the front and back of the body. The treatment course may be continuous for four to five weeks, or it may be divided into two 2,000-unit courses with an interval of several weeks between each course.

The kidneys, portions of the liver, the intestines, and the stomach are shielded from unnecessary radiation. The radiation treatment field includes the adjacent lymph nodes.

Side Effects of Radiation

Many people undergo radiation treatment to the pancreas and experience only moderate side effects. Some may experience nausea and heartburn, but these side effects are easily controlled with medication (such as Compazine and antacids). Most patients use a trial-and-error method to determine which foods must be avoided. Generally speaking, low-fat, bland foods are best (see Chapter 3). Commercial liquid dietary preparations (Sustical, Ensure, Carnation, Vivonex) are often excellent food sources because they contain needed calories as well as vitamins and minerals but require little effort to ingest. These liquid-meals are available in pharmacies and food markets. Liquid vitamin and mineral supplements are advisable for people who prefer regular foods but are unable to consume enough to provide adequate nutrition.

Side Effects of Chemotherapy

Side effects of chemotherapy include nausea, vomiting, diarrhea, hair loss, mouth sores, and fatigue. Chemotherapy affects the blood counts, especially the white blood-cell counts, so there may be an increased risk of infection. However, when compared to many other chemotherapy drugs, gemcitabine is generally better tolerated.

Follow-Up and Outlook

Treatment results can best be evaluated by performing a CT scan of the abdomen. This test will also help determine if there has been re-growth of the cancer and whether it has spread to neighboring organs. CEA levels are also taken to measure tumor activity. A drop in CEA values is a good sign; rising values indicate that the cancer is recurring.

When used in combination, radiation therapy and chemotherapy often reverse the jaundice, pain, and weight loss caused by the cancer. However, by the time most patients are diagnosed, pancreatic cancer is usually in an advanced stage, so survival rates are low. Cures do occur, so when indicated, treatment should be aggressive.

New drugs are being developed for treatment of pancreatic cancer. These include targeted agents that work by inhibiting growth factors, blood supply, and enzymes needed for the cancer to grow. It is especially important for pancreatic cancer patients to find out if they may be eligible to participate in clinical trials.

Prostate Cancer

The prostate gland, an organ of the male reproductive system, is situated at the base of the bladder. The urethra is a tube-like structure through which urine passes; it begins in the bladder, traverses the middle of the prostate, and ends at the tip of the penis. In young men the prostate is about the size of a small walnut, but it increases in size as men age and undergo hormonal changes.

The normal enlargement is called *benign prostatic hypertrophy* (BPH) and may cause changes, such as urinary frequency, nocturia (the need to get up at night several times to urinate), urgency (the sense of needing to go *now*), narrowing and slowing of the urinary stream, and hesitancy (stand and wait). These symptoms are most commonly caused by BPH, but prostate cancer may cause the same symptoms, which is why it is so important to distinguish between cancer and BPH.

Prostate cancer is the most common cancer occurring in men. In most cases it is a slow-growing, highly curable cancer; however, high-grade aggressive cancers are not uncommon, particularly in younger men. In the past, the only means we had for screening for this disease was a digital rectal exam. If a physician found a hard mass or nodule on the prostate, then a biopsy would be performed. At one time, it was not uncommon for prostate cancer to be discovered as an incidental finding during surgery for urinary obstruction, presumably caused by BPH. Unfortunately, in too many cases it was discovered after it had spread.

Early-stage diagnosis is possible primarily due to a simple blood test that measures prostate specific antigen (PSA). As its name implies, PSA is a protein specific to prostate cells, and, apparently, cancer cells produce a greater amount of this protein than normal cells. The test results are expressed in numbers, with most physicians believing that the normal value should be under 4. However, some in the field believe that age should be taken into account when evaluating a patient's score. They suggest that for men under the age of sixty, the upper limit should be 3, and for men over the age of seventy, a normal number may be higher than 4.

An elevated PSA does not necessarily mean cancer is present, because infection or enlarged prostate can cause an elevated value. However, the PSA test is now a routine screening test and an elevated number raises the possibility of cancer and indicates the need for further evaluation or biopsy.

An extension of this test measures Free PSA, and the values are expressed in percentages. For example, the normal value for Free PSA is greater than 25 percent; a lower value on this test further raises the possibility for cancer.

If men have an elevated PSA and their physicians suspect *prostatitis* (a prostate infection), they may prescribe a course of antibiotics and then repeat the PSA test. If the PSA returns to the normal range and the symptoms go away, then it is presumed that the cause of the initial elevated PSA was the infection. However, if the PSA remains elevated or symptoms remain, then a biopsy will likely be suggested.

A biopsy is the only way to definitively diagnose prostate cancer. It is an outpatient procedure and performed under ultrasound guidance. An ultrasound probe is inserted into the rectum, and a spring-loaded needle-within-a-needle is inserted through the probe a few millimeters into the prostate. The spring is released and the inner needle quickly enters the prostate and extracts a core of tissue (usually twelve cores are obtained). Based on this description, the procedure probably sounds as if it is painful, but because this core extraction is so quick, most patients find that it isn't particularly painful. Patients are generally free to go home almost immediately.

A pathologist then examines the tissue and determines whether cancer is present. Depending on symptoms and circumstances, appropriate follow-up will be suggested if the tissue is benign, meaning that no cancerous cells are found.

The pathologist's report may come back with the diagnosis of a high prostatic intraepithelial neoplasm (PIN) number. While this is not cancer, it is believed to be a *precancerous* condition. At this time, we can't be certain what percentage of men with a high PIN number will develop cancer or in what period of time it will develop. However, in general, men with a high PIN number are watched more closely.

If the biopsy results in a diagnosis of cancer, then the pathologist grades the cancer, using what is known as the *Gleason score*. The tumor is graded from one to ten; the higher the number, the more aggressive the cancer. A score of four or lower is considered a low grade; five to seven is an intermediate grade; and eight to ten a high grade.

Once the diagnosis is established, the next step is to do a metastatic workup, meaning that we conduct appropriate tests to see if the cancer has spread. Some believe that if the PSA is under 10 and the Gleason score is 6 or under, then a metastatic workup is not necessary because spread is unlikely. However, we generally recommend getting a bone scan because it establishes a baseline for future reference. In addition, we recommend having a CAT scan of the abdomen and pelvis, which can be used for treatment planning and occasionally it may pick up a more serious abnormality.

If a patient has a high Gleason score (8, 9, or 10) or a PSA over 20, the chance for metastasis is greatly increased, and we recommend a bone scan, a CAT scan, and a PET scan.

Treatment

When preliminary testing suggests that the cancer is localized, that is, confined to the prostate, the patient may undergo surgery or a course of radiation. No study has demonstrated the superiority of one treatment over the other: they give equally good results. Ongoing studies are factoring in the PSA, the Gleason score, patient's age, and/or the presence of a nodule on digital rectal exam, and we hope to arrive at a formula that can be used to make a determination about the best treatment for individual patients.

More than many other cancers, a number of treatments for prostate cancer exist, but not all are suitable for all patients. Ultimately, patients must make the choice after carefully examining the options, which include watchful waiting, surgery, and radiation treatment. Obviously, this situation presents a difficult dilemma for men with prostate cancer because no one can absolutely predict the outcome of any treatment. Certainly, physicians and patients are guided by research data, but some treatments are relatively new and long-term results cannot be predicted as accurately. The information presented here is based on current knowledge, which is always changing and improving as more data accumulate. Always ask your doctor about the most recent information available about each type of treatment.

Watchful Waiting. As the name implies, this option involves forgoing aggressive treatment in favor of ongoing observation. Prostate cancer is relatively slow growing, so some patients will decide to gamble, based on a range of probabilities, which include the likelihood that some other disease will cause death. For example, elderly men in poor health may find the cancer treatments too physically taxing. In other cases, when the cancer has spread, there may be a belief that the metastasized cancers at other sites are likely to cause death.

Watchful waiting is considered an option based on a large Swedish study that concluded that there was no survival benefit for men over age seventy who received treatment for the disease versus those who did not undergo treatment. However, this study did not factor in the Gleason score, nor did it consider the health status of all the subjects.

Other researchers have since gone back to studies performed in the United States and have reanalyzed the data. They have found that there was a survival benefit for men with a Gleason score of 6 or more who received treatment. This analysis also showed a slight survival benefit for men with a Gleason score under 6 who also received treatment.

Unfortunately, making decisions about cancer treatment often involves weighing options, all of which appear to have disadvantages. Watchful waiting is no different. Of course, the chance that the cancer may spread and, therefore, cause pain and other adverse effects must be considered too.

Surgery. A radical prostatectomy involves removing the entire prostate gland and surrounding tissues and lymph nodes. This surgery once invariably caused impotency, but today a nerve-sparing prostatectomy is often performed. The phrase "nerve-sparing" means that at least one of the nerve bundles that supplies the prostate gland is left intact. This procedure is not appropriate for all men, but it may be recommended for men who have localized or lower-grade disease.

The surgery has some complications, including blood loss, anemia, and the risks associated with anesthetic use. (Twenty percent of men undergoing the procedure require a blood transfusion.) There is also significant risk of incontinence and other urinary symptoms. When cancer is confined to the prostate gland, surgery is associated with a high cure rate. However, such factors as age and overall health are considered, because the surgery is extensive.

With the traditional surgical procedure there is a very high rate of impotency, but with nerve-sparing surgical procedures, the rate of impotency has been reduced to 30 to 50 percent. However, not all patients are candidates for the nerve-sparing procedure.

External Radiation Therapy. Radiation treatment also is associated with high cure rates. This treatment uses x-rays directed at the prostate. Facilities with state-of-the-art equipment use what is called 3-D conformal technique. CT scan, or other tests that allow visualization, obtains the 3-D imaging of the prostate. A beam is shaped to conform to the outline of the prostate and is delivered to the prostate from a number of angles. This method spares surrounding tissues from excessive radiation exposure. Usually, thirty-five to forty treatments are delivered over an eight-week period.

Side effects include urinary frequency, including nocturnal urinary frequency, burning upon urination, diarrhea, and rectal irritation. Lasting complications of treatment may include impotency (affecting 30 to 50 percent of men treated), rectal symptoms, urinary symptoms, and a slight chance of incontinence. (This occurs in less than 10 to 15 percent of men.) External radiation treatment has the lowest incidence of incontinence of all treatments.

Patients considered good candidates for surgery and who choose the surgical procedure also may be advised to undergo a course of radiation if the pathologist finds tumor close to the margins on the surgical specimen or if the patient's PSA doesn't drop to 0 after three to four months.

The usual dose delivered is 6,500 to 7,000 units of radiation in thirty-five to forty daily treatments. Studies have shown that higher doses yield higher cure rates. Using IMRT (see Chapter 1), some researchers are attempting to deliver 8,000-plus units. Their work of evaluating results, including assessing side effects and complications, continues. In other words, will this treatment increase the cure rate, or will it cause unacceptable rectal and urinary complications? Thus far, no definitive results have been published.

Seed Implant. Also known as *brachytherapy*, low-energy radioactive seeds are implanted in the prostate gland. This procedure was first tried many years ago, but the results at that time were unsatisfactory. However, for several reasons, current results show great improvement in this treatment. We can use ultrasound to guide our needle placement and advanced computer technology to guide placement of the seeds.

The procedure is performed under a spinal or general anesthesia, and patients are generally able to return home the same day. Rarely is more than a mild analgesic required to relieve the two or three days of discomfort resulting from the procedure.

The side effects of brachytherapy include urinary symptoms, but only rarely do rectal symptoms appear. Permanent urinary symptoms and impotence are possible; however, of all prostate cancer treatments, this therapy reportedly results in the lowest incidence of impotence.

One study has demonstrated that patients with a Gleason greater than 7 or PSA over 10 did not do as well with a seed implant as with surgery or external radiation. For patients with these values, we usually recommend combination treatment.

Combination Treatment. Combination treatment evolved when studies began to show that patients with high-grade tumors did not fare as well with a seed implant. Combination treatment involves a modified course of external radiation, usually 4,500 to 5,000 units in twenty-five to thirty daily treatments, plus a modified seed implant to deliver an additonal 10,000 units. One report, with a twelve-year follow-up on these patients with high-grade disease, demonstrated a 75 percent disease-free survival rate. The combination approach is frequently administered in conjunction with drugs that temporarily block production of male hormones for a period of three months to a year.

The side effects and potential complications with this combination treatment are similar to external radiation or implant alone.

Positron Radiation Therapy. This is a form of radiation therapy in which positively charged radioactive particles are propelled at a high rate to the prostate. Although this sounds contradictory, it is both new and not new. A process known as *cyclotron-produced radioactive particle treatment* has been performed intermittently over the past fifty years. In the past, results have not been satisfactory. However, with newer equipment and improved techniques, this form of radiation treatment may improve cure rates. At this time, however, we do not have meaningful data about short- or long-term results or complications.

Cryosurgery. This is a treatment that uses ultrasound technology to guide insertion of needles into the prostate in order to release gases that freeze the tissue. Until recently, cryosurgery had primarily been used to treat men who had failed to show improvement with radiation and who had only local disease. Cryosurgery also carried a very high risk of incontinence. Recently the FDA approved its use as a primary treatment, and over time our experience with the treatment has reduced the risk of incontinence. However, this risk is still greater than with other treatments.

Hormonal Therapy. Although hormone strategies can be used early on, hormonal therapy is more commonly instituted when it has been documented that the prostate cancer has metastasized. The male hormone testosterone is known to stimulate prostate cancer growth, and removing testicular tissue (orchiectomy) decreases production of this hormone. In past years, estrogen, the female hormone, was used to suppress testosterone.

Currently, we have medications that block the production and activity of testosterone and effectively suppress cancerous prostate cells. These androgen deprivation strategies can be used at the time of diagnosis to shrink the tumor before radiation or surgery. However, more commonly, androgen deprivation is used after completion of radiation or surgery in patients whose disease has spread.

Hormone drugs that cause androgen deprivation can be given by injection or orally. Luteinizing hormone-releasing hormone (LHRH) agonists inhibit production of testosterone by influencing hormonal regulation in the pituitary gland (located in the brain). These hormones include leuprolide (Lupron) and goserelin (Zoladex). These are given as injections, usually into the abdominal wall; they come in forms that last for one month or for three months. Antiandrogens block the binding of testosterone to androgen receptors on the cancer cells; bicalutamide (Casodex) is a pill that works this way. Sometimes both hormone strategies are combined to inhibit both the production of testosterone and the binding of testosterone to androgen receptors.

Other hormonal agents sometimes used include steroids; estrogens; finasteride (Proscar), which blocks an enzyme used in the conversion of testosterone; and ketoconazole, an antifungal medication that has an antiandrogen effect.

Initially we almost always see a decrease in the PSA level as a result of hormonal treatment. We also see a reduction in the size of the prostate, and, if patients have bone metastases that are causing pain, patients experience significant pain relief, too. These results can last for as little as one year or for as long as ten years. Most patients experience three to five years of benefit, and then the cancer cells become resistant to this therapy.

In the past, hormone treatments were usually given continuously until they stopped working. However, a new strategy involves using hormone treatments intermittently. This may help to reduce side effects and may possibly allow patients to respond to hormone treatments over a longer period of time. Clinical trials will help determine if this is a superior way to treat prostate cancer.

Chemotherapy. When hormone therapy ceases to be effective, chemotherapy is recommended. A number of different chemotherapy drugs are used to treat prostate cancer and include both oral and intravenous medicines. The drugs include mitoxantrone, docetaxel (Taxotere), paclitaxel (Taxol), doxorubicin (Adriamycin), and liposomal doxorubicin (Doxil), cyclophosphamide (Cytoxan), and estramustine (Emcyt). These drugs may be given alone or in combination.

Other Treatments. If prostate cancer has spread to the bones, pamidronate (Aredia) or zolendronic acid (Zometa) are generally recommended along with hormonal medicines and chemotherapy. These medicines are given intravenously once a month to help to reduce bone pain and risk of fracture. Currently, the medication flutamide (Eulexin), in combination with a hormone, has been shown to depress tumor cell activity by blocking the effect of testosterone on the cancer cells. In addition to being very expensive, the drug also leads to problematic weight gain.

Clinical trials are looking at new targeted agents and vaccines against prostate cancer cells, but as yet, we do not have preliminary reported results.

Making Decisions

Both surgery and external radiation therapy have been used for a long time, and the ten-year cure rates for each are about the same. Many surgeons believe that cure rates for surgery are superior to cure rates for radiation therapy. Radiotherapists disagree, and believe that the apparent ten-year survival benefits of surgery are primarily due to patient selection, that is, taking earlier-stage cases and healthier patients. To date, no prospective long-term study has been initiated.

For patients treated with seed implant alone, we have follow-up data covering ten years that shows that the seed implant alone gives similar survival rates as surgery or radiation for patients with a Gleason score of 6 or under.

Using 3-D technology, we can deliver extremely high doses of radiation to the prostate gland while sparing surrounding tissues and controlling radiation exposure to the urethra. In the short term, this treatment does not appear to have increased complication rates, and, because most difficulties occur during the first two or three years following treatment, it is presumed that there will not be long-term complications. We assume that the high doses will improve the cure rate, while not increasing complication rates.

At this time, hormonal treatment is not curative, although there are benefits when hormonal therapies are combined with seed implants. Some clinicians believe that combining hormonal treatment with external radiation therapy will improve survival rates. Patients with advanced disease most certainly benefit from hormonal treatment. However, the benefits are limited because the tumor cells eventually overcome the suppression of the hormonal agents.

Further Uses for Radiation Therapy

If metastases occur, they usually appear in the skeleton, although most organs can be affected (see Chapter 5). The spread of metastatic prostate cancer to the spine and the spinal cord may constitute a radiation therapy emergency, in that it must be done immediately to prevent permanent neurological damage.

External beam radiation therapy is very effective in reducing bone pain from metastatic prostate cancer (see Chapter 5). Recently, the addition of an isotope (a radioactive substance) called strontium 89, given by injection into the bloodstream, has been found to be valuable in treating bone pain and prostate cancer. This treatment is usually used when the disease affects multiple bones. Pain relief usually begins ten to twenty days after therapy is started with maximum relief occurring in about six weeks. There may be a transient increase in bone pain approximately one week after therapy has begun, followed by the beneficial effect that occurs in about 80 percent of patients.

The isotope goes specifically to the diseased areas and spares the normal bones of unnecessary levels of radiation. Within one week of administration, 90 percent of the isotope is excreted from the body. The pain relief benefit of this treatment generally lasts between seven and twelve months. It may also be used in conjunction with external beam radiation therapy to enhance pain relief. Patients will have blood counts checked during and after treatment because the platelet count occasionally decreases. As long as the blood count remains stable, strontium 89 treatment may be repeated. For example, in some patients, pain relief is not satisfactory or does not last for the expected period of time. These patients may then receive additional strontium 89 treatments, with significant pain relief often resulting.

Average survival is unfortunately only one to three years after the discovery of metastatic prostate cancer. Patients who die of metastatic prostate cancer often had no evidence of their original prostate disease.

Side Effects of Radiation

Because high doses of radiation are required, most patients will experience side effects. The radiation to the intestines will cause cramping and diarrhea, beginning by the end of the second week or early into the third week of treatment. Medications such as Lomotil, paregoric, or Imodium A-D will usually reduce these intestinal symptoms when combined with dietary modification. The diet should be low in fat, and fried foods and raw fruits and vegetables should also be avoided. All food and liquids should be caffeine-free (see Chapter 3). The medication and diet modification must be continued throughout the course of the treatment or symptoms will return.

The bladder is also affected by the high doses of radiation. Urinary urgency and frequency, beginning in the third or fourth week of treatment, are the result of irritation to the bladder. Fortunately, medications (Pyridium, for example) are available to soothe the bladder. Sitting in a warm bath twice a day, particularly before going to bed at night, is quite helpful.

Slight blistering and reddening in the rectal area and between the folds of the buttocks are quite common, and generally begin around the fourth or fifth week of treatment. Hydrocortisone cream and Anusol HC suppositories relieve these symptoms. The symptoms experienced are predictable, meaning that most people undergoing high-dose radiation therapy for this length of time report similar side effects. Discuss the symptoms with your radiation oncologist as soon as you begin to notice them. There is no need to suffer in silence, because over the years we have found that various medications and dietary modifications can greatly relieve these unpleasant side effects of treatment.

Fortunately, these symptoms disappear within six to twelve weeks after radiation therapy is complete. It is an unusual patient whose symptoms persist for longer periods. Patients with such underlying medical conditions as ileitis and colitis will be more prone to intestinal side effects, both in the acute stage and over the long term. It is advantageous to stay on the medications and maintain the dietary modifications for at least a week after radiation therapy is complete, because the symptoms diminish gradually rather than disappearing all at once.

About 10 percent of patients will experience transient episodes of bleeding from the rectum or the bladder in the two years following treatment. It is unclear why some patients' intestinal tracts and bladders are more prone to the delayed effects of radiation than others. Bleeding may be slight to moderate and usually subsides spontaneously; however, on occasion, cauterization may be needed to stop the episodes of bleeding.

Impotency, if it is to occur at all as a result of radiation treatment, usually begins within six months after treatment has been completed. Statistically, we know that approximately 15 to 30 percent of previously potent patients develop impotency within two years of completion of treatment. Recently, the new nerve-sparing surgical techniques that attempt to preserve potency and decrease the incidence of incontinence have been favorable factors that allow some men to choose surgery over radiation. Viagra and newer potency-enhancing drugs are effective in many of these cases. Traditional surgery causes almost 100 percent loss of the ability to obtain an erection, but the nerve-sparing techniques significantly reduce this result.

As with all types of cancer, there are normal emotional reactions to both having the disease and the side effects of treatment (see Chapters 2 and 3). Both patients and family members may need help to cope with the inevitable difficulties that arise.

Side Effects of Hormonal Therapy and Chemotherapy

The most common complaints with hormonal therapy are hot flashes, fatigue, and, over time, muscle wasting and thinning of the bones (osteoporosis). Some men may experience headache, nausea, or enlargement of the breast tissue. They may experience difficulty with erection, difficulty controlling urination, and loss of sexual desire.

Chemotherapy drugs used to treat metastatic prostate cancer may be associated with low blood counts, especially low white blood-cell count, which increases risk of infection, and with anemia. Certain chemotherapy drugs such as Taxol and Taxotere may be associated with numbness and tingling of the fingers and toes and muscle or joint pains. Nausea, vomiting, hair loss, and mouth sores may be seen with Adriamycin and mitoxantrone. Estramustine may cause leg cramps, edema, nausea, diarrhea, or breast tenderness.

Follow-Up and Outlook

It is mandatory that you see your urologist frequently following completion of treatment. For example, patients will undergo periodic rectal examinations. Digital rectal examinations and PSA tests are done approximately every six months for the first five years, then yearly after that. In some situations, repeat biopsy of the prostate may also be done one year after diagnosis.

Bone scans are done if the PSA is rising or if a person is experiencing symptoms such as bone or muscle pain. Bone scans can help differentiate the pain of arthritis from the pain of cancer. Other tests used in follow-up include CT scans to monitor lymph node areas and MRIs. If the PSA is rising, repeat biopsy of the prostate area may also be done. Chest x-rays are also routinely performed, because prostate cancer may spread to the lungs.

Because the incidence of prostate cancer increases dramatically with age, it is important for men fifty and older to undergo annual prostate examinations, including rectal examinations and PSA blood tests. Researchers are currently trying to develop tumor markers that are more sensitive and specific than PSA for our use in the future.

Skin Cancer

There are many types of skin cancer, the most common of all cancers, and most are treated by surgical removal. Those for which radiation treatments may be recommended include basal cell and squamous cell cancer. Melanoma, a very serious form of skin cancer, is usually not effectively treated with radiation unless it has spread to the bones. After surgery some patients with melanoma may receive extra systemic treatments to reduce risk of recurrence.

Treatment

At one time, radiation therapy, surgery, or a combination of both, were the usual methods of treating skin cancer. However, we now have new treatment techniques available, including electrodesiccation, cryosurgery, laser surgery, Mohs micrographic surgery, and topical (local) chemotherapy. Nowadays, those patients referred for radiation therapy for basal or squamous cell cancers are generally elderly persons who may not be willing or able to undergo surgery. Others are treated with radiation therapy if residual disease is present following surgery. Radiation oncologists are currently treating fewer skin cancers because these new therapies are available.

When tumors are large, radiation therapy is advantageous because it eliminates the need for complicated surgical procedures, which may require skin grafts. For this reason, it is often the preferred treatment for cancers occurring on the nose or ear or near the eyes.

Following a diagnostic biopsy, treatment for basal cell cancers is delivered with either superficial radiation therapy machines or with electron beam (see Chapter 1). This particular energy of radiation therapy predominantly affects the skin and minimizes radiation to underlying tissues. Doses of 4,000 to 5,000 units of radiation may be delivered over a three- to four-week period of daily treatments. However, doses and treatment schedules vary widely.

The skin being treated eventually reddens, a desirable sign because it indicates that sufficient radiation is reaching the cancer. Some patients have an ulceration of the skin that is caused by the cancer or is the result of the biopsy. A scab, known as an *eschar*, is often present over the area of ulceration. When treatment is complete, the scab will gradually be shed as the underlying skin heals after the cancer is destroyed.

There are similar treatment plans for squamous cell cancer, although a higher total dose of radiation may be necessary. If the basal or squamous cell cancer is very extensive, and particularly if it extends to underlying bone or cartilage, a modification of the daily and total dose may be indicated to reduce radiation-therapy complications. Treatments are individualized, and your radiation oncologist will make recommendations based on his or her experience and judgment.

Melanoma is treated by surgical removal of the skin lesion along with enough surrounding normal tissue (margin) to assure it is all out. If the tumor is found to extend deep into the skin, then lymph nodes in the area may be removed. If the melanoma has spread to the lymph nodes, then extra systemic treatment may be recommended to prevent recurrence of melanoma. These treatments move throughout the bloodstream to reduce the risk of melanoma recurring either at the original site or at distant sites.

Unlike most cancers, where this extra treatment means taking chemotherapy drugs, with melanoma, the treatment is *biologic* (immunotherapy). Interferon alpha-2b is the most commonly recommended immunotherapy for melanoma. It is given as a subcutaneous injection three to five times per week for approximately six months.

In patients with melanoma that has spread, Interleukin-2 (IL-2), another form of immunotherapy, is sometimes given intravenously, and sometimes in high doses. In addition, chemotherapy is sometimes given as well. A number of melanoma vaccines are currently being studied and are available to those patients participating in clinical trials.

Side Effects of Radiation

Patients are often surprised when a skin reaction does not appear immediately. However, it is only toward the end of treatment, usually after three to four weeks, that the skin shows a sunburnlike reaction, which is technically known as an *erythema*. The erythema persists for many weeks following the end of therapy. Ask your doctor about an appropriate skin cream, usually one that contains vitamins A and E, to alleviate discomfort.

A raw wound (ulcer) often caused by the cancer will heal within several weeks following radiation treatment, and careful follow-up with the radiation oncologist and a dermatologist is necessary. As a rule, the skin is healed two months after treatment is completed.

The skin reactions experienced by fair-skinned people will be more intense than those experienced by darker-skinned people. Following completion of radiation therapy, a gradual darkening of the skin may occur, along with some scaling and itching. Ointments and creams are applied as needed by the individual. For the most part, the skin returns to its normal appearance in three to six months following completion of radiation therapy. There is, however, great variation among individuals.

Side Effects of Chemotherapy and Immunotherapy

Interferon treatment may cause lowered white blood-cell and platelet counts; allergic reactions, such as fever or chills; or flu-like symptoms, such as fatigue, headache, and muscle aches. Blood counts are done regularly to monitor blood cells and liver function. Some people may experience mood changes including depression or even—rarely—delirium.

Side effects of high-dose IL-2 can be serious and include drops in blood pressure, fluid accumulation in the body (especially the lungs), along with the flu-like symptoms and possible allergic reactions mentioned above. IL-2 is generally administered in a monitored setting, such as in the hospital.

Follow-Up and Outlook

Cure rates are quite high for primary basal cell cancer treated with radiation. However, skin cancer patients must see a dermatologist on a routine basis. This is absolutely necessary, because new tumors arise within a year in 20 to 30 percent of cases. Patients are also advised to avoid excessive exposure to the sun, and they should regularly apply a strong sun block. In some cases, complications may arise. Patients may develop extensive scarring or chronic radiation dermatitis (itching, scaling, and change in pigmentation).

Follow-up for squamous cell cancer is particularly important because this type of cancer has a greater tendency than basal cell cancer to spread both locally and to distant sites.

Patients with melanoma are also closely monitored following completion of treatment. The frequency of checkups for recurrence depends on the stage of the melanoma, with individuals at higher risk of recurrence being monitored more closely. Those who had lymph node involvement may also have follow-up blood tests, chest x-rays, and CT scans, if indicated. Any patient who has had melanoma should also have thorough, regular skin examinations for life, because individuals who have developed one skin cancer may be at higher risk of developing a second one in another area.

Testicular Cancer

Testicular cancers (also known as *germ cell tumors*) are rare. However, they are among the most common cancers affecting young men. Two major types of testicular cancers are recognized based on how they look under the microscope. The first is known as *seminoma* and is almost always curable with radiation therapy; the second is categorized as nonseminomatous germ cell tumors (NSGCT) and is treated with chemotherapy. Because treatments of seminomas and nonseminomatous germ cell tumors are quite different, each will be discussed separately.

Treatment for Seminomas

Following a biopsy that confirms the presence of cancer, surgery is performed. The testicle, its attachments, and the local lymph nodes are removed. There is generally a step-by-step progression of seminomas from the testicle to adjacent lymph nodes. These lymph nodes extend from the pelvis to the abdomen and then into the chest. Following surgery, radiation therapy is administered to treat the lymph-node pathways of the pelvis and abdomen. Should cancer be discovered to have spread to the lymph nodes of the abdomen, then radiation may also be given to those in the chest.

Seminoma cancers are very sensitive to radiation, and only 2,000 to 3,000 units of radiation may be required to cure the disease. This is usually given in two to three weeks. Treatments are usually administered through the front and the back of the body, and the remaining testicle is carefully shielded to protect it from the radiation. Many lymph nodes are involved in treatment, particularly those situated adjacent to the major blood vessels of the pelvis and abdomen. Therefore, it is necessary that the treatment field be quite large.

Chemotherapy is used in patients with seminoma whose cancer is advanced or has recurred. The most commonly used drugs are cisplatin and etoposide (EP) and bleomycin, etoposide, and cisplatin (BEP).

Treatment for Nonseminomatous Germ Cell Tumors (NSGCT)

Treatment for nonseminomatous germ cell tumors (NSGCT) includes surgery and chemotherapy. Prior to determining the optimal treatment, the treatment team carefully reviews the pathology slides, the CAT scans, and blood tests which include tumor markers beta HCG and alpha fetoprotein (AFP).

For patients with Stage I NSGCT, the three treatment options following removal of the testicle are: observation; chemotherapy; or further surgery to remove lymph nodes, a procedure called a *retroperitoneal lymph node dissection* (RPLND). This particular surgery needs to be done by a surgeon (urologist) experienced in doing a nerve-sparing procedure because the most significant potential risk associated with the surgery is retrograde ejaculation, which results in infertility. If you choose observation, this means being examined by your doctor every three months, along with having CT scans done.

Patients with Stage II disease may receive surgery (RPLND), chemotherapy, or both. If surgery reveals disease in the lymph nodes, then chemotherapy is given.

Chemotherapy is the main treatment for advanced testicular cancer. The combinations of chemotherapy most commonly used today include EP and BEP. In patients whose disease does not respond to these treatments, drugs such as ifosfamide, paclitaxel, carboplatin, and vinblastine can also be used.

Side Effects of Radiation

Radiation dosages may adversely affect the opposite normal testicle, in spite of appropriate shielding. Sperm counts and motility will generally be depressed, and radiation may also cause damage to genetic material, i.e., chromosomes. This can lead to infertility and may harm future offspring. Because of this, men are advised to store sperm before initiating treatments.

Because the total radiation doses are low, patients usually do not experience significant side effects. If mild nausea occurs, it can be controlled easily with medication such as Compazine. On rare occasions, bone marrow may be affected by radiation treatments, and blood counts may be lowered. Although this situation is the exception, weekly blood counts are obtained as a precaution.

Side Effects of Chemotherapy

Chemotherapy used to treat testicular cancers may cause low blood counts, which may predispose patients to infection. Other side effects include hair loss, nausea, vomiting, diarrhea, fever, coughing, shortness of breath, mouth sores, or rash. These occur right after treatment and generally resolve completely once treatment is done. Some of the drugs, such as cisplatin or carboplatin, may cause numbness and tingling in the fingers or toes, dizziness, or hearing loss that may be noted after treatment has been completed.

In addition, chemotherapy may interfere with sperm production. As with radiation treatments, patients may want to consider sperm banking. Although extremely rare (less than one percent), the possibility exists of later developing a blood disease or leukemia.

Follow-Up and Outlook

Testicular cancers have an excellent prognosis overall, with cure rates of over 90 percent. It is important that patients undergo regular follow-up tests. Chest x-rays and CT scans of the abdomen and pelvis are extremely important to determine whether residual disease exists or new disease has occurred. Specialized blood tests (tumor markers beta HCG and AFP) are followed in patients with NSGCT.

Patients whose disease has come back or has spread to distant sites may be considered for high-dose chemotherapy and stem cell transplant (bone marrow transplant). Sometimes, when disease has come back in distant sites, the cancer may be surgically removed (resected) from that site.

Like Hodgkin's disease, testicular cancer is an example of a cancer with high cure rates, and current research focuses on ways to maintain high cure rates but minimize side effects of treatment.

Uterine Cancer

The uterus is the medical term for the womb; the outlet of the uterus that leads to the vagina is called the cervix. The cancers that originate in the uterus and cervix have different biological characteristics, and therefore, they require different treatments and are discussed separately.

The most common uterine cancer begins in the endometrium, or lining, of the organ. Eventually it extends to the underlying muscle wall of the uterus, and it may extend to the cervix. If the cancer progresses to more advanced stages, it will spread to the ovaries, the vagina, the bladder, the rectum, or other adjacent sites.

About 75 percent of patients have localized disease at the time of discovery. When the cancer is confined to the uterine wall, as is often the case, there is a relatively good chance of a cure.

Treatment

Treatment for endometrial cancer is highly individualized. However, surgery—in which the uterus, the fallopian tubes, and the ovaries are removed—is the mainstay of early and moderately advanced uterine cancer. Most women who develop this type of cancer are beyond childbearing years, and so the emotional response to losing the uterus may be less severe than experienced by younger women. (Seventy-five percent of uterine cancer occurs after age fifty.)

External radiation therapy is often used with patients who are at high risk for recurrent cancer after surgery. Specifically, these patients have aggressive cancer cell types, and the cancer has involved a good part of the uterine muscle wall, or has spread to the cervix, or is suspected or discovered to have spread to adjacent lymph nodes. (The human body has thousands of lymph nodes, which filter elements foreign to the body. Because they are so widely distributed, lymph nodes are often affected when cancer spreads from its original site.) The combination of radiation therapy and surgery provides the best survival rates.

Radiation may precede or follow surgery, and no evidence exists showing that one method is better than the other. Radiation oncologists see most patients postoperatively, because only patients who have significant muscle invasion and high-grade tumors or cervix involvement benefit from radiation, and often this cannot be determined until the specimen is examined by the pathologist after the uterus has been removed. The usual dose of radiation is 4,000 to 5,000 units delivered in twenty-five to thirty daily treatments.

In some cases, rather than external treatments, the patient may be advised to have a vaginal insertion only, a procedure in which radioactive sources are inserted into the vagina. (The radioactive source is enclosed in a specialized instrument.) There are many situations in which the patient may be advised to have both external radiation as well as a vaginal insertion.

The radioactive insertion can be performed in either of two ways. In the traditional method, radioactive cesium is placed in a tamponlike device, inserted into the vagina, and left in for twenty-four to forty-eight hours. This method doesn't require anesthesia, but it does require hospitalization during the time of treatment. The second method uses a high-intensity after-loading device (see Chapter 1). This is done as an outpatient procedure two or three times, taking between thirty and ninety minutes, including set-up time. The two procedures give equal results. It is difficult to say if one procedure that requires hospitalization is more or less uncomfortable and difficult for the patient than two or three procedures performed while an outpatient. Discuss this with your doctor in order to reach the best decision for you.

Some patients are not able to undergo surgery either because their health does not allow it or because of the stage of their disease, and radiation therapy will be their only treatment. Radiation therapy has been found to be effective in both curing and controlling this cancer, but not as effective as when combined with surgery. Patients who receive only radiation are usually given external treatment first, followed by internal treatment to both the uterus and the vagina.

Patients are considered to have very advanced cancer when it has spread out of the uterus to the adjacent organs and pelvic tissues. These patients may be treated with radiation therapy only or radiation along with hormonal therapy or chemotherapy. Hormone therapy is usually in the form of the female hormone progesterone, given as an oral medication. Chemotherapy is given intravenously and can be given as a single drug or in combinations. The most commonly used medications include doxorubicin (Adriamycin), cisplatin, carboplatin, and paclitaxel (Taxol). One combination sometimes used is cisplatin and doxorubicin, with or without cyclophosphamide. The goal is to palliate, that is, to arrest the disease and make the patient more comfortable.

Side Effects of Radiation

The side effects of internal radiation treatment are moderate rectal and bladder irritation, which are controlled with medication. Generally speaking, patients are not in too much pain during this treatment because mild narcotic medication is prescribed. Internal radiation treatment may be performed in two sessions, requiring two hospital admissions.

Most women treated with external radiation are able to tolerate the treatments quite well, and side effects, while annoying, are not of serious concern. Mild to moderate side effects include some diarrhea, urinary frequency, and mild reddening of the skin over the areas being treated. These symptoms usually begin within the second or third week of treatment. All symptoms can be easily controlled with appropriate medication. Diarrhea can be treated with Lomotil or Imodium A-D; urinary frequency is treated with medications such as Pyridium and Ditropan; skin irritation is treated with soothing skin creams, including cortisone ointments if necessary.

Side Effects of Chemotherapy and Hormonal Therapy

Side effects of the hormone progesterone include fluid retention and weight gain; some women may experience nausea or headache. Side effects of chemotherapy used in the treatment of this cancer include lowering of the white blood cells, which increases risk of infection; nausea; vomiting; diarrhea; numbness in the fingers and toes; and hair loss. During treatment with cisplatin, kidney function is monitored closely, and *rarely* hearing loss may occur.

Follow-Up and Outlook

After treatment is completed, a woman is evaluated periodically by a gynecologist because it is absolutely essential that the pelvis and the vagina be checked for recurrent cancer. Chest x-rays, CT scans of the pelvis, and IVP examinations may be ordered to check for recurrent disease (see Chapter 8).

5

If Cancer Has Spread

In the previous chapter we discussed treatment of primary cancers, that is, those originating in specific organs. This section deals with the treatment of cancers once they have traveled from the organ of origin to a distant site. This spread of disease is technically known as *metastasis*. The term also refers to the secondary growth itself. There is an in-between stage in which cancers invade the tissues surrounding the site of origin. This is referred to as *local invasion*.

Cancers begin as a cluster of cells multiplying in an out-of-control manner, unlike the body's normal cycle of cell destruction and replenishment. This uncontrolled growth rate is caused by alterations in the cell's DNA makeup, and these cancerous cells have the ability to locally penetrate and invade the surrounding tissue. This is distinctly different from benign tumors, which only push or displace adjacent tissue.

As cancerous tumors invade tissues, they enter the lymph system and can then spread by way of the lymph ducts. (The lymph system is a network of ducts that carry a clear protein fluid that leaks from capillaries and cells called lymph fluid. These ducts are interrupted by lymph nodes, which act like filters that strain out bacteria viruses and cancerous cells in an attempt to control spread.) This process is called *lymphatic spread* and usually progresses in an orderly pattern. For example, sometimes a breast cancer spreads first to low-level axillary (armpit) nodes, then upper-level nodes, and then to nodes above the collarbone or neck.

Cancerous cells may also invade arteries or veins and spread via this route. When this occurs, cancer can appear anywhere in the body. This usually is a more aggressive type of spread, and certain cancers have a predilection for it. For example, it is not uncommon for a small one-inch lung tumor to have spread to the brain, while adjacent nodes in the center of the chest test negative for tumor.

When metastasis occurs and cancer has spread outside the primary site and lymph node region, most tumors are no longer curable. However, some patients will have a prolonged survival despite the continued presence of cancer; thus, the cancer is treated as a chronic disease, similar to diabetes. The primary goals of treatment are to prolong survival; however, preserving the best possible quality of life is most important.

Systemic therapy—chemotherapy, hormones, or biologic agents—is the primary treatment for metastatic disease; radiation therapy and surgery are reserved for alleviating pain, preventing complications, and maintaining the best quality of life possible. When radiation therapy, chemotherapy, or surgery is administered in the setting of metastatic cancer, we generally refer to it as *palliative* treatment. This means we are attempting to control the disease by relieving symptoms such as pain, neurological problems, and the effects of pressure on vital organs, rather than attempting to cure the disease.

Treatment of metastatic cancer can result in the cancer shrinking (partial remission), sometimes to the point that it is no longer detectable (complete remission). However, for most of the common cancers, such as breast, colon, or lung, ultimately the disease comes back. At that point, further treatment may include different chemotherapy drugs and treatment directed at relieving any symptoms a patient may experience.

The chemotherapy drugs that are recommended for metastatic cancer include drugs used in the treatment of early-stage disease as described in the previous chapter. A breast cancer that is metastatic to the lungs (started in the breast but spread to the lungs) is treated using drugs that are active against breast cancer, not lung cancer. For this reason, you should first refer to the particular site of origin of the cancer to learn what drugs are considered active. This chapter will help you understand the additional treatments you can consider.

Metastasis to Bones

Over 50 percent of patients with breast, lung, and prostate cancer that have metastatic disease develop metastases to the bone. Other primary cancers may also spread to the bone, but this occurs less frequently. Patients experience symptoms that include pain and limited motion caused by destruction of the bone and/or stretching of associated nerve fibers. (Although the vertebrae of the spine are considered bone, we have included a separate section on the spine, because the spinal cord and its nerves warrant individual discussion.)

Treatment

The amount of radiation delivered to skeletal areas depends on the size of the disease and its location. Radiation therapy is usually the most effective and rapid way to relieve bone pain caused by cancer. (Hormonal therapy for breast and prostate cancer metastases to the bone can be very effective, and it is generally recommended when the cancer in the bones is widespread.) The pain is completely alleviated in 75 to 90 percent of cases, depending on the site of the original disease. The amount of radiation and duration of treatment are guided by the alleviation of pain. However, clinical experience allows radiation oncologists to predict fairly accurately how quickly and completely a metastatic cancer will respond to a particular treatment schedule. Therefore, depending on where the cancer originated, bones affected by cancer will require differing amounts of radiation over variable periods of time.

Weight-bearing bones of the leg often require more radiation than non-weight-bearing bones. When more than one-third of the width of one of these long bones is affected, it is weakened to the point that fractures could occur. When your physicians suspect that such a fracture will take place, an orthopedic device (a metal rod) may be inserted. This procedure limits further damage to the bone and provides pain relief. Radiation therapy is started after the orthopedic procedure is performed.

Patients help the radiation oncologist design an area of treatment, because the area of bone pain generally corresponds quite accurately to the site of the disease. Physical examination will also help determine the areas to be treated. X-rays and nuclear bone scans (see Chapter 8) are extremely helpful in designing the portal to be used. The diminishing pain is usually a reliable indicator that cancer in the area being treated has been destroyed.

In general, excellent results will be achieved after ten to fifteen treatments delivered over a period of two to three weeks. This relatively short treatment time, in which the radiation oncologist delivers a high dose of radiation, is possible because bones of the arms and legs can tolerate a higher dose of radiation than, for example, the more sensitive soft tissues of the abdomen. Because of the adjacent soft tissues, the bones of the spine, skull, and pelvis are treated less rapidly.

The patient's response will help guide the exact level of the dosage, and the radiation oncologist notes subsiding pain and return of motion to the affected structures. Once a sufficient dose of radiation has been delivered to a particular area, it is unlikely that the pain and disease will return to the same location. A total dose of 3,000 to 5,000 units of radiation is usually sufficient; the average is about 4,000 units.

Bone pain disappears because the cancer in the bone has been eradicated or its growth arrested by the radiation treatments. As a rule, pain decreases within the first two weeks of treatment, and it may begin to subside after the first few treatments. The response varies among individuals, but the greatest variation depends upon the primary site of the cancer. For example, bones affected by prostate cancers generally respond quickly to radiation therapy within the first two weeks. Bones affected by lung cancer may take longer to improve, and the response of bones affected by breast cancer is somewhere in between. However, response also varies among individuals with the same cancer. Therefore, there is no hard-and-fast rule concerning how quickly pain will be relieved.

Patients tend to fall into one of four pain-response groups. The first are patients who have immediate pain relief, often beginning within a week or two after treatment is initiated. The second group includes patients who obtain relief toward the end of the treatment course. In the third group are patients, fortunately in the minority, who do not get pain relief until several weeks after treatment is completed. Approximately 5 to 10 percent of patients never experience sufficient pain relief. These patients require continued pain medication or a surgical procedure to block the nerve fibers responsible for the pain.

As pain lessens, patients describe it as changing from sharp to dull. Mobility of the affected area improves, and patients experience psychological relief as well. They look and feel better and are able to follow a more normal lifestyle because of their renewed feeling of well-being. Sleep patterns usually return to normal; appetite improves. Many people are able to eliminate pain medication, and even those taking strong narcotics are able to reduce the dosage or switch to over-the-counter pain-relief medications.

Care is taken not to treat too many bones simultaneously, because radiation may affect the bone marrow's ability to manufacture blood cells.

Drugs called *bisphosphonates* also are used in the treatment of cancer that has spread to the bones. These are not chemotherapy medicines, but rather they are bone strengthening medications, similar to but much more potent than those commonly used to treat osteoporosis.

Pamedronate (Aredia) and zoledronic acid (Zometa) are the two most frequently used drugs to treat cancer that has spread to the bone. Pamidronate is given as a ninety-minute intravenous infusion once a month; zoledronic acid is given intravenously over fifteen minutes once a month. Both drugs have been shown to improve survival in patients with breast cancer or myeloma who have bone involvement, and they help to reduce complications related to cancer in the bones, such as fracture. They also help reduce pain and may reduce the need for radiation to the bones. In patients with prostate cancer, these drugs may slow down the progression of cancer in the bones, and they are also being studied in other cancers, such as lung cancer with bone involvement.

Side Effects

Pamidronate and zoledronic acid may be associated with transient bone discomfort the day after treatment; this symptom is more common after the first treatment. Patients being treated with Zoledronic acid need to have their kidney function monitored, and, if needed, the infusion may need to be given more slowly, over a period of up to sixty minutes.

The side effects encountered when delivering radiation to the bones vary greatly, depending on the location of the bones being treated. Blood counts may need to be monitored if several bone sites are being treated or if a large area of bone that contains significant bone marrow—the hip, for example—is being treated. There are generally no side effects from radiation treatments to the long bones of the arms and legs because the soft tissues in the path of the radiation beam do not react. Side effects are experienced when the bones being treated are next to sensitive organs. For example, treating pelvic bones will result in radiation to the intestines, which may cause diarrhea and nausea. Treating the bones of the neck will affect the esophagus, causing sore throat and difficulty in swallowing. These side effects are temporary and can be controlled with medication and dietary modifications. They usually disappear within a week or two after radiation treatment has been completed.

Follow-Up and Outlook

Follow-up x-rays and nuclear bone scans (see Chapter 8) often reveal improvement because the cancer has been destroyed or arrested. These tests are also used to detect new areas of disease.

Metastasis to the Brain

The radiation treatment described here is that given to patients whose original cancer has metastasized to the brain. (See Chapter 4 for an explanation of the radiation treatment that is delivered when the brain is the site of the primary cancer.) Your radiation oncologist will design the treatment field after reviewing tests (generally CT scans and MRIs) that reveal the location of the metastatic disease (see Chapter 8). However, in most cases, the entire brain is treated, because metastatic disease usually produces multiple tumors. Even when only one or two tumor deposits are revealed in the imaging tests, physicians generally believe that additional disease is present but the deposits are too small to be imaged. Therefore, treatment portals are designed to include all the important areas that need radiation treatment.

Currently, clinical trials show that surgery for some types of brain metastases can prolong survival, although it does not cure the disease. Chemotherapy is not recommended as the sole treatment for cancer that has spread to the brain, because the drugs often do not penetrate well into the brain. Most patients however, who have disease that has spread to the brain, will also likely have other sites of spread outside the brain, thus chemotherapy is used to treat the cancer in general.

Treatment

A patient's clinical situation will affect the total dose of radiation administered as well as the length of treatment. Some cancer specialists favor rapid high-dose treatment (approximately 3,000 units in two-and-a-half weeks), and others favor treatment doses administered over a longer period of time (approximately 5,000 units in five-and-a-half weeks). However, the extent of the disease in the brain, the site of the primary cancer, and the patient's over-all condition are the major considerations when the treatment plan is designed.

Cortisone medication (most commonly, the steroid dexamethasone) is given along with radiation therapy to reduce the swelling of the brain tissues, a con-dition called *edema*. The edema is often caused by the tumors, but it may also be aggravated by the radiation treatments. Anticonvulsant medications are also sometimes prescribed.

Radiosurgery is most commonly used as a treatment for cancer that has metastasized to the brain from another primary site. The purpose of radio-surgery is to deliver a high dose of radiation to a specific tumor location while minimizing the exposure to the surrounding tissues. (It is sometimes used to treat primary cancer occurring in the brain.) It may increase chances for sur-vival, but cure is rare. Radiosurgery for metastasized cancer in the brain is used when the disease in the original site is under control or in remission.

In addition, survival benefits have been shown only when certain criteria are met. For example, currently radiosurgery is considered when no more than three lesions are present, and these lesions are no larger than approximately 1.5 inches (3.5 cm). These criteria are subject to change, of course, but are determined by the likelihood of achieving any positive survival benefit.

Three types of equipment are used to perform radiosurgery. We mention them only so that you are familiar with the terms if you hear your physi-cian use them. It is not necessary to understand the technology. If a cobalt source is used, the term *gamma knife* is used. A *linear accelerator* may be used, or the procedure may use heavy, charged particles produced by *cyclotrons* or *synchrotrons*.

Unfortunately, radiosurgery has not resulted in increased survival rates for malignant gliomas, which are tumors occurring in the supporting tissues of the brain, those tissues that intermingle with the neurological structures. Some studies are looking at the use of radiosurgery on primary tumor sites, but so far, the results have been disappointing.

Side Effects

Two common side effects of radiation to the brain are drowsiness and dis-orientation, sometimes occurring one to two hours after treatment. For this reason, we usually advise patients to sleep and rest after each treatment. These symptoms can be alarming to the patient because, quite naturally, people associate the brain with the functions that make them alert and able to participate in life. However, there is no medical cause for concern, and mental functioning returns to normal after a short period of time. Some patients experience mild nausea and headaches, both of which can be controlled with medication. Fatigue may begin some time during treatment. Nausea can be alleviated with Compazine; headaches with over-the-counter pain-relief medications.

Severe headaches, projectile vomiting, and vision changes are rare symptoms, but when they occur they signal an increase in pressure inside the brain. Radiation therapy may be temporarily stopped or the dosage of cortisone medication increased.

Hair loss can cause a significant emotional side effect. The amount of hair loss is related to the amount of radiation given; the higher the dose, the more likely the hair loss. Generally, an excess of 3,000 units (a very common dose) will result in some hair loss, but only in the area receiving the treatment. Although some people do not experience hair loss because of especially strong hair follicles, patients should expect it and prepare for it in advance. We advise patients to obtain a hairpiece before any loss occurs. In this way, they will never undergo a period of baldness, and a sense of self and body image can be preserved.

Hair loss usually starts about two weeks after the beginning of treatment, and in many cases the hair will not grow back. For those whose hair does grow back, the new growth is usually sparse and the texture is altered. If smaller areas are treated, rather than the whole brain, then hair loss will occur only at the site receiving radiation. The scalp may become irritated, and a soothing skin cream will usually alleviate the discomfort.

Follow-Up and Outlook

When radiation is administered to the brain for metastatic disease, it is considered palliative, in that it temporarily arrests the growth of the cancer and relieves pain. Unfortunately, cures are rare. Six to eight weeks following completion of radiation therapy, MRIs and CT scans may be performed to evaluate results (see Chapter 8).

Metastasis to the Chest

Metastases to the chest, which includes the lung and its covering (known as the *pleura*), and rib cage can cause a variety of symptoms. These include pain, pressure, cough, bleeding, or shortness of breath. When metastases involve the rib cage, pain is the usual symptom. Radiation therapy is very effective in rapidly reducing bone pain. Chest x-rays and CT scans (see Chapter 8) are performed to locate the areas of disease and to follow up on the results of treatment.

Treatment

A dose of 3,000 to 4,000 units may be delivered over two to three weeks and is usually sufficient to alleviate rib pain.

When fluid accumulates in the space around the lung (pleural effusion) or in the space around the heart (pericardial effusion), it is removed, sometimes under CT scan or ultrasound guidance. In order to drain the fluid, a tube is placed in the chest; it may be large (chest tube) or may be a small flexible catheter. Once the fluid has drained out, a chemotherapy medicine, or talc, or an antibiotic is instilled into the space to cause a reaction that seals the space. This procedure generally prevents the fluid from accumulating again. The procedure can be uncomfortable, so pain medication is often necessary.

In some situations, radiation therapy is of limited value in treating metastatic cancer in the chest area. For example, fluid around the lung or heart does not respond well to radiation, and the procedures described above are used. Radiation may be helpful in treating obstruction of the airways caused by tumor. Radiation therapy has not been shown to be of much value for treating multiple metastases in the lungs. Depending on the type of primary cancer, chemotherapy may be effective for this condition.

If cancer has spread into the small lymph vessels in the lung (lymphangitic spread), steroids are sometimes recommended in addition to chemotherapy to treat the underlying specific cancer.

Side Effects

When small areas of the ribs or pleura are being treated, there are generally no side effects. However, when larger areas of the chest are treated, the patient may experience some nausea, which can be controlled with Compazine.

Follow-Up and Outlook

Radiation is usually effective in alleviating pain and bleeding; results are not as good for relieving obstruction. There is also great variation in patients' response to treatment. Chest x-rays and CT scans are very accurate in evaluating the results of radiation therapy.

Metastasis to the Lymph Nodes

Cancer discovered in lymph nodes has metastasized from a primary site. Although Hodgkin's disease and non-Hodgkin's lymphomas are thought to originate in the lymph nodes, the presence of these cancers in many lymph nodes can be considered metastases, because the disease has spread from one lymph node to another. The human body contains thousands of lymph nodes, distributed throughout the body. The lymph nodes are part of the lymphatic system, which is a component of the body's immune system. Lymph nodes filter foreign elements in the body—infections and cancer, for example.

Physicians can evaluate by touch and sight those lymph nodes that are close to the surface of the body. Those that are suspicious for cancer can then be biopsied to confirm the diagnosis. Lymph nodes that lie deep in the body require imaging tests, such as CT scans or MRIs, to detect and evaluate possible cancers. Lymph nodes that contain cancer do not usually cause pain unless an infection exists concurrently. As a rule, large lymph nodes that contain cancer are more difficult to treat than small lymph nodes.

Treatment

The path of lymph-node involvement in various cancers is often predictable, and treatment plans are designed according to what is known about each pathway of spread. (There are notable exceptions to this, which cancer specialists take into consideration when they design treatment plans.) Radiation therapy dosages for lymph nodes vary according to the origin of the cancer and the size of the lymph node being treated. Therefore, cancerous lymph nodes from prostate cancer will require a different dose than cancerous lymph nodes caused by Hodgkin's lymphoma.

Radiation treatments to lymph nodes often begin at the time the primary cancer is discovered if it is suspected (even if not yet proven) that the lymph nodes are cancerous. It is also delivered to lymph nodes when imaging tests such as CT scans or MRIs identify lymph-node enlargement considered to be caused by cancer. Radiation therapy is also commonly performed after surgery has removed the primary cancer, and it is proven that the lymph nodes contain cancer.

Lymph nodes may require additional treatment if the original radiation therapy was unsuccessful. Chemotherapy may later be added. For some cancers, particularly the lymphomas, chemotherapy is often the initial treatment and radiation follows to treat residual disease.

As a rule, cancers originating in the brain do not spread to lymph nodes, and therefore radiation treatment is delivered only to the primary site.

Cancers of the head and neck can spread to the local lymph nodes of the neck. Surgery is often performed to remove these metastases, and is followed by radiation or chemotherapy. Disease in these lymph nodes can often be evaluated by sight and touch; lymph nodes located deeper in the tissues are evaluated by CT scans or MRIs. Lymph nodes of the head and neck are often difficult to cure because of their size and number at the time the cancer is discovered. Moreover, it is often the appearance of these lymph nodes that first suggests an undiscovered cancer is present in the area. The size and number of lymph nodes, as well as the cancer's natural resistance to being easily destroyed, means that radiation treatment portals will be large and the dosages high. In addition, infections often exist in these lymph-node metastases and must be treated with antibiotics.

Breast cancer will often metastasize to local lymph nodes. The underarm region, known as the *axilla*, is the most frequent, and often the first site of spread. Generally, it is necessary to biopsy the lymph nodes to determine if cancer is present, although if they are large, the lymph nodes may be detected through a physical examination. Breast cancer may also spread to lymph nodes in the chest wall, behind the breast, and beneath the breastbone. As a rule, lymph nodes in these areas can be neither imaged nor felt. Therefore, radiation and chemotherapy are administered when the presence of cancer is likely.

Enough information is known about the spread of the disease to establish a degree of probability that can help guide treatment decisions. The tendency for the cancer to spread to adjacent lymph-node groups is one reason that radiation therapy for breast cancer requires a large treatment field.

Cancer of the lung and esophagus will usually spread to lymph nodes in the chest, and it may also extend to the lower neck and upper abdomen. The deep lymph nodes of the chest can be evaluated only by imaging tests such as x-rays, MRIs, and CT scans (see Chapter 8). CT scan is the most effective test for this purpose because the number and size of lymph nodes are shown in great detail. Treatment can then be planned to include all the chains of diseased lymph nodes that are discovered on the CT scan. By the time they are discovered, many lung and esophageal cancers have already spread to the nearby lymph node groups, which is why radiation treatment portals are large. Both the primary cancer and the adjacent lymph nodes can be treated simultaneously.

Cancers of the pancreas rapidly spread to the adjacent lymph-node groups, which then require radiation treatment. These lymph nodes are deep within the body, and a CT scan is the best way to evaluate them for disease.

Treatment of cancers in the pelvic region—the prostate, uterus, cervix, bladder, testicle, and rectosigmoid colon—usually includes the lymph nodes next to the organ that contains the primary cancer. At the time these cancers are discovered, they may have already spread to the surrounding lymph node groups. The treatment portals will be large, allowing the primary cancer and the nearby lymph nodes to be treated simultaneously. Chemotherapy is of additional value in treating lymph node cancers in this region, particularly testicular and colon cancers.

Cancers that are thought to originate in lymph nodes (Hodgkin's disease and non-Hodgkin's lymphoma) spread from one group, or chain of lymph nodes to another. The radiation doses needed to cure or control these lymph-node cancers are not usually as high as those delivered for other cancers. However, the area being treated is large in order to include all the lymph nodes that are potentially affected by the cancer. This is particularly true in the case of Hodgkin's disease, where, for example, a known lymph-node cancer in one side of the neck will require that lymph node groups in both sides of the neck, the underarm area, and the chest be included in the treatment (see Chapter 4).

Side Effects

The side effects of radiation therapy directed to lymph nodes correspond to the area of the body being treated. For example, when radiation is directed to the pelvic region, side effects may include cramping, diarrhea, and urinary frequency and urgency. Treatment to the upper abdomen primarily causes nausea and indigestion. The side effects of chemotherapy depend on the drugs used. Refer to Chapter 2 for a discussion of treating the expected side effects of radiation and chemotherapy.

Follow-Up and Outlook

Results of treatment are evaluated by physical examination if the lymph nodes are close to the surface of the body. The lymph nodes should shrink to a very small size after radiation therapy. However, they generally do not completely disappear because scar tissue forms and is felt as a small nodule. If physicians suspect that cancer still remains in a lymph node, it is necessary to physically monitor changes in the lymph node over a prolonged period of time, or a biopsy may be required.

Lymph nodes that are located deep in the body can be evaluated only by imaging tests. Size and number should decrease following either radiation or chemotherapy, and periodic testing will show whether the treatments were effective. On occasion, it may be necessary to perform a biopsy to confirm that the disease has been arrested.

Metastases to the lymph nodes is generally the second step of cancer progression after the initial growth. Although there are exceptions, the next step is generally dissemination throughout the body. Therefore, lymph-node metastases should be treated aggressively, especially when a cure is considered possible.

Metastasis to the Skin

Metastases to the chest wall (skin and underlying soft tissues) may occur months or years following a mastectomy for breast cancer. Radiation is used to treat this metastatic disease, which is not necessarily life threatening. However, skin metastases resulting from other kinds of cancer, such as lung cancer, are generally considered to be a sign of very advanced disease. Five to 15 percent of patients who have had a radical or modified radical mastectomy experience metastases to the skin. This is referred to as local disease because the chest wall and breast are in the same location. Because a recurrence in the skin following mastectomy may be a harbinger of disease at distant sites in up to 25 to 30 percent of patients, systemic therapy (hormonal or chemotherapy) may be recommended along with radiation. When the breast cancer is more advanced at the time of diagnosis, the percentages of skin metastases are higher. While the situation is serious, it is by no means hopeless.

Treatment

Many patients who develop these local recurrences but show no evidence of distant metastases have a relatively good overall prognosis. However, if these cancerous lesions are left untreated, they will progress into painful, infected ulcerations. One or two local deposits may be easily surgically removed. However, when multiple deposits are present, as is often the case, radiation therapy is delivered to the entire chest wall to prevent later problems with ulceration, bleeding, and pain. Approximately 5,000 units of radiation are delivered to the entire chest wall in five to six weeks. Most patients are seen during the early stage and cured of their local disease. Patients with more advanced disease may require different dose and time schedules. Radiation may still help heal the ulcers, stop the bleeding, and arrest the infection. Many radiation oncologists advocate treating the entire chest wall as soon as even one metastatic growth develops, because of the probability that cancers will appear in other areas.

Side Effects

These radiation treatments do not cause significant side effects, except for mild reddening of the skin, more common among fair-skinned individuals. Occasionally, patients develop scarring of that portion of the lung, which, despite efforts to keep exposure to a minimum, has received some radiation.

Some patients may develop an inflammation of the lung tissue (pneumonitis), which is treated with cortisone and sometimes antibiotics.

Follow-Up and Outlook

Depending on the stage of the cancer, radiation therapy administered to the chest wall immediately after the mastectomy or lumpectomy will reduce the incidence of skin recurrences. Women developing skin metastases shortly after surgery (within a year or two) do not have as good five-year survival rates as those whose skin metastases occur two years or longer after surgery.

Metastasis to the Spine

The spine consists of seven vertebrae in the neck (the cervical area), twelve in the upper and middle back (the thoracic area), five in the lower back (the lumbar region), and approximately ten in the tailbone (sacrum and coccyx). The bony vertebrae enclose the spinal cord and the nerves that exit from it. The spinal cord, originating in the upper neck, is connected to the lower part of the brain and ends at the lower thoracic vertebrae. The spinal cord is bathed by spinal fluid and is surrounded and contained by a membrane known as the *dura*.

Tumors may spread to the vertebral bone or to the spaces around the dura, or to both areas simultaneously. When the bone is involved, pain and limited motion are frequent symptoms. When the dural spaces are involved, with or without bone involvement, a common result is loss of motor or sensory function. These symptoms occur because as the tumor enlarges, it creates pressure on the spinal cord and the adjacent nerves. How much motor or sensory function is lost depends on the tumor's location and the extent to which the spinal cord and nerves are involved. Most cancers can extend to the spine; however, lung, breast, prostate cancers, and lymphomas are the most likely primary cancers to affect this region of the body.

A variety of tests may be used to evaluate the extent of the disease. For example, bone x-rays may reveal bone destruction, which often results in fractures of the vertebrae. A nuclear bone scan is a very sensitive means of detecting bone metastases. CT scans and MRIs (see Chapter 8) may also be performed to further evaluate the extent of the disease, particularly when the cancer involves the dural tissues around the spinal cord.

Treatment

When it is found that only bone tissue is involved in the disease, radiation therapy is given to reduce pain, improve limited motion, and prevent further spread of the cancer to the spinal cord and adjacent nerves. A dose of 3,000 to 5,000 units of radiation may be delivered over a two- to four-week period. The total dosage and treatment time depend on how quickly the pain disappears, the origin of the primary cancer, the extent of the disease, and the patient's overall physical condition. Most patients experience significant pain relief.

Cancer involving the spinal cord and nerves (with or without bone disease) may result in one of the few radiation-therapy emergencies. The loss of nerve function must be treated immediately; if it is not, normal function will not return. A short course of radiation with relatively high daily doses is often necessary to reduce acute symptoms. The exact level of radiation and the total daily dose are tailored to the cancer's site of origin, the extent of the disease, and the patient's response to treatment. In addition to radiation therapy, cortisone medication (prednisone or Decadron) is given simultaneously to help relieve pressure on the spinal cord caused by swelling of the tissues.

On occasion, some bone tissue is surgically removed to relieve pressure on the spinal cord (laminectomy). Radiation therapy is then administered to treat the remaining tumor deposits.

Side Effects

The location of the disease will determine the kind of side effects experienced. Radiation therapy to the cervical vertebrae may cause throat pain; radiation delivered to the mid-back may cause nausea and heartburn; radiation to the lower spine may cause nausea and diarrhea. These side effects occur because as the radiation beam goes through the spine, the soft tissues of the neck, chest, and abdomen are in its path. (For further discussion of side effects, see Chapter 2.)

Follow-Up and Outlook

If neurological symptoms are caught early (within approximately twenty-four hours), radiation treatment may reverse the damage in many patients or at least halt its progress. This is the reason that delivering radiation therapy to the spine is often considered urgent. Unfortunately, the treatment is not always effective, no matter how aggressive the effort, and the patient's symptoms will progress. In other cases, the cancer is detected too late for treatments to be effective. These patients will experience varying degrees of neurologic impairment that are not reversible.

If Cancer Has Spread and Treatment Stops Working

If cancer has spread despite surgery, radiation, and chemotherapy, and treatment has stopped working, patients and their doctors need to carefully redefine goals. We know how difficult it can be to switch gears, so to speak, when cure has been the goal, and patients have endured months or years of treatment. However, new goals may include a desire to remain pain free, spending as much time as possible at home, or maintaining a certain level of functioning. Quality of life becomes the issue, and even if treatment of the cancer is not possible, it *is* possible to treat symptoms related to the cancer and help people to live better.

Although these discussions may be painful and difficult, it is important to talk about death. Making plans does not mean giving up, but we have seen that planning can reduce some of the inevitable stress on patients and families.

End-of-life care can focus on pain relief and reducing fear. Support from a hospice or palliative care program allows individuals to be cared for at home or in a medical facility.

For more information on hospice programs, access the home page of the National Hospice and Palliative Care organization at nhpco.org.

6

More Treatments for Cancer

In addition to surgery, radiation, and chemotherapy, additional substances and procedures are used in cancer treatment. Some are relatively new; others have been used for several years—even decades. We include a brief discussion of these other cancer treatments because your doctors may mention them to you at the time of diagnosis or during treatment. In each case, current basic scientific research and clinical trials are underway in an attempt to establish efficacy of these treatments for certain cancers and discover additional uses for them. Many people consider that participating in a clinical trial can be the best treatment option.

Bone Marrow Transplantation

Bone marrow transplantation is used in the treatment of blood diseases, genetic diseases, and cancer. Bone marrow *stem cells* are the parent cells of red and white blood cells and platelets. Most of these stem cells are located in the bone marrow, the liquid part in the bones; however, some stem cells may circulate in the peripheral blood.

When used as a treatment for cancer, high-dose chemotherapy is administered first, followed by infusion of bone marrow stem cells in order to regenerate the bone marrow eradicated from the chemotherapy. With diseases such as lymphoma or leukemia, where the bone marrow cells may be diseased, the high-dose chemotherapy is important in eliminating the cancerous cells. The transplanted bone marrow cells are given to repopulate the diseased bone marrow eradicated by the chemotherapy. Sometimes total-body irradiation (radiation delivered to the whole body) is also used to eliminate any cancerous cells in bone marrow.

The bone marrow given back to patients is known as the *donor marrow*. The two main types of bone marrow transplant are *autologous* and *allogeneic*. *Allogeneic* bone marrow transplants are done using either a related donor or an unrelated donor with matching features on their cells. Siblings are related donors most likely to be a complete match. Unrelated donors are identified through the National Bone Marrow Transplant Registry, but it may take weeks to months to identify a donor. Under anesthesia, bone marrow is removed from the donor's iliac bones (the bones in the back of the hips) and is stored. When it is time for the transplant, the marrow is given to the patient by vein. Allogeneic transplant is used to treat leukemia more frequently than it is used to treat other cancers.

In *autologous* bone marrow transplants, the bone marrow stem cells are collected from the patient prior to giving the high doses of chemotherapy. Then the cells are infused back into the patient. This procedure is also known as a *peripheral blood stem cell transplant* because the cells collected for the procedure are known as *peripheral blood stem cells*. They are collected using a procedure similar to that used when donating blood. This type of transplant can be done when the patient's bone marrow is normal, either because the disease is in remission or because the disease has not affected the bone marrow. This type of transplant is done for patients with breast or testicular cancer, for example; it is also done for lymphoma or myeloma in order to allow the patient to receive higher doses of chemotherapy.

Possible side effects of bone marrow transplant depend on the chemotherapy drugs used prior to giving back the stem cells. Major side effects are those related to the severe and prolonged periods of low blood counts. Risk of infection is highest in patients who have had allogeneic transplant because the period of low blood counts is the longest, which increases the risk of not only bacterial infection but viral and fungal infections as well. During the period of low blood counts, patients need red blood cell and platelet transfusions. Growth factors (granulocyte-colony stimulating factors) also are used to help improve recovery time for white blood cells.

Nausea and vomiting may occur early on, and painful mouth sores may sometimes limit patients' ability to eat, thereby requiring intravenous feeding and pain medicines. Sometimes sores appear throughout the intestinal tract, which may be associated with diarrhea and risk of infection.

One possible side effect unique to transplantation is known as *graft fail-ure*, meaning that the bone marrow given back to the patient has difficulty producing new blood cells. Although rare, this may mean that not enough cells were transplanted.

Graft versus host disease, a side effect unique to allogeneic transplant, occurs when the new, donor marrow takes over and recognizes the patient's own cells as being foreign. Skin rash, liver abnormalities, and other organ damage may develop. In order to prevent graft vs. host disease, the patient is given a med-ication that suppresses the immune system; however, this can also lead to a higher risk of infection. However, for patients with leukemia, having a little bit of graft vs. host disease (sometimes called *graft versus leukemia effect*) can actually be a good thing because the donor cells also become enlisted in an immunologic war against any residual leukemia cells.

Patients may be at risk of organ damage, particularly to the heart, liver, or lungs, depending on the chemotherapy drugs used and whether graft vs. host disease develops.

When the technology for bone marrow transplant was first developed, these treatments were limited to younger patients. Now that treating the compli-cations of transplant has significantly improved, autologous transplants may be done in individuals in their sixties if they are otherwise healthy. Allogeneic transplant, because it has potentially greater side effects, notably graft vs. host disease, is generally done up to age fifty. However, as posttransplant care becomes more refined, the upper age limits keep changing.

Bone marrow transplantation may be curative for certain cancers, such as leukemia, Hodgkin's and non-Hodgkin's lymphomas. For other cancers, such as breast cancer, the results have been disappointing. In other cancers, such as testicular cancer, the results are promising. Finally, in a number of other cancers, such as kidney cancer and melanoma, bone marrow transplant is still investigational.

Other Anticancer Substances

The cortisone (steroid) drugs prednisone and Decadron are sometimes used for breast cancer, multiple myeloma, Hodgkin's disease, and non-Hodgkin's lymphoma because they retard the growth of cancer cells. The drugs are also used to decrease swelling of brain or spinal tissues caused by tumors in these areas. High doses of cortisone medications are effective in treating leukemia and lymphomas because they have a direct destructive effect on the cancer cells and retard their proliferation. Decadron is also a highly effective anti-nausea medicine.

Steroids may cause weight gain, fluid retention in body tissues, heartburn, ulcers, and increased appetite. (These side effects are also common when these drugs are used to treat conditions other than cancer.) They may also produce a sense of well-being—obviously a positive side effect. However, long-term use of steroids may cause loss of bone mass (osteoporosis).

Bisphosphonates are a group of medications that help to strengthen bones that have been affected by cancer. Although more potent, they belong to the same class of drugs used to treat osteoporosis. These drugs include pamidronate (Aredia) and zoledronic acid (Zometa), both of which are given intravenously once a month. They help to reduce complications that may be seen when cancer spreads to the bone, they decrease bone pain, decrease the risk of fracture, and reduce the need to have radiation treatments to painful bone sites. They have been shown to help extend life in patients with myeloma and metastatic breast cancer, and they are helpful in patients with prostate cancer that has spread to bones. Bisphosphonates are being studied for use in treating lung cancer and other cancers that involve bony sites. In addition, they are being studied to see if their use *before* cancer has spread will work to prevent the spread of cancer to the bones.

Gene Therapy

Gene therapy may hold the key to developing an eventual cure for cancer. To understand how gene therapy works, you need basic information about what causes a cell to transform from a healthy, normal state to a cancerous state. As you know, our bodies are comprised of cells, each of which contains chromosomes. Half our chromosomes come from our mother, half from our father. Chromosomes contain only four molecules, called nucleotides; normal life processes are controlled by the arrangement of these nucleotides.

Areas on the chromosomes control seemingly unimportant genetic information such as our hair color, body type, and our height. There are also areas on the chromosomes that tell each cell what kind of cell it should be. So, while a brain cell has the same chromosome pattern as a rectal cell, for example, these cells have entirely different functions.

Certain areas on the chromosomes tell the cell how to reproduce. When we are young and our bodies are growing and developing, all our cells reproduce at a rapid rate. The cell turnover slows as we move into adulthood, but certain cells are more active than others. For example, adult bone-marrow cells are more active than adult brain cells. Cells also need to "stay put," so to speak. A liver cell should stay in the liver; a lung cell should stay in the lung.

The word *gene* applies to the areas of the chromosome that control specific functions. Imagine that a chromosome is a street, and the genes are specific houses on the street, with each house designated to control a specific function.

When Something Goes Wrong

A cell may become cancerous when something goes wrong with its genetic pattern. The "something" that can trigger abnormal changes in cells includes such things as viruses, chemicals in the environment, and genetic defects. A cancer cell is by definition dangerous because it is able to reproduce rapidly, but also because of its inability to stay in its designated site. Metastasis occurs because cancer cells invade adjacent organs or travel through the bloodstream and settle in distant sites.

Our current treatments—surgery, radiation, and chemotherapy—are most effective when the cancer cells are localized; chances for remission or cure are reduced when metastasis occurs. As you know, all three types of treatment have inherent limits. For example, chemotherapeutic agents act as a poison directed at the most actively growing cells—the cancer cells. These abnormal cells are the most sensitive to the drug. However, bone-marrow cells, for example, are active cells, too. Hence, almost all the chemotherapy drugs in use today affect them. Radiation therapy affects both normal and cancerous cells, and we are limited in our ability to deliver higher doses of radiation because we must avoid, to the extent we can, damage to healthy adjacent cells.

Targeting the Ultimate Cause

Gene therapy can be used to correct an abnormality in the cell *or* to attack the specific abnormality in the cell. To correct an abnormality, gene therapy implies the transfer of genetic material directly to the cell. Currently, the most commonly used mechanism is a process by which a virus is modified and it invades the cell and carries new genetic coding.

This new therapy is in its infancy, and thus far the goals are modest. However, current approaches involve transferring genetic codes to the chromosomes in order to reduce their growth rate or to make them more responsive—sensitive—to other radiation and chemotherapy, as well as immunotherapy. It is true that gene therapy is somewhat limited, too, in that normal cells are affected when genetic codes are altered. Ideally, future gene therapy will involve isolating the specific genetic abnormality on the chromosome and transferring genetic material through viruses, or other means that become available, to correct the abnormality.

Gene therapy can also imply the use of targeted treatments to attack the cause of cancer, the gene itself. Because tumor cells may grow differently than normal cells, this approach aims to select only cancerous cells and leave healthy cells alone.

Specific targets include the cancer-causing genes, growth factors and their receptors, and enzymes that control cell growth. An example of a cancer-causing gene, bcl-2, prevents cell death and is abnormal in certain cancers like lymphoma. Therapy targeted at bcl-2 is being investigated as a treatment for lymphoma.

Growth factors are proteins that stimulate cell growth, and there are specific types of growth factors for specific cells. For example, vascular endothelial growth factor (VEGF) is needed for blood vessel growth.

Cancerous tumors rely on a process known as *angiogenesis* to develop their own blood supply, which is needed in order to grow. *Antiangiogenesis* drugs are agents that reduce the blood supply to the cancer in an attempt to inhibit growth. These agents are most effective when used in combination with chemotherapy. The drug bevacizumab (Avastin) targets VEGF and is used in the treatment of solid tumors such as colon cancer.

For epidermal cells, *epidermal growth factor* is needed. Erbitux is a monoclonal antibody targeted against the epidermal growth factor receptor EGFR.

Targeted treatments against epidermal growth factor are being studied for use in treating colorectal cancer, lung cancer, and other solid tumors. These agents may be used alone or with chemotherapy.

Trastuzumab (Herceptin) is a monoclonal antibody and an example of treatment targeted against a growth factor receptor, specifically against breast cancers that have too much of the *Her-2 neu* protein, which is associated with the potential for rapid growth. Only about 20 percent of all breast cancers have excessive amounts of this protein on their surface, so it is used only in selected patients.

Enzymes are needed to speed up cell reactions. One family of enzymes called *tyrosine kinases* is important in cancer treatment. For example, the drug Imatinib (Gleevec) is targeted against the specific tyrosine kinase abnormality associated with chronic myelogenous leukemia and has been responsible for dramatic improvement in the prognosis for these patients. A similar molecular abnormality has been found in other cancers, such as a very rare type of stomach cancer. So, even though the diseases are quite different, Imatinib has been useful because of a shared molecular abnormality. Other drugs that target different tyrosine kinases include Iressa (used to treat lung, head and neck, colon, and prostate cancers) and Tarceva (used for pancreatic, head and neck, and esophageal cancers).

Monoclonal Antibody Therapy

Our bodies have the ability to recognize foreign bacteria because areas on bacteria cells have chemical configurations that are different from normal cells. These areas—sites—are called *antigens*. The body protects itself by making proteins to attack the bacteria, and these proteins attach to the antigen sites. We call the proteins *antibodies*; antibody therapy attempts to help the body recognize a foreign invader. Our bodies are designed to protect us against abnormal cells, which of course include cancer cells. However, our immune system is not universally able to differentiate between normal and cancerous cells. A more recent approach to cancer treatment is to inject a patient with an antibody that has an affinity for cancer cells. The body then recognizes the foreign antibody and attacks it, which means it attacks the cancerous cells, too.

It is also possible to "tag" the antitumor antibodies with either a chemotherapeutic agent or radioactive material, which will then be carried to the cancer cells in order to kill them directly. Two examples of this type of agent use the principle of targeting the lymphoma cells using a monoclonal antibody directed against the CD20 protein that carries with it a radioactive isotope right to those cells. Ibritumomab tiuxetan (Zevelin) is a monoclonal antibody combined with the radioactive isotope yttrium 90. Tositumomab (Bexxar) combines an anti-CD20 monoclonal antibody with the radioactive isotope iodine 131. These strategies do have side effects, and their use is cumbersome due to special precautions needed when using the radioactive isotopes. However, they have shown promise in relapsed lymphoma cases when other treatments have not been effective.

Vaccines are in development to treat certain cancers, such as melanoma, renal cell cancer, and breast cancer. This is an area in which it may be valuable to seek participation in clinical trials.

Genetic Predisposition and Preventing Cancer

Over the years, there has been some consideration of, in a sense, stopping cancer before it starts. For example, women with a strong familial history of breast and/or ovarian cancer, particularly occurring at a young age, are often very concerned about their genetic predisposition to these diseases. This means that they are possible carriers of the altered genes that increase risk.

There remains considerable controversy over who should be tested. Individuals must ask themselves what they are prepared to do if they test positive. Are they willing to accept treatment options, limited though these options are at the present time? Currently, for women at increased risk of breast cancer, the choices include more intensive surveillance, bilateral mastectomy, or removing the ovaries (oophorectomy). If family history of breast cancer is strong, then absence of the known genes should not alter a woman's decision to increase surveillance. Only about one-third of patients with a strong family history of breast cancer actually carry the BRCA-1 or BRCA-2 genes, two genes that are identified with a much higher than normal risk for developing the disease.

The more drastic option is to undergo a prophylactic bilateral mastectomy, which means removing both breasts. Even with immediate reconstruction, this option may be unacceptable to many women. In addition, the surgery does not guarantee that a woman will not develop breast cancer in the residual glandular tissue that may be left behind. Removing the ovaries reduces the risk of ovarian cancer and partially reduces the risk of breast cancer, making it a more acceptable option, particularly for women who have completed childbearing.

Chemoprevention using tamoxifen (see Chapter 4) is another choice currently under discussion. A recent national study found that tamoxifen decreased incidence of breast cancer in high-risk women by 50 percent. Ongoing studies include comparison of tamoxifen with raloxifene (a drug used in the treatment of osteoporosis) and with a new class of hormonal agents known as *aromatase inhibitors*.

Chemoprevention, often using aspirin (an antiprostaglandin), is considered for patients with strong family histories of multiple polyps and colon cancer (familial adenomatous polyposis). Other agents, such as celecoxib (Celebrex), could be recommended because they inhibit COX-2, which is part of the prostaglandin pathway. (Prostaglandins are important in the body's response to inflammation. An antiprostaglandin is a substance that blocks—inhibits—their production.)

Genetic testing has serious potential disadvantages that remind us of the "brave new world" we inevitably face in the twenty-first century. For example, genetic predisposition is not an absolute, and most of us have predisposition to diseases we never develop. Furthermore, we cannot underestimate certain risks with this testing. For example, some individuals may be denied insurance coverage or even employment opportunities based on results of genetic testing. Remember, too, that genetic testing is being carried out to identify risk for diseases other than cancer. We may learn, of course, that a significant portion of the population carries predisposing factors to one disease or another.

Looking to the Future

Important goals for the future of cancer treatment involve not just curing cancer, but also sparing individuals from the agony of the diagnosis and the intensity of the current treatments. Future treatments for cancer will aim to predict and prevent. Specifically, we will strive to identify those who are at higher risk of developing cancer, and then direct those individuals to specific strategies to reduce the risk of developing the disease at all. In order to do this, we need to foster research in the lab to identify specific abnormalities, then use translational research to bring these strategies into the clinical arena, first through clinical trials and then ultimately, as the standard of care.

7

Treating Pain

At some point, about one-third of all patients undergoing treatment for cancer require medication to control pain. For patients with advanced disease, the figure rises to more than two-thirds. As the survival rates for cancer improve, many more patients have been afflicted with pain from the disease. In other words, because of advances in treatment, patients with cancers that were at one time fatal now have their lives extended, and they may experience periodic flare-ups that cause pain.

Pain can be classified by type. *Acute pain* is what someone may experience immediately after surgery or after an injury. *Chronic pain* is pain that lasts longer, and is what may be seen in individuals with metastatic cancer. Chronic pain may be *intermittent*, meaning that it occurs from time to time. Chronic pain may be *continuous* or persistent. This type of pain requires consideration of use of long-acting pain medications. Finally, with chronic pain that is continuous there may be periods of *breakthrough pain*, meaning that control is good for most of the day but that there are periods of episodic pain despite long-acting medication.

Why Is Cancer Painful?

The origin of most cancer pain is related to tumors causing pressure and destruction of bone. Pain will also occur as the result of nerve compression, infiltration of the cancer into soft tissues and organs, and pressure on or blockage of the gastrointestinal tract. Pain resulting from cancer treatments affects only a minority of patients (approximately 10 percent).

Pain is strongly influenced by emotions, and people react differently to the same pain stimuli. Some patients feel distraught as a result of their fear of disability or death and worry about financial matters as well as a sense of isolation and loneliness. The level of emotional concerns a patient has will affect their perception of pain intensity. Because the brain is capable of producing its own painkillers (endorphins), techniques to stimulate their production can be effective. Meditation, imaging, and biofeedback are examples of these techniques.

In addition, the fear of pain may increase the perception of the pain itself. In other words, a host of physical and emotional factors interplay, and your physician will evaluate all of them when treating you.

Pain Relief Medications

Your physician must consider many factors when prescribing pain medication. First, the origin of the pain (bone, muscle, or nerve) must be determined. Each site may require different treatment regimens. Cancer pain that is caused by muscle spasm or swelling of tissues is different from that caused by bone disease. In practical terms, medication that is effective for one kind of pain may be ineffective for another.

For acute pain—that following surgery, for example—medications such as acetaminophen (Tylenol) or nonsteroidal anti-inflammatory drugs such as ibuprofen may be recommended. Fast-acting narcotic analgesics, such as codeine or oxycodone may be added. These medications come in preparations that are already in combination, such as Tylenol with codeine or Percocet (oxycodone and acetaminophen). These medications are prescribed "as needed," meaning that if you feel the pain, you should take the medicine. For neuropathic pain, a burning type of pain, anticonvulsant drugs such as gabapentin (Neurontin) or antidepressant drugs such as amitriptyline (Elavil) are sometimes recommended.

For chronic pain, meaning pain that lasts for most of the day, a round-the-clock medication is preferred. This means taking the medication to prevent pain, rather than waiting for the pain and then taking medication to relieve it. In this situation, long-acting pain medicines are preferred; these include long-acting forms of morphine (MS Contin) or the long-acting form of oxycodone (OxyContin). The analgesic fentanyl, often used in anesthesia, is available in a patch that is changed every three days and may provide good long-acting pain control. In addition, methadone may sometimes be used. In some situations, narcotic medication can be given as continuous intravenous pump.

For breakthrough pain—that is, short bursts of pain—the medications used work more quickly than the long-acting preparations, but their effects are temporary. Examples include immediate-release morphine, oxycodone, hydromorphone (Dilaudid), or levorphanol (Levo-Dromoran). Anti-inflammatory drugs or steroids may be added. Anticonvulsants and antidepressants also have a role in pain management.

When discussing narcotics, it is essential for patients and family members to understand the meaning of the terms *tolerance, physical dependency,* and *psychological dependency.* By *tolerance* we mean that a particular dosage of pain medication that was satisfactory for a while eventually becomes less effective. In other words, the body has accustomed itself to a level of medication, and therefore its effect is reduced. When this happens, your doctor should not hesitate to increase the dose to make you more comfortable. When pain is severe, medication should be administered around the clock rather than on an "as needed" basis. Although some patients stay on the same dose for long periods of time, other patients reach tolerance more quickly. Doctors know this has happened when patients note that the effect of the medication wears off more quickly, hence the time needed between doses decreases.

When medications must be increased because of tolerance, patients often begin to worry about physical dependency—addiction. They are also concerned about developing a psychological craving for the drug. Most cancer specialists agree that psychological dependency—another characteristic of addiction—is extremely rare. Patients should not suffer pain because of a fear of dependency, and dosages of narcotics should be adequate to control pain. For the majority of patients, the use of narcotics decreases as radiation therapy successfully reduces pain. Remember, people who are experiencing pain do not get addicted to pain medication. Rather, people who take these medicines that have no pain are the ones who are vulnerable.

The most common side effects of narcotic medication are constipation, nausea, and oversedation. Your physician will suggest laxatives, stool softeners, and dietary changes that can relieve constipation. Most patients on long-acting narcotic pain medicines will experience constipation, so prevention is key, and patients will often be advised to take something on a daily basis to prevent constipation. Medications to reduce nausea are available and may be useful if the nausea does not gradually disappear on its own. Sedation is an unfortunate side effect, because cancer patients may already have low energy levels and feel fatigued. Stimulants, such as methylphenidate (Ritalin), may be helpful for some patients to help them stay awake during the day. Itching is another, less common side effect of pain medications, and may be relieved with antihistamines.

Generally, radiation oncologists prescribe pain medications, but their knowledge of those medications may not be as extensive as that of medical oncologists. We usually leave it to these specialists to fine-tune the use and dosage of narcotic medications. However, radiation oncologists are always aware of the medications you are taking and monitor their effectiveness. During the course of radiation therapy, you will be asked about pain, and as it decreases, decisions about reducing medications can be made. Your family physician will also be aware of other conditions that your radiation and medical oncologists should be told about, because these conditions will influence the types of medication used during your treatment.

Treating the Disease

Treating the cancer causing the pain is a priority. With some cancers, such as lymphoma, pain relief may come shortly after the first dose of chemotherapy. In patients with hormonally responsive, advanced breast cancer or prostate cancer, hormone medication can provide good pain relief; however, it may take some time to take full effect. If cancer has spread to the bones, radiation may be the fastest and most effective way to obtain pain relief, in particular, if there are only one or two main sites of involvement.

Radiation therapy is most effective when used to treat bone pain, and relief is generally accompanied by arrest or eradication of the cancer in the bone under treatment. (X-rays and nuclear bone scans often document this.) In the majority of cancer patients, pain is caused by cancer invading the skeleton or adjacent nerve endings.

Another important strategy in reducing pain due to cancer that has spread to the bone, is the use of medicines called *bisphosphonates*. These medications are "cousins" of the commonly used drugs that treat osteoporosis; they include pamidronate (Aredia) and zoledronic acid (Zometa). These medications have been best studied in patients with myeloma and breast cancer who have disease that is involving the bones. In these patients, pamidronate and zoledronic acid have been shown to reduce bone pain, reduce the risk of fracture, reduce the need for radiation, and overall make the bones an "unfriendly" place for cancer cells to be. These medications are administered intravenously on a monthly basis.

Surgery is effective only in specialized situations, such as the relief of intestinal blockage or to relieve the pressure on the spinal cord and its nerves caused by the cancer. Cancers that cause pressure on nerves are often more effectively treated with cortisone and narcotics.

Pain Assessment

Good communication with your doctor is the key to successful pain management. You should be regularly assessed, with a plan put in place, and then follow-up to see how the plan is working. Your doctor will ask you to describe your pain. Is it a burning discomfort or is it a sharp pain? Is it a dull ache, like a toothache? They will often ask you to rate your pain on a scale from zero to ten, with zero being pain-free and ten being the worst imaginable pain. They will want to know what seems to bring the pain on. Do you wake up with it? Does it appear to come on after walking? Is the pain intermittent or is it a constant pain? How does the pain interfere with your day-to-day activities and your mood? Does it keep you from doing what you want to do?

Understanding your pain will help your physician make the best recommendations for you. The goal is to have you pain-free and able to function without limitations.

Once you are on medication, your doctor will ask the same questions to see if the plan is working. Doses may be increased and at other times reduced. If you are on a long-acting medication, you will be asked if the dose is completely relieving the pain. If it does, but the effect does not last until the next dose is due (breakthrough pain), then your doctor may recommend changing the interval of your medicine. He or she may also recommend adding a fast-acting pain medicine to take in between.

Additional Strategies

In addition to taking medication, a number of other strategies may be helpful in controlling pain. For example, relaxation techniques, massage, hot or cold packs, and physical therapy may be helpful. Some individuals may find meditation, prayer, and guided imagery helpful in managing pain. Currently, acupuncture is being studied as a possible additional strategy to relieve cancer pain.

If pain control is difficult to achieve, referral to a pain specialist is recommended. Some pain specialists may recommend injections of medicines into painful areas. When all else fails, specialized neurosurgical procedures may be required to block pain. One procedure is to inject chemicals into the nerves, another is to sever the nerve fibers. Surgery may also be used to reduce tumor size and thus relieve pressure on nerve fibers.

Pain is not necessarily a sign of advanced cancer; curable cancers also may cause pain. It is important for you to remember that pain is not a sign of weakness or something to be ashamed of. When you experience pain or reactions to medications, don't hesitate to talk about what is happening to you. In almost all cases, something can be done to make you more comfortable.

Although it may not currently be possible to cure all cancers, the ability to treat pain as it arises is a reasonable goal. Be sure to communicate with your doctor about the presence or absence of pain, and, beyond that, how pain may be affecting the way you live day to day. You and your doctors can work as a team to achieve the important goal of relief. For more information, log on to the American Pain Foundation website, painfoundation.org.

PART 3

Other Issues in Cancer Treatment

This section describes some of the many tests used to establish a diagnosis of cancer and for follow-up evaluations that determine the results of treatment. Some of the tests are redundant, and choosing the appropriate ones involves both accuracy and cost considerations. Some of the tests listed here are time-proven standards; others (PET and MRI) are high-tech and may not be readily available in some locales in the United States and other countries.

8

Diagnostic Testing

When patients describe symptoms that suggest the presence of cancer, physicians take the necessary steps to either rule out the condition or offer a definitive diagnosis. Some cancers, such as skin cancers, can be seen by a physician trained to recognize them; cancers of the prostate gland, testicles, rectum, lymph nodes, the female reproductive organs, breast, the thyroid gland, and the mouth can often be detected by physical examination. Physicians palpate—feel—the affected area and determine if an irregularity may be a cancer. Throat and intestinal cancers can be diagnosed with endoscopes, specialized tubes that allow areas within these internal structures to be viewed. Laboratory tests may provide additional diagnostic information, and some of these tests—the Pap smear, for example—provide a definitive diagnosis of cancer.

Because of their size and location, many other cancers may not be detected without using imaging tests that allow physicians to see structures and tissues inside of the body. The results of these tests are often so suggestive of cancer that a biopsy is performed subsequently to confirm or disprove the initial suspicion of cancer.

Test results are used to design appropriate treatment plans, monitor progress during therapy, and as part of the follow-up care. Although some general guidelines exist, the treatment plan for each patient is individualized. The amount and kind of testing ordered for one person with colon cancer, for example, may not be the same as that recommended for another with the same disease. The person's age, other coexisting conditions, and the stage of the disease are always considered.

Choosing the Test to Use

If your primary-care physician believes that a particular type of cancer may be present, he or she will refer you to other specialists who will perform the examinations necessary to confirm the diagnosis. Radiologists perform imaging tests, which include x-rays, nuclear scans, CT scans, ultrasound, MRIs, and PET scans. The radiologist determines which test is best able to substantiate or disprove the primary-care physician's initial impression. A positive test result means the presence of disease; a negative result means that disease is not present or has not been detected.

For many reasons, cost certainly being one of them, radiologists attempt to choose the test that is likely to be the most accurate and decisive, thereby eliminating the need for additional tests. The most technologically sophisticated—and therefore the most expensive—test may *not* always be the best choice. A simple x-ray test may diagnose a particular cancer as accurately as the more complex MRI examination. On the other hand, one MRI may be less expensive than a battery of the more simple tests. Be sure to ask for explanations about the reasons certain tests are recommended. Remember, too, that x-ray tests and other imaging examinations included in this section are also used to diagnose diseases other than cancer.

Review of Test Results Prior to Treatment

Once a diagnosis of cancer has been established (through biopsy) and your physicians have determined that radiation treatment is appropriate, your radiation oncologist will plan your course of treatment. Imaging tests performed during the diagnostic process are then reviewed in order to design the size and shape of the treatment field, or portal. The tumor is part of the treatment field, which may also include the usual pathways by which the particular cancer is known to spread. The imaging tests indicate the patterns of spread as well as the depth of the tumor inside the body. Thus, the tests are used both to design the size of the treatment field and to determine the depth of treatment necessary in each individual case.

Testing During Treatment

Based on the patient's unique situation, physical examinations and imaging tests may be necessary to evaluate results. Imaging tests make it possible to determine the effect of radiation and/or chemotherapy on the tumor, thereby allowing the treatment plan to be modified, if necessary. The treatment portal size may be reduced or reshaped, and the dosage may also be changed. Patients can be encouraged that treatment is working. In addition, this testing can evaluate new conditions or clarify symptoms. For example, when bone pain arises in areas not treated, x-rays or nuclear bone scans may be performed to differentiate between cancer and arthritis. Patients may develop gastrointestinal (GI) problems that cannot be explained as side effects of the radiation therapy or chemotherapy, and a GI series or barium enema may be performed to evaluate this separate complaint.

Testing After Completion of Radiation Therapy and Chemotherapy

The established guidelines for posttreatment testing are arbitrary and serve as *recommendations* based on studies that included large numbers of patients with similar cancers. However, most physicians individualize each patient's treatment plan and follow-up care, based on the presence or absence of symptoms and physical examination. The type of cancer treated and its stage at the time of its detection will greatly influence decisions about follow-up testing. When patients are free of their disease, the interval between imaging tests usually lengthens.

Types of Tests

The following tests, briefly described below, are arranged in order of their technological complexity, from low-tech to high-tech. They include bone x-ray, chest x-ray, gastrointestinal examination (GI series), barium enema, colo-noscopy, small-bowel series, intravenous pyelogram examination (IVP), mam-mogram, nuclear scanning, ultrasound, computed axial tomography scanning (CT scan), magnetic resonance imaging (MRI), and PET (positron emission tomography).

An extensive discussion of the reasons these tests are performed, what patients must do to prepare for them, and what patients can expect during the test are outside the scope of this book. The information below provides only a general overview of the most frequently used imaging tests. Talk with your physicians about your specific questions and concerns.

Bone X-Ray

Bone x-rays are usually performed when a fracture is suspected. On x-rays, fractures appear as lines across the bone; when the injury is severe, the break appears as fragments of bone. Bone x-rays are also used to evaluate infections and tumors.

Bone x-rays are generally not as accurate as nuclear bone scans in reveal-ing early signs of infection or tumors. When they have progressed past the early stage, tumors and infections may appear on x-rays as irregular black holes. (Bone tumors usually are the result of the spread of cancer from dis-tant sites.) These conditions often weaken the bone and cause it to fracture. Cancer spread to bone may also show up as spots of increased bone forma-tion, or increased whiteness, rather than holes. Both effects may coexist. After treatment, the reappearance of normal bone may be seen on the x-ray, thus confirming the beneficial results of radiation therapy.

Chest X-Ray

A chest x-ray is ordered when symptoms such as cough or difficulty breath-ing suggest lung or heart problems. The routine chest x-ray also is sometimes used as a screening tool, that is, to detect diseases for which symptoms have not yet appeared. Lung cancer often fits into this category. Unfortunately, by the time a lung cancer is seen on a chest x-ray, the cancer often is advanced or has spread. Studies have failed to demonstrate significant survival benefit with annual or even semiannual chest x-rays in high-risk groups.

We now have a new CT scan procedure called a *spiral CT*, which can reveal tumors less than one centimeter in size. This test takes less than five minutes, is painless, and requires no preparation. Currently, it is recommended as a screening procedure for only those in high-risk categories, such as current or recent ex-smokers. At this time, the spiral CT is not covered by insurance or Medicare, but studies are currently underway to see if detecting smaller lung cancers will mean increased cure rates. We believe it will.

Despite its limitations, the chest x-ray remains a valuable test because it is quick, inexpensive, and can find many abnormalities. It allows radiologists to evaluate the lung fields for abnormalities, and, if present, determine their size, number, and shape. Certain characteristics differentiate cancers from benign diseases, and in order to arrive at a specific diagnosis, further tests (usually a CT scan and a biopsy) are needed. A chest x-ray also allows the radiologist to analyze potential abnormalities in the heart, blood vessels, and lymph nodes; and it reveals fluid that has collected in the spaces around the lungs (pleural tissues).

Although a chest x-ray may detect an abnormality, other tests may differentiate among similar conditions. For example, bacterial, viral, or fungal pneumonias may look like one another, and cancers may sometimes lurk under a pneumonia. Furthermore, a small spot or even a large mass may be nonspecific for the diagnosis of cancer. Comparing recent x-rays with earlier ones helps to determine if changes are of recent origin, indicating acute disease (infection or cancer, for example), or have been present a long time, indicating old disease, which would suggest a benign cause.

Gastrointestinal Examination

The upper gastrointestinal series, referred to as a GI series, examines the esophagus (swallowing tube), the stomach, and a portion of the small intestine called the duodenum. It is common for symptoms from these three areas to mimic one another, and the entire GI series is usually performed to determine which structure is causing the difficulty.

Some symptoms are specific to the esophagus, and when these occur, only an esophagram is performed. These include swallowing problems, experienced as lumps or sticking sensations in the throat or chest, or regurgitation, a sensation of food coming up from the stomach to the esophagus or throat. Generally, however, symptoms such as bloating, pain, nausea, and indigestion are evaluated with the entire GI series.

Patients are given instructions about preparing for this test, which involves overnight fasting. Patients drink a barium-sulfate solution, the *contrast agent* that creates greater contrast between the filled organ and the surrounding tissues, enabling abnormalities caused by disease to be identified.

The GI series is considered fairly accurate in the diagnosis of ulcer diseases and cancers. With the advent of endoscopy, a procedure that uses flexible tubing to allow direct visualization of the stomach and duodenum, diseases can be diagnosed even more accurately. Many patients now undergo endoscopy alone or after an abnormality has been detected on the GI series, particularly when cancer is suspected. The biopsy may be performed through the endoscope and a diagnosis arrived at directly.

Barium Enema

This is a valuable diagnostic tool for detecting diseases of the large bowel (large intestine) and actually is not as nasty as it is reputed to be. A barium-sulfate solution is introduced into the bowel through a tube inserted in the rectum. The complete filling of the bowel is monitored by fluoroscopy, the use of x-rays to create an image of internal organs and to visualize their motion. Diverticulae (saclike protrusions), inflammatory disease (colitis), polyps (mushroomlike growths), and cancers can all be detected with a barium enema. This test is also used to determine the effects of abnormalities of adjacent organs on the bowel.

Symptoms of large-bowel disease may include: rectal bleeding; cramping; steady or intermittent abdominal pain; and changes in normal bowel habits, such as diarrhea, constipation, or alternating periods of each. When infection is present, fever may accompany the bowel symptoms; if bleeding is prolonged or extensive, anemia will result.

Polyps may be benign or malignant. Larger polyps are more likely to be malignant than smaller ones, and they sometimes cause rectal bleeding. Cancers can appear as polyps on the barium enema. Large, cancerous irregularities of the bowel wall may lead to obstruction.

Colonoscopy

Colonoscopy allows direct visualization of the colon. It has largely replaced the barium enema because it can detect smaller lesions and the physician can remove a small polyp, or biopsy a tumor, at the time of the procedure. A bowel preparation (a strong laxative) is used to insure the bowel is free of stool. The patient is sedated and a flexible tube is inserted into the colon, which allows the physician to view the inside of this internal structure. Sometimes, if there are too many kinks or bends, the procedure may be limited to visualizing only a portion of the colon. If the study is incomplete, a barium enema is then performed. The procedure requires sedation and the patient may have an adverse reaction to the drugs used. On rare occasions, the colon may be perforated.

A recently developed CT scan procedure, *virtual colonoscopy*, eliminates the risks of sedation and bowel perforation. The procedure still requires a bowel preparation. However, this procedure can detect polyps or tumors smaller than a centimeter. If an abnormality is seen, the patient will require a colonoscopy for a biopsy or removal of a small polyp. One study demonstrated this test to be as sensitive as a colonoscopy, but another study disputes this finding, so at this time controversy remains.

Small-Bowel Series

This test may be performed by itself or as part of the GI series, depending upon symptoms, and is commonly recommended to detect inflammatory diseases, such as ileitis, and cancers. It is also used to determine if an obstruction of the small bowel is present. Patients undergoing radiation therapy to the abdomen or pelvis occasionally require this examination if the side effects are unusually severe and suggest inflammation or obstruction. Tumors in the small intestine are uncommon. The small-bowel study is occasionally used to detect rare conditions caused by various parasites and to evaluate certain disease states causing impaired absorption of nutrients, also called *malabsorption.*

Small-bowel examinations are often performed for cancer patients when symptoms due to radiation therapy arise. The test allows us to differentiate the side effects of the treatment from the onset of infectious diseases that results from immunosuppression.

The small-bowel series is a time-consuming examination (an average of two hours) because approximately twenty to twenty-five feet of intestine must be filled with barium and examined. The examination is usually performed at half-hour intervals, and the test is completed when the entire small bowel has been filled.

Intravenous Pyelogram Examination (IVP)

The intravenous pyelogram (IVP) is a test of kidney function as well as an evaluation of the size and shape of the urinary system. It is a painless examination.

Infection of the kidneys may cause pain in the small of the back (flank pain); and bladder infections often cause urinary frequency (increased urination), urgency (the sensation of needing to urinate even when the bladder is empty), and burning sensations. Radiation therapy to the pelvis can cause similar symptoms.

A kidney stone lodged in one of the ureters may result in obstruction of the urinary tract. The ureters, one on each side, constitute the major collecting system of the urinary tract and serve as drainage pipes leading out of the kidneys to the bladder. The ureters may also be obstructed because of kidney tumors.

In males, benign enlargement and cancer of the prostate gland are both frequent causes of bladder obstruction. In females, benign or malignant tumors of the uterus and ovaries may cause obstruction of the ureters. Depending on the location, obstruction causes a backup situation similar to clogged plumbing, which results in a dilatation, or widening, of the system behind the obstruction. Obstruction of the ureters may be severe and shut down kidney function.

Blood in the urine may be caused by an infection, an obstruction caused by stones, or by tumors. Infection may alter the size and shape of the ureters and may, in advanced stages, alter the size and shape of the kidneys as well. Tumors will also alter the size and shape of the involved organs, often causing irregularities in the contour of those organs.

The IVP requires a contrast agent, which is an organic iodine compound that is injected into a vein in the arm and travels through the bloodstream directly to the kidneys; it then passes through the kidneys and the ureters. From the ureters, the contrast agent then empties into the bladder. The fluid appears white on an x-ray, contrasting with the grayish and black appearance of surrounding organs, and thus provides a picture of the kidneys, the ureters, and the bladder.

Before the contrast agent is injected, an ordinary x-ray of the abdomen is obtained. Occasionally, a specialized x-ray of the kidneys—called a *tomogram*—is added. This x-ray technique "slices" the kidney, focusing on a layer that is usually a quarter of an inch thick. By obtaining both of these pictures, calcified stones in the kidneys and ureters can be detected.

Although rare, moderate to severe allergic reactions may occur within one to three minutes after the beginning of the injection; more mild reactions appear in the first ten minutes. (The attending doctor or nurse almost always asks about your history of allergies, but if they overlook this question, bring it up yourself.) In the event an allergic reaction occurs, specific drugs are administered to counter it. However, severe allergies are medical emergencies, which is why it is important to discuss the issue of allergic reactions prior to the test.

The IVP examination is the best test for detecting obstruction from many causes, but it is less accurate for imaging tumors of the bladder and kidneys. Therefore, a CT scan or an ultrasound examination may be used in addition to the IVP. CT scans are fast replacing the IVP as the examination of choice when investigating conditions involving the urinary tract.

Mammogram

A mammogram is an x-ray examination of the breast, and is usually done for the purpose of detecting or excluding the presence of cancer. There are two types of mammograms: a *screening mammogram* and a *diagnostic mammogram*. Unlike many other diagnostic tests, screening mammography is done even when no symptoms are present.

Being intelligent about breast care means combining monthly breast self-examinations with yearly breast examinations by a physician and mammograms at appropriate intervals. The American Cancer Society recommends monthly breast self-exams to begin at age twenty, yearly clinical breast exam after age thirty, and yearly screening mammography starting at age forty.

Two views of the breast are generally obtained for routine screening. In the first, the woman is seated and the x-ray beam traverses from top to bottom, the *cranial-caudal* view. The second is a side view, with the x-ray beam traversing from one side of the breast to the other. Mammography generally lasts three to five minutes. The breast is slightly compressed for the examination by a plastic plate, to make the thickness of the breast tissue as uniform as possible and thus enhance photographic quality. This compression causes moderate discomfort. If breasts are very painful to begin with, this compression may be unpleasant, although it does not last more than the setup time of approximately thirty seconds. It makes sense, if possible, to have your mammogram done at a time of the month when your breasts are less tender—that is, the first two weeks of the menstrual cycle—and avoid the week just before the onset of your period. This allows for optimal compression.

Mammography may reveal, in decreasing order of frequency, the presence of inflammation, noncancerous masses, or cancer. The inflammation referred to is usually called *fibrocystic change* or *fibrocystic condition*. These are general terms used to describe a condition consisting of overgrowth of the cells lining the mammary ducts, the milk-producing channels. This condition is often associated with scarring (fibrosis) of the breast tissue and fluid collections called *cysts*—thus, the term *fibrocystic*. Radiologists are able to recognize the patterns of fibrocystic change and differentiate these from other breast conditions.

Breast cancers have their own specific pattern. On an x-ray, they are generally seen as irregularly shaped masses. Often the edges of the masses have linear strands much like a picture of sunrays. In about 50 percent of the cancers, the mammogram will reveal small particles of calcium associated with the tumor. Called *microcalcifications*, they help confirm the diagnosis. On occasion, cancers are detected solely by the presence of these microcalcifications because the calcium deposits are too small to be felt and so no mass is evident. In order to help the surgeon biopsy and confirm a suspected cancer that can't be felt, the radiologist will place a needle in the breast, a procedure called *needle localization*, to guide the surgeon to the proper spot.

A *diagnostic* mammogram is done to evaluate a problem and includes three or more views as well as possible magnification. A woman should have her previous films available for comparison when having a new mammogram done and should always make a note where she had her last mammogram performed. When the radiologist has the opportunity to compare a current mammogram with a previous one, this will decrease the likelihood of a false positive reading or the possibility of having to come back for extra films.

Diagnostic mammograms include additional views taken from other angles and sometimes magnification views to home in on an area. Other breast imaging studies may be used along with diagnostic mammography to further evaluate an abnormal finding in the breast. These include breast ultrasound and breast MRI, which are detailed in the following sections.

For women who have had a diagnosis of breast cancer, mammography is the single most valuable test they have as part of follow-up after completing treatment. For women who have been treated with breast-conserving therapy, mammography is done of the treated breast, generally six months after completing radiation. This allows comparison between the original appearance of the breast and that following treatment, as it is expected that there will be postsurgical and postradiation changes noted in the breast. Additional follow-up mammograms are generally recommended every six to twelve months for the first two years, then yearly. Women will continue yearly screening mammography of the opposite breast.

For women who have had a mastectomy, the breast tissue has been removed so mammography is done of the opposite breast only in routine annual screening.

Nuclear Scanning

Nuclear scanning involves the imaging of organs such as the liver, bones, heart, or lungs that have been made to temporarily emit x-rays (gamma rays).

This is accomplished by injecting radioactive substances, or isotopes. The image that results is called a *scan*. Over the past several decades, newer and safer isotopes have been developed, resulting in decreased radiation dosage while increasing the accuracy of the examination.

Biochemists have devised ways to combine certain chemicals with these isotopes in a process called *labeling*, so that the scanning agents seek out the particular organ, referred to as the *target organ*, to be examined. For example, combining the technetium 99 isotope with sulfur colloid will trap most of the isotope in certain liver cells. By using a device that can detect and record the radioactivity emitted from the liver, an image of the liver can be transcribed to x-ray film as a permanent record. When we combine the same technetium 99 isotope with methylene diphosphonate, the isotope seeks bone rather than liver.

Various combinations of chemical substances labeled with different isotopes allow the body's organs to be visualized and disease states identified. Other individual isotopes seek out organs by virtue of an organ's inherent biological activity. For example, because the thyroid gland is involved in iodine storage, swallowing radioactive iodine will reveal this gland for imaging.

Once the scanning agent has been injected or ingested, it travels through the bloodstream and then reaches the target organ. This organ gradually accumulates radioactivity over a period of time. The rate of accumulation depends on the isotope used and the biological properties of the particular organ. So that the needed accumulation can take place, there is an interval of several hours between the administration of the agent and the performance of the test.

When the isotope has accumulated, the patient lies or sits, depending on the test, in front of an instrument that detects the radioactivity. This instrument is called a *gamma camera*, and it never touches the patient at any point during this painless test. The camera is able to detect and "collect" the gamma rays emitted from the target organ. This process is recorded on a video monitor by the nuclear-medicine technician. When enough activity has been recorded to obtain an accurate image, it is transferred onto x-ray film for the radiologist to interpret.

Few of these tests involve side effects or aftereffects from the isotopes. However, because most isotopes are excreted in human milk, a nursing mother should substitute formula feedings for a period of time suggested by her physician.

The following types of nuclear scanning tests appear alphabetically.

Bone Scan. The bone scan is the most frequently performed isotope scan for diagnosing cancer. The scanning agent is injected into an arm vein.

The bone scan is extremely useful for detecting injury and also in determining the age of an injury. For example, a patient may complain of back pain, and x-rays reveal a fractured vertebra; however, the fracture may have been present for years. Thus, the bone scan may indicate if the injury is recent or old. With infections or arthritis, the bone scan will often reveal the abnormality before the conditions appear on an x-ray.

Bone scanning is of greatest value and most often performed for the detection of metastatic cancer, that is, cancer that has spread from a distant site. The bone scan provides information that reveals the extent of the disease involving one or a group of bones. This is of great help in staging the cancer, as well as planning the location and extent of treatment. It is also of great use in assessing the results of radiation therapy or chemotherapy, because abnormal areas may revert to normal after treatment. Although almost any cancer can spread to the bone, the most common cancers to be evaluated are those originating in the lung, breast, and the prostate gland.

Some cancers spread to the bone but do not always show up on a bone scan. These include myeloma, thyroid cancer, kidney cancer, some breast cancers, and lung cancers. In these cases, other tests, such as plain x-rays, CT scans, or MRIs are used.

Although the scan is very sensitive in detecting bone disease, it is nonspecific. Arthritis, infection, fractures, and cancer may all look the same. Thus, x-rays of the affected bones are often obtained to assist in differentiating these conditions. The patient's history, together with the x-rays, then clarifies the situation.

Liver Scan. A radioactive substance is used in a liver scan. After an intravenous injection of the agent, imaging is immediately performed in multiple projections in order to visualize all the surfaces of the liver. The scanning is a painless procedure.

The primary reason a liver scan is performed is to detect metastatic cancer, although in facilities with advanced technologies available, the CT scan has largely replaced the liver nuclear scan for this diagnostic purpose. The liver scan is also used to evaluate the liver for cirrhosis, an inflammation that is often associated with alcoholism.

Lung Scan (Pulmonary Scan). Nuclear imaging of the lung is primarily used to evaluate blood clots (emboli). We include this test because some cancers may be associated with pulmonary emboli as a presenting symptom. These clots may form as the result of inflammation in distal veins, usually in the legs (phlebitis); if dislodged from the vein, they may travel to the lungs. Abdominal, pelvic, and hip surgery may cause clots to form in the veins. These clots may then travel to the lungs. Occasionally, cancers may predispose a patient to the formation of clots. However, blood clots may also form in the lungs for no obvious reason. The scan is also used to evaluate lung function in patients with lung cancer, emphysema, and other chronic pulmonary diseases where some obstruction of the airway or blood flow may be present.

Another test, the *ventilation scan*, uses a different isotope and evaluates how clear the bronchial airways are. Abnormal ventilation scans are common in patients with emphysema, asthma, and obstruction caused by cancer. The ventilation scan is performed by inhaling a radioactive gas called xenon 133.

Ultrasound

No radiation is involved in an ultrasound examination. Using a device called a *transducer*, inaudible high-frequency sound waves are beamed through solid and fluid-filled structures of the body. The echoes bounce off the structures and are returned and collected by the transducer, which is in contact with the patient's body. The series of sound signals are processed electronically, and a display of the anatomical sound image is made on a screen. These images are then transferred to x-ray film for a permanent record. The images formed are anatomical representations of the body's organs and disease processes.

Modern ultrasound scanners use so-called "real time" technology, meaning that the pictures analyze not only structures, but their motion as well. This is analogous to the fluoroscopic examination, except in this case sound waves are used, rather than x-rays, to obtain the images.

Normal organs and their tissues reveal specific ultrasound patterns; conversely, diseases have their own characteristic echo patterns. The ultrasound technician beams the sound waves and collects these echoes with the transducer. A jelly substance is applied to the transducer and the skin to act as a contact so that air does not form a barrier to the sound waves. The pictures obtained are sections or slices (tomographic images) of the area examined. Thus, multiple images must be acquired in order to image the entire organ.

An ultrasound test is painless. A patient will feel only moderate pressure as the technician passes the transducer over the skin.

The following ultrasound tests are listed alphabetically.

Breast Ultrasound. Breast ultrasound is commonly used for further evaluation of a breast lump because it can distinguish a simple cyst from a complex cyst, and cysts from solid masses. Ultrasound-guided biopsy can then determine exactly what type of solid mass is seen. Breast ultrasound is generally not used for screening, but it is being studied as a possible screening tool in women who have dense breasts.

Cardiac Ultrasonography (Echocardiogram). This is an effective means of visualizing heart valves, the heart chambers, and the space around the heart. It is sometimes used to assess how well the heart pumps; a nuclear scan of the heart is another way. Heart function may need to be monitored when certain chemotherapy drugs are used, such as anthracyclines (for example, Adriamycin). In addition, this test may be used to evaluate fluid around the heart, *pericardial effusion*, which can be a site of metastatic cancer.

Gynecological Ultrasonography. Noncancerous and cancerous ovarian and uterine masses are best examined with ultrasound because it is highly accurate for detecting their size, location, and whether they are solid or fluid filled. Abnormal fluid around these organs will also be clearly seen. However, the test's ability to make a definitive diagnosis is limited because many infectious and cancerous conditions look the same on ultrasound. Thus, a benign cyst of the ovary may look exactly like an infected cyst caused by pelvic inflammatory disease (PID). Similar abnormalities may be seen with cancers. In order to make the examination more specific, a physical examination and the patient's history are extremely important. Follow-up ultrasound examinations may also clarify the diagnosis by showing the evolution of the disease process.

Ultrasound is often used as a screening test, followed by a CT scan, to obtain a more accurate diagnosis. Because ultrasound does not involve the use of radiation, it is an ideal test for women of childbearing age.

Kidney Ultrasonography. Because the size, shape, and structure of the kidneys are well visualized, ultrasound is a good screening examination to evaluate the size of the kidneys and to detect obstruction (blockage of the urine flow), cysts, and cancers. Further testing is usually not required after a normal ultrasound examination unless symptoms dictate continued investigation. In many situations, a CT scan may be necessary to evaluate suspicious masses that could be cancerous.

Liver Ultrasonography. Since the advent of modern CT scan examinations, liver ultrasonography is not performed as often as in the past. However, because it costs less than CT scans and is accurate, it is still extensively used as a screening test to detect abnormalities. It is also performed to supplement information where results of a CT scan are equivocal. One of the prime reasons for performing ultrasonography of the liver is to detect metastatic disease, most commonly metastatic cancers of the lung, breast, and colon.

Pancreatic Ultrasonography. Because jaundice (yellowing of the skin) may occur as a result of bile duct obstruction, a pancreatic scan is often performed in conjunction with a liver ultrasound scan in order to evaluate the entire bile duct system. Infections of the pancreas (pancreatitis) and cancer of the pancreas may also be clearly visualized with ultrasound.

Rectal Ultrasonography. This is used in the evaluation of rectal masses to determine local spreading. It is also used to evaluate masses in the prostate gland.

Computed Axial Tomography Scanning (CT Scan or CAT Scan)

Computed axial tomography—or as it is more commonly known, CT or CAT scanning—allows for the precise visualization of many abnormalities in the body. The development of the CT scan represented a major step in technology, allowing for the accurate display of disease processes and organ anatomy.

The CT images are created by the interaction of x-rays with body tissues. Specialized detectors installed in a doughnut-shaped machine surround the part of the body to be examined. When focused x-rays pass through the body, the density differences in the various tissues (such as bone, lung, or muscle) are perceived by the detectors, and the signals are analyzed by the computer. As the body passes through the detector site, a series of images are displayed in the form of slices, also called *tomographic sections*. These pictures are obtained to reveal different views (perpendicular, transverse, etc.) of the organ to be examined The examination table moves slowly into the detection "doughnut" to obtain the picture slices.

The CT scan is a painless test during which the patient lies on a comfortable examination couch. Many CT scans must be performed with the use of intravenous contrast agents in order to highlight certain abnormalities.

The following types of CT scans are listed alphabetically.

Abdomen and Pelvis. CT scans of the abdomen clearly visualize the internal organs and their relationships to one another. The stomach and other parts of the intestinal tract (including the esophagus, located in the chest) are imaged by administering an oral contrast agent. This fills the gastrointestinal tract to prevent these structures from being confused with abnormal masses. Infections and cancers in the abdominal and pelvic regions are often clearly visualized, and frequently no additional imaging tests are needed.

CT scans often result in a specific diagnosis, therefore making it an efficient and cost-effective tool. However, ultrasound for gynecological conditions is often used because it does not involve radiation.

Cancers affecting the liver, kidneys, pancreas, lymph nodes, and bile ducts are generally well demonstrated on CT scans. This is often the only type of imaging that detects these diseases. In the pelvis, the CT scan is primarily used to diagnose cancer and its local extensions. CT scanning is used when lymph-node enlargement is suspected or to evaluate the result of lymph-node treatment.

Central Nervous System (Brain and Spine). MRIs have largely replaced CT scans as the best test for neurologic (brain and spine) abnormalities. Cancers, strokes, and herniated discs are best detected with MRIs, but when this technology is not available, or to minimize cost, the CT scan is a very effective alternative. For example, neurological (brain and spine) abnormalities are often clearly depicted on a CT scan, and the size, location, and extent of the disease seen then allows for precise medical and surgical treatment. The CT scan frequently detects neurological disease without specifically indicating its cause. In such cases, a list of possible conditions, called a *differential diagnosis*, may be offered. By following the evolution of the abnormality, the specific diagnosis becomes apparent. A biopsy may be performed when the diagnosis remains doubtful.

Injuries to the brain and, to a lesser extent, the spinal cord are well diagnosed with a CT scan. For example, even in the absence of fractures, the skull may sustain severe injury. Thus, a negative skull x-ray does not preclude an extensive CT scan workup of the brain. Collections of blood trapped between the skull and the brain (subdural and epidural hematomas), as well as bleeding into the brain substance, may be rapidly diagnosed using this technique, and lifesaving procedures instituted. Spinal injuries also are well imaged with CT scanning. This test is usually ordered for complicated spinal fractures that cannot be fully revealed through conventional x-rays.

CT scanning can effectively image infections of the brain and spine. However, MRIs and biopsies may also be necessary in order to distinguish between infections and cancer. CT scans of the brain are commonly performed to detect and evaluate strokes.

The CT scan is a good initial test to evaluate a suspected brain cancer, either originating there or spreading from a distant site. MRIs may then be used to further clarify the extent and nature of the cancer. In most situations, however, the CT scan is an excellent test to diagnose cancer and to evaluate the results of radiation treatment.

Chest. Although chest x-rays are valuable, when more information is necessary to confirm a diagnosis or to evaluate lymph nodes, CT scans are of inestimable value. The CT scan is particularly useful in evaluating the lymph nodes of the central chest tissues, or mediastinum. Often, pneumonias mask underlying cancers, and the CT scan greatly helps in differentiating one from the other. Furthermore, this test is used to plan biopsy procedures of the mediastinal lymph nodes or lung masses as well as surgery.

Precise evaluation of the results of treatment for lung cancer can also be monitored by CT scanning, because ordinary chest x-rays are often not accurate or sensitive enough to perform this function. CT scanning for trauma to the chest is often lifesaving, because the extent of injury to the lungs, bronchial tubes, and major blood vessels can be rapidly evaluated.

Head and Neck. In the evaluation of head and neck diseases, particularly those due to injury and tumor, the CT scan is usually far superior to all conventional x-ray techniques. Cancer surgeons may use the CT scan to evaluate the extent of disease prior to surgery, and radiation oncologists plan patients' treatment using the results of the scan. Radiation oncologists also use the scans after surgery to determine the location of residual cancer. MRIs (see below) may eventually be the test of choice for head and neck evaluation because it more accurately images the soft tissues in the neck.

Magnetic Resonance Imaging (MRI)

Magnetic resonance imaging (MRI) is one of the newer high-tech tests. It is unique because it provides precise and detailed anatomic information without exposing the patient to x-rays. To date, no biological ill effects resulting from MRI have been discovered; however, MRI remains expensive, so if physicians believe that a CT scan will provide sufficient information in a particular situation, they tend to use it instead.

Although MRI technology is extremely complicated, the general principle on which it is based can be simply stated. Atoms (specifically their nuclei) in the body can be made to act like bar magnets with north and south poles. This occurs when the magnetic field of the MRI machine is applied to the body. The nuclei of the hydrogen atoms in the body line up in relation to the magnetic field applied. When radio waves are transmitted into the patient, these atoms, acting as tiny magnets, tilt on their axes, resulting in some absorption of the radio waves. Hence, the term *resonance*. When the radio signal is shut off, the atoms, again acting as little magnets, return to their original state and send back the signal they absorbed. An antenna detects this rebroadcast, and a computer processes the signal into an image. The magnetic field of the machine is very powerful, thousands of times greater than that of the Earth's magnetic field.

MRI images are processed as "slices" on x-ray film. These slices can be obtained in many different views, referred to as projections. The MRI is a sensitive test, but it is not very specific in, for example, differentiating between cancer and infections of the brain. Therefore, the patient's history and physical findings are important in establishing a definite diagnosis. On occasion, a biopsy may be necessary to clear up any doubts.

MRI images are more detailed than those obtained with CT scans and MRI is more versatile than the CT scan, in that images may be obtained in many more geometric planes. The most common planes used are the axial (perpendicular to the long axis of the body, as in slicing a loaf of bread) and the sagittal (parallel to the long axis of the body, as in slicing carrot sticks).

The following types of MRI are reviewed alphabetically.

Abdomen and Pelvis. MRI and CT scans are approximately equal in accuracy for evaluating conditions of the abdomen and pelvis. As a rule, CT scans are performed because they are less expensive. Eventually, however, MRI may become the ideal test for the staging of cancer.

MRI technology is currently unable to detect small calcifications seen in kidney stones, gallstones, and certain tumors. The image is also affected by normal biological motion such as intestinal activity and breathing, so the ability of MRI to evaluate the gastrointestinal tract and small masses in the lung is somewhat reduced.

Brain and Spine. For diseases of the brain and spine, the MRI is superior to the CT scan, especially for strokes, most brain tumors, and diseases such as multiple sclerosis. The MRI is usually superior for diagnosis of conditions of the spine because it can image the entire spinal cord in its long axis (it looks like a tube). The spine's coverings and surrounding fluid (cerebrospinal fluid) are also well imaged. MRI has decreased the need for CT scans in diseases affecting the spine.

Breast. Optimal MRI of the breast requires a special *breast coil accessory* used with an MRI unit. Breast MRI is an important problem-solving tool for radiologists when routine breast imaging studies such as mammography and ultrasound have not determined the exact nature of an abnormality. Breast MRI also can be used in women with known breast cancer to see the extent of the cancer or to determine if there are any other suspicious areas in that breast.

After surgery, it can determine if and to what extent the margins are involved. MRI is being studied as a screening test in women with dense breast tissue, who have a family history of breast cancer, and may need to begin screening tests at an earlier age. There are special nonmetal attachments that can be used to perform biopsies, despite the magnetic forces of the MRI, if an abnormality is seen that needs further evaluation.

In July 2004, the *New England Journal of Medicine* published the results of a study conducted in the Netherlands that investigated the value of using MRI as a screening tool for women with a familial, or genetic, predisposition to breast cancer. The researchers concluded that MRI appears to be more sensitive than mammography in detecting tumors in those women who, because of inherited susceptibility, are considered at high risk of developing breast cancer. We expect this study to lead to an expanded discussion of the role of MRI in breast cancer screening.

Chest. The role of MRI in detecting and evaluating lung cancer is currently being investigated. At the present time, however, the CT scan is less expensive and very accurate.

Head and Neck. Because of its ability to visualize small differences in soft tissues, MRI appears to be the ideal test to evaluate cancers of the head and neck. While these cancers can be examined visually, their extensions into the deeper tissues are best evaluated with MRI.

Joints. MRI is currently the best imaging test for the diagnosis of joint disease. However, certain conditions contraindicate the use of MRI imaging. Specifically, pacemakers may be shut down and surgical clips in the head or eyes may dislodge. In addition, patients requiring life-support systems that contain metal cannot be examined because the metal is attracted to the magnet.

Positron Emission Tomography (PET) Scanning

The PET scan is unique in its ability to image disease at the cellular level, making PET scanning the premier test for the *early* detection of cancer in lymph nodes. It helps us evaluate the way the cells function. As such, it represents a significant advance in diagnostic technology. PET scans take advantage of the increased activity of most cancer cells, because many (but not all) cancers have higher than normal metabolic activity. This means that they use more glucose (sugar) to maintain their activity than that used by noncancerous cells.

To perform the test, a sugar molecule (glucose) is chemically bound to a radioactive atom and injected into the patient. Because there is more activity in cancer cells, a greater concentration of the radioactive element occurs in cancerous tissue. We can think of the PET scan as a "Geiger counter"–type of instrument that generates a picture of cellular activity, and it can do it in thin slices or sections like CT and MRI. Recently, PET and CT scans have been combined into a PET/CT unit that allows the two technologies to complement each other. In this way, even cancers as small as 1 cm (⅕ of an inch) can be seen.

PET scans help us precisely identify an appropriate biopsy site, stage the cancer, grade the tumor, and determine if the disease has spread to distant sites. It is also used to monitor treatment and evaluate the results during follow-up care. To date, PET scan is the optimal test for cancers of the esophagus, pancreas, testes, uterus, cervix, ovary, lung, and colon as well as lymphoma. It shows promise in evaluating melanomas, breast cancer (recurrent or metastatic disease in particular), and cancers of the head and neck. This testing will eventually be used to investigate noncancerous conditions such as the heart muscle following a heart attack.

Currently, the test requires a six-hour fast prior to the scan, although fluid is allowed. Patients are also instructed to limit physical activity before the test in order to minimize normal muscular uptake of the isotope, which might affect the sensitivity and quality of the scan. The patient's blood-sugar level also is tested. The test takes approximately an hour.

Although this test is extremely valuable, its cost and limited availability have reduced its current use. We expect this situation will soon change.

9

Frequently Asked Questions About Cancer and Treatment

The following group of questions includes those that patients frequently ask before, during, and after treatment. However, we realize that some readers may have lingering concerns or specific topics they would like to explore further. For that reason, we have listed many books and websites in the Additional Resources section.

Will I Become Radioactive as a Result of Radiation Therapy?

If you are receiving external radiation therapy, you do not become radioactive. The radiation passes through you and causes biochemical changes in the tissue that receives the radiation, but there is no residual retention of radioactivity. If you receive an injection of radioactive material, such as radioactive iodine 131, used in the treatment of thyroid cancer, or if you have a radioactive seed implant, most commonly used in the treatment of prostate cancer, you will be radioactive because your body contains radioactive material.

The length of time that you will be radioactive depends on the half-life of the radioactive material used. In this context, the half-life means the time it takes for the radioactivity to be reduced by half. For example, the Paladium 03 for prostate seed implants has a half-life of twenty days. This means that every twenty days the radioactivity is reduced by one-half. As a rule of thumb, five half-lives are considered nonactive. Thus a patient with this implant will be nonradioactive in one hundred days. However, patients with prostate implants are released the same day of the procedure because the radioactivity emanating from them is so low that others are not in danger. Patients who receive a high dose of a high-energy radioactive material are kept isolated in the hospital until they no longer pose a danger to others.

Am I Dangerous to Others as a Result of Radiation Therapy?

As stated previously, if you are receiving external radiation, you certainly pose no danger to anyone else. However, if you receive an injection of radioactive material or an implant, you will be advised as to what precautions you should take. Your doctor will inform you about the strict Federal and State regulations that must be followed when radioactive material is used in treatment. In some cases, patients may be required to stay in the hospital until their radioactivity falls to a safe level. The length of time depends on the half-life and the dose of the radioactive material used.

Is My Cancer Contagious?

As far as we know, cancer is not a disease that can be transmitted to another person. This is most often a concern to people who have a cancer in a reproductive organ and wonder if a sexual partner could possibly catch the disease. It is not surprising that people wonder about this because we still have so much to learn about the causes of cancer. It remains a disease with an aura of mystery, and it is perhaps the most feared disease we contend with.

Certain viruses may be associated with cancer. For example, human papillomavirus is associated with cancer of the cervix, and the HIV virus predisposes a person to certain cancers, such as non-Hodgkin's lymphoma and Kaposi's sarcoma. However, while these viruses may be transmitted, the cancers can not.

Will I Die from the Cancer I Have?

Fifty percent of all people who have contracted cancer in the past ten years will survive the disease and live a normal life span. This statistic will undoubtedly improve as new discoveries are made relating to prevention and early detection. Treatment methods are also steadily improving, and this progress will further help increase cure rates. Some cancers already have very high cure rates—better than 85 percent. These include breast cancer (when detected in its early stages), early cancer of the vocal cords, early Hodgkin's disease, some testicular cancers, and most skin cancers.

People often view cancer as a death sentence because they have known people who died from the disease. Therefore, they think that a similar fate is inevitable. This fear of death—sometimes even an assumption of death—is one of the stages that people with cancer often go through. It is wise to admit to having the fear, talk about it, and seek help if necessary. (Cancer support groups serve an important function for many people.) Over the years, we have found that people feel better in the long run by examining their fears and dealing with the realities of cancer. By contrast, retreating into a silent denial or forcing yourself to be unrelentingly positive actually may be detrimental.

Neither you nor your physicians know when you are going to die or what the cause will be. We've observed that, ultimately, most people try to achieve the best life they can regardless of how long they will live. It seems to us that this is more important than the impersonal estimates of how much time is left. The statistics given, even for advanced cancers, need not prevent you from defying the odds, because cures abound. Cure rates are dependent on primary tumor stage of disease and initial response to treatment, but remember, nothing in life is 100 percent; even in apparently hopeless cases we see cures.

My Doctor Told Me That My Cancer Is Advanced. Can I Still Achieve a Good Quality of Life?

Most likely there are many things that can be done to make daily life as pleasant and comfortable as possible. Radiation therapy, chemotherapy, and/or surgery are often used to help control the cancer and prevent unpleasant symptoms. Medication can control the pain, diet can be modified, and emotional support systems can be developed. We have seen individuals with very advanced cancers live relatively full lives even when the disease itself was considered hopeless. Naturally, a person's age and overall medical condition affect quality of life, but a person's spirit is important, too.

If I Start to Take Pain Medication, Will I Become Addicted to It?

There is no evidence that cancer patients become addicted to the pain-relief medication they take, at least in the way an addict is defined in today's society. That is, patients do not begin to crave the drugs for their euphoric or hallucinatory effects. Patients may, however, become physically dependent on the pain medication to do what the drug is intended to do—relieve pain. Drug dosages may be increased or decreased as warranted, and most patients stay on the same medication for long periods of time. However, medications are often reduced when cancer treatments lessen the pain.

When the disease improves, the need for medication usually decreases markedly. Either the medication is decreased in dosage, or a less potent medication is prescribed. For example, people who have been on morphine switch to aspirin or Tylenol. Patients who are cured or who undergo long-term remissions may not need any medication. We emphasize that narcotic medication, when indicated and necessary for the patient's comfort, should be taken as needed for as long as it is required.

Will I Lose My Hair from Radiation Treatment and Chemotherapy?

As a rule, radiation treatment results in scalp hair loss if the whole head is treated with doses greater than 3,000 to 4,000 units. Local scalp hair loss will occur over just the areas treated. The hair may eventually grow back, but the texture may change, so the hair when it returns may be finer or coarser than it was before treatment. Radiation delivered to other parts of the body may also cause local hair loss. A popular misconception is that scalp hair loss occurs regardless of the area being irradiated. However, the generalized hair loss that occurs with chemotherapy does not occur with radiation treatment.

With chemotherapy, hair loss depends on the drug and dosage used. Some drugs always cause hair loss, some cause thinning, and others do not affect hair at all. In addition, sometimes body hair, including eyebrows and eyelashes, may be lost. Hair will always grow back after chemotherapy has been completed, although sometimes hair may grow back curlier than it was previously.

What Will Happen to My Skin During Radiation Therapy?

Fortunately, the technology of radiation therapy has improved in the last fifty or so years, and today's newer machines spare the skin to a great degree. In the first half of the twentieth century, cancer patients undergoing treatment often experienced extensive skin reactions. However, with today's technology, mild reddening and irritation of the skin is experienced only in the area under treatment. This irritation may particularly occur in areas where skin rubs against skin—under the arms and the folds in the buttocks, for example. No adverse skin effects are present outside the area of treatment.

When high radiation doses are necessary, particularly in fair-skinned individuals, the skin may crack and blister. Skin creams are effective for their soothing and healing effects. These symptoms are temporary and disappear in two to four weeks after treatment is completed. The skin will darken gradually and then peel to reveal normal underlying skin, much like the effects of sunburn. In general, darker-skinned people experience less intense skin reactions than those with very fair skin.

Should I Seek Complementary or Alternative Therapies Such as Nutritional Supplements, Herbal Remedies, Meditation Programs, and So Forth?

At least 30 to 40 percent of cancer patients use complementary or alternative therapies. Usually, the term *complementary therapy* refers to treatments used along with standard therapy. Therapies considered complementary cover a wide range and include such diverse things as relaxation therapy, massage, yoga, art therapy, or acupuncture.

On the other hand, *alternative therapy* implies the use of treatment in the place of standard therapy. This usually means declining treatments with demonstrated efficacy to take unproven treatments instead. Unfortunately, most have unrealistic expectations about the benefits of these treatments. No form of alternative therapy has been shown to be curative or beneficial, despite testimonials you might see on TV or the Internet. In addition, some of the substances promoted may actually be harmful.

Integrative therapy, a term frequently used today, implies using other approaches along with a standard treatment plan, thus integrating a total approach. We believe it is extremely important that you keep your physicians informed about what you may be doing or taking in addition to the standard treatments offered to you. For example, the benefits of a certain radiation treatment or chemotherapy drug may not be the same in the presence of an additional substance.

Without studying the agents together, one can not be sure as to whether a substance may enhance the effects of chemotherapy, detract from it, or have no effect at all. Many people are interested in considering herbal substances, which they think are "natural." However, herbal preparations can have adverse effects.

Memorial Sloan-Kettering Cancer Center's website includes information about herbs and supplements (see Additional Resources). You can also get information from the U.S. Food and Drug Administration (FDA). The National Center for Complementary and Alternative Medicine also has health information fact sheets on their website (see Additional Resources).

Although vitamin and mineral supplements in amounts in line with the Recommended Daily Allowance (RDA) may be helpful, we do not recommend that you take large amounts of any vitamin, mineral, or herb without seeking your doctor's advice. Many hospitals and treatment centers offer nutritional consultations with a trained dietitian; many also offer support groups that give patients the opportunity to exchange information about complementary treatments they have found helpful.

Why Do I Need So Many Blood Tests During Treatment?

During chemotherapy and radiation, blood counts are monitored on a regular basis. Because radiation can affect the blood counts, radiation doses may be delayed when the counts are low. Similarly, chemotherapy also affects the blood counts, especially the white blood cells. For this reason, before each cycle of chemotherapy is given, we do blood tests to be sure that the blood counts are high enough. Sometimes, blood counts may be checked in the middle of the cycle to see how low the white blood-cell count may have dropped (also called the *nadir* count). If you develop a fever in the middle of the chemotherapy cycle, the white blood-cell count is checked to determine the risk of infection and, if necessary, the choice of antibiotics.

The red blood-cell count (including the hemoglobin and hematocrit) is also followed during treatment to determine the need for blood transfusion or if the medication, erythropoietin, is required. (Erythropoietin is a hormone that stimulates red cell production.) If levels are low, we give doses of erythropoietin to boost the red blood-cell count to prevent the necessity of blood transfusions.

Will I Lose My Ability to Function Sexually as a Result of Treatment?

Some specific cancer treatments to the reproductive organs, such as radiation therapy to the prostate, may eventually lead to sexual dysfunction in a percentage of patients. Prostate surgery, for example, may result in impotence, especially when it is characterized as radical. This also applies to many pelvic cancers, specifically bladder and prostate in men. In women, external radiation therapy to the pelvis may irritate the vaginal tissues and cause enough discomfort so that intercourse is avoided temporarily. Internal radiation for cervical or uterine cancer may result in scarring of the vaginal tissues. Stretching of the tissues may be needed, and in some cases, a degree of dysfunction may be permanent. Chemotherapy may cause symptoms of early menopause, which could include vaginal dryness. This can be treated, however, and normal sexual activity can continue.

In many cancer patients, however, sexual functioning is not directly affected. Sexual relations may continue if the patient feels well enough and depression, fatigue, and other side effects do not interfere with the desire for sexual contact.

The loss of sexual function or desire among some patients may occur as a result of feelings of shame or unattractiveness. These feelings are more common among patients who have undergone mutilating surgeries. Support groups, individual counseling, and loving relationships with sexual partners will help minimize these feelings.

Have I Done Something Wrong to Develop the Cancer?

When individuals are newly diagnosed with cancer, natural questions come up: Why this? Why me? Was it something in my diet, where I grew up, or something I did wrong?

Cancer develops because a number of "checkpoints" in the cells' protective mechanisms have failed. Smoking or alcohol use influences some cancers; other cancers occur in part because of a genetic predisposition. However, some cancers occur without any clearly defined predisposing factor.

Although controversial, some studies have demonstrated that certain personality traits or the occurrence of a catastrophic life event may predispose a person to develop cancer. They seem to show that a major stressful life event or a predisposition to chronic feelings of helplessness and an impaired ability to communicate can, in some people, stimulate the development of cancer or other major illnesses. This may be related to a generalized weakening of the immune system that makes the body more prone to disease processes of all kinds, from infections to cancers. However, there is no known psychological connection for the majority of cancer patients.

I Am So Depressed That I'm Unable to Cope. Is This Common?

It is perfectly normal to be depressed because a diagnosis of cancer is so overwhelming. People often see it as their body's betrayal, and they have taken normal good health, up to this point, for granted. Unfortunately, some patients do not *seem* depressed, nor do they talk about how they feel. However, depression may exacerbate a person's condition, and to some degree, even interfere with the treatments. Although a positive attitude is helpful, this does not mean that you should attempt to deny either the diagnosis or the feelings that go along with it.

Again, it is important that patients not internalize their fears, but rather find a way to express them and deal with the situation realistically. Counseling and support groups may also be very helpful. The will to live and beat the odds has been found to be an important part of stimulating the body's defenses to fight the cancer and promote healing.

What Exactly Are the Lymph Nodes?

Lymph nodes are small, rounded structures found throughout the body. They are part of the lymph system, which contains fluid and forms a continuous channel. This channel connects to our bloodstream by an opening in a large vein in the upper chest.

The lymph nodes (often mistakenly referred to as lymph glands) and lymph channels contain a clear fluid in which white blood cells and nutrients float. The lymph nodes and channels are part of the body's defense system against disease. The nodes act as biological filters, trapping elements foreign to the body, such as infections or cancers. When a person develops tonsillitis, for example, the painful swellings felt in the neck are the lymph nodes containing the infection, which has drained through the lymphatic system from the tonsils. Similarly, cancers of various organs will drain through the lymph channels into the neighboring lymph nodes.

Once the infection or cancer is contained by the lymph nodes, there is a chance for cure, if appropriate, and adequate treatment stops further spread. Because the lymph-channel system connects with the bloodstream, it is easy to see why unsuccessfully treated infections and cancers can spread to distant sites in the body. Lymph nodes are part of the solution for resisting disease, but become part of the problem when overwhelmed. Thus, what starts as a local infection or cancer may in time spread elsewhere.

Can Radiation Therapy Be Given to an Organ Structure More Than Once?

The answer depends on the type of cancer and its location. Generally speaking, cancers localized to one organ, without evidence of spread beyond that organ or the adjacent lymph nodes, are given a maximum dose with the hope that the cancer will not recur in that region. The maximum dose is determined based on knowledge of what dose is effective to cure or arrest the cancer, as well as the tolerance of the normal tissues to the radiation. In these situations, it would be unusual for the radiation oncologist to deliver additional radiation to the region.

When bones are involved, usually as a result of spread from a distant region, they may be retreated. This applies particularly to bones of the arms and legs, because these surrounding soft tissues may tolerate high doses of radiation. Each person's situation is different, and decisions are made based upon the particular clinical picture and the radiation oncologist's judgment.

When cancer remains after radiation has been administered, the radiation oncologist will often work with a medical oncologist because drugs such as those used in chemotherapy may eradicate disease not completely destroyed by radiation.

Can I Shield the Rest of My Body During Treatment to Protect It from Radiation?

Radiation treatments are delivered in a precisely focused way so that tissues outside those in the path of the treatment beam do not become directly irradiated. Once internal, some radiation may be deflected sideways, and this is known as *scatter*. If scatter occurs close to the reproductive organs, it can cause harm to these tissues. For example, young men undergoing treatment for cancer of the testicle may need to have a protective shield applied to the remaining testicle. The ovaries of young women may be surgically moved out of the way of the treatment beam in a procedure called *oopheropexy*.

How Should I Tell My Family Members That I Have Cancer?

Discussing cancer is much like discussing any serious illness. We believe that a frank and honest discussion is all that is necessary, and in most cases, family members and friends quickly rally around to provide practical and emotional support. There are obvious exceptions to this general rule. For example, very young children may not understand that a disease can be simultaneously very serious and curable, and it may be better not to give them detailed explanations of the illness. Similarly, if a relative is older, very ill, or emotionally fragile, he or she may not be able to handle the information about a loved one. Common sense usually dictates when this is the case.

Describing a realistic but hopeful picture usually helps alleviate anxiety in patients and in loved ones alike. Older children should not be excluded from information and discussions about treatment, side effects, and outlook. They generally handle knowledge of a loved one's illness far better than we give them credit for.

My Doctor Recommended a Clinical Trial. I Don't Like the Idea of Being a Guinea Pig, but Should I Consider It?

Look carefully at who is sponsoring the study and what its aims are. Clinical trials are always reviewed by a hospital's internal review board and must meet certain guidelines before they can be discussed with patients. You will need to sign an informed consent form that details why the study is being done, what your role in it will be, what to expect from the treatment, and what possible side effects to be aware of.

Most cancer clinical trials are well designed, carefully thought out, and very closely scrutinized. The most common ones compare new treatments to those previously considered standard. Many trials are randomized, meaning that you will be randomly assigned to receive one of several treatments. Before you decide to enroll (in consultation with your doctor), you need to be comfortable with all the treatment possibilities.

One advantage of participating in a clinical trial is that you may be able to receive new treatments before they are commercially available. In addition, you may be more closely monitored when taking a new treatment. Even if you decide not to participate, you can learn a great deal about standard treatments for a particular cancer. Just by reading the consent form, you can discover the unanswered questions about the proposed treatment, so clinical trials are always worth considering.

You need not wait for your doctor to raise the idea of a clinical trial. You can take the initiative and ask about these possibilities. You can also research clinical trials on your own. (See the Additional Resources.)

Just How Safe Is Radiation Therapy?

It is always best not to be exposed to x-rays of any kind unless it is considered absolutely necessary. Radiologists and x-ray technicians always reduce their own occupational exposure to radiation as much as possible. However, x-ray testing is sometimes the only way to definitively diagnose a disease; radiation therapy is often the most effective treatment for cancer. In these cases, radiation can be considered lifesaving.

What Exactly Are Hospice Centers, and How Can I Locate Them?

By definition, hospice helps terminally ill patients and their families. Hospice facilities sometimes house patients and family members and take physical care of a dying patient while offering emotional support. Sometimes the help is offered to patients in their own homes. Hospice nurses visit on a regular basis and help family caretakers and patients live as comfortably as possible during the difficult last stages of an illness. We advise talking with your doctors about hospice services or contacting a local chapter of the American Cancer Society to learn more about these facilities in your area. You can also check the website for the National Hospice and Palliative Care Organization at nhpco.org.

•

I Am Not Experiencing Any Side Effects from My Radiation Treatments and/or Chemotherapy. Does That Mean They Are Ineffective?

There is a common belief that if a treatment isn't unpleasant, it must not work—not unlike the belief that if medicine is foul-tasting, it must be effective. Nothing could be further from the truth. It often surprises patients that they feel well throughout their treatment, but there is no correlation between the side effects of treatment and the results.

How Long Do the Beneficial Effects of Radiation Therapy Last?

Treatment is often administered because a cure is possible. If a cure is subsequently achieved, the effects of the radiation last for the duration of that person's life. When treatment is administered for palliation—that is, to arrest the disease and alleviate symptoms rather than to eradicate the tumor—the effects may last from months to years.

Radiation therapy often shows a lag effect. The biological changes resulting from radiation are still active in the body long after treatments are completed. For example, patients receiving radiation to bone may experience pain relief long after the course of treatment is over. In addition, chest x-rays and CT scans often show that tumors become smaller weeks or months following treatment. This is the reason follow-up x-rays and other tests should be performed in the weeks and months after treatment has been completed.

I Have Heard Stories About Mistakes in Administering Medications. How Can I Be Certain That an Error Won't Occur During My Chemotherapy Treatments?

Chemotherapy doses are different based on the disease and the particular protocol. These doses and schedules have been determined from extensive research and confirmed in clinical trails. Most chemotherapy medications do not come in just one dose. The doses are calculated based on an individual's height and weight and may be further adjusted based on kidney and liver function.

Once the medical oncologist calculates the dose, there are often several checkpoints to minimize risk of error. A specially trained pharmacist or nurse will prepare the chemotherapy drug by mixing it into an appropriate fluid to be given intravenously. The pharmacist will recalculate the dosage. A specially trained oncology nurse, who also recalculates the dose, gives the patient the chemotherapy agent. When you go to the facility where you will receive your treatments, ask what systems are in place to minimize medication error. Medical oncologists' offices and hospitals take these safety issues very seriously, and they understand why you want specific answers to these safety-related questions.

Where Can I Read About the Latest Medical Studies of Cancer Treatments and Cures?

In recent years, many new resources have become available to patients in their quest to educate themselves and make informed choices about their care. For example, The National Consortium of Cancer Centers has treatment practice guidelines that cover all major cancers, with versions written for patients. These guidelines outline standard treatment options and are available in printed form or online at nccn.org.

We have also listed websites in this book that can help you understand and cope with your diagnosis. As a cautionary note, keep in mind that while many useful resources are available on the Internet today, this vast amount of information also contains potential misinformation, thus confusing an already difficult situation. For example, a rumor was started on the Internet claiming that deodorant use was associated with breast cancer. No scientific articles existed to substantiate this claim, which was only speculation. It appears that websites selling "natural" antiperspirant may have perpetuated the rumor. So, try to get your information from well-recognized sites, avoid many chat rooms, and avoid sites that may have something to sell. Always check with your doctor about the accuracy of information you find and to make sure it applies to your specific situation.

Will I See My Radiation and Medical Oncologists After Treatment?

It is customary to see your radiation oncologist at least once following completion of treatment, although facilities have varying policies about this. For example, you may see your radiation oncologist three to four weeks after completion of radiation treatment to answer remaining questions, to examine you for any residual side effects, and to evaluate treatment results.

Medical oncologists generally continue to see their patients for at least five years to monitor for recurrence. After that, some may continue to see their patients on a yearly basis—indefinitely. There are several reasons for this, including the need to screen some patients for the possibility of developing second cancers. Even if you are believed to be cancer-free and have an excellent prognosis, your oncologist may wish to help you with a long-term strategy to maintain overall good health. In addition, you may have specific health concerns unique to cancer survivors that your doctor wants to review. For example, women who experience early menopause following breast cancer may need to attend to osteoporosis prevention.

Fortunately, today, there are more and more cancer survivors. As a result, more attention is directed to specific needs and concerns of cancer survivors. (See the Additional Resources for relevant websites.)

Glossary

Adjuvant chemotherapy: The use of chemotherapy to prevent the growth and spread of cancer that is not detected but is judged to possibly be present.

Benign: Tumor tissues that do not have the capability of spreading locally or metastasizing; the opposite of malignant.

Biopsy: A tissue sample obtained by surgery to evaluate the presence or absence of cancer. A biopsy is almost always necessary in order to plan appropriate treatment.

Bone marrow: A soft substance within the bone in which red and white blood cells and platelets are produced. Radiation therapy and chemotherapy may cause a decrease in blood-cell production, which is one reason frequent blood counts are taken during cancer treatment.

Brachytherapy (internal radiation therapy): Implanting a radioactive seed into a tumor, allowing a high dose of radiation to be delivered directly to the cancer cells but sparing surrounding tissue from significant amounts of radiation energy.

Chemotherapy: The use of anticancer drugs to treat the disease by either killing the cells or preventing them from growing.

Contrast agent: A chemical that is used to highlight disease processes on x-ray tests, allowing them to be seen in clear contrasting to normal tissues.

Cure: An outcome of treatment that leaves the patient disease-free, with no likelihood of recurrence.

Diagnostic workup: Performing x-ray and other imaging tests, blood tests, and physical examinations in order to establish a diagnosis.

Differential diagnosis: A list of the most likely diagnoses for a particular set of symptoms and x-ray findings. The use of different imaging techniques often narrows the differential diagnosis to one most likely disease.

Dose-time relationship: The relationship between the total amount of radiation delivered in the course of treatment and the period of time over which it is administered. This relationship is vital in determining the best treatment plan for a particular cancer patient. The radiation oncologist is trained to judge what is the best dose to be delivered in the most advantageous time to achieve the best chance for cure or palliation. In determining the doses and times, the radiation oncologist also considers how well surrounding tissue will tolerate treatment.

-ectomy: The suffix to indicate removal of, as in pneumonectomy, the removal of a lung; cystectomy, the removal of the bladder; mastectomy, the removal of a breast; colectomy, the removal of the intestine.

Electron beam: Linear accelerator machines are capable of delivering radiation with photons (x-rays) and electrons. Each is a different type of radiation. Photons, in the energies used with linear accelerators, are very powerful, traversing great depths of tissues. Electrons may travel only for a limited distance, depending on the energy used to propel them.

Fractionation: The daily dose of radiation based on the total dose divided into a particular number of daily treatments.

Gamma rays: Radiation originating from unstable atomic nuclei. One example is the production of gamma rays from the isotope cobalt 60. Gamma rays have particular energies depending on the specific isotope from which they are emitted. For those derived from cobalt, this is approximately one million electron volts.

Grade: In reference to tumors, the aggressiveness of the cell type, from very low aggressiveness with a slow growth pattern to very aggressive with rapid spread. Tumor grading classifications vary according to tumors.

Isotope: A radioactive substance used in diagnosis or treatment of cancer.

Local invasion: The spread of cancer from an original site to the surrounding tissues.

Localized tumors: Tumors that are contained in one particular site and have not yet spread.

Malignant cells: Cancer cells that have the ability to spread locally in an uncontrolled fashion and may also spread to distant sites.

Medical oncologist: A physician whose specialty is diagnosing and treating cancer. Medical oncologists are first trained in internal medicine and then do subspecialty training in oncology. Many oncologists are also trained in hematology, a field concerned with blood, including blood cancers.

Metastasis: The spread of cancer from its original site to other parts of the body. Cancer cells from the primary site travel through the lymph system or the bloodstream and attach to the new site.

Palliation: Treatment delivered not to cure but to arrest the disease. This may focus on issues such as eradicating pain or bleeding.

Portal film: An x-ray film of the anatomic area that is designated to be treated with radiation.

Primary tumor: The place where the cancer originates, which is referred to regardless of the site of its eventual spread. Prostate cancer that spreads to the bones is still prostate cancer and is not referred to as bone cancer.

Prognosis: The outcome, or outlook, for a patient's condition based on the type of tumor, the stage, the available treatments, and other factors such as the person's overall health status.

Radiation dose: The amount of x-ray or other energy absorbed by an irradiated object. This dose is recorded as grays (GY) or as centigrays (CGY). Ten GY equal 1,000 CGY. For simplification, we refer to centigrays as "units." When we say 1,000 units, this means 1,000 CGY.

Radiation oncologist: A physician whose specialty is radiology and who is further trained in the science and art of radiation treatment. Some radiation oncologists are also certified in diagnostic radiology.

Radiation portal or radiation field: The area under treatment with radiation.

Radiation scatter: A change in the forward direction of particles of photons as a result of collision and interaction with tissues.

Radiation sensitivity: The response of the cell to radiation. Cancer cells that are very sensitive to radiation include seminomas and some lymphomas.

Radiation therapist: A person who is trained to operate the specialized radiation treatment machinery. Once commonly known as a radiation technologist, this person is involved in the hands-on work of delivering treatment.

Regional involvement: The spread of cancer to areas near the original site and not to distant areas of the body.

Remission: A period during which the disease is regressing and symptoms are improving.

Resistance: The opposite of radiation sensitivity (see above). Cancer cells that are particularly resistant to radiation include melanoma, a type of skin cancer. Resistance also means that a particular cancer does not respond to chemotherapy drugs or that the drugs that once worked to control that cancer no longer do so.

Serial examination: Obtaining x-rays sequentially to document the activity of a disease process. For example, a density in the lung field may be due to infection or tumor. So, while the patient is taking antibiotics, serial examinations will enable the physician to determine which of the two is most likely.

Side effects: Symptoms directly related to treatment, such as the nausea that results from treatment in the vicinity of the stomach. Side effects are considered acute when they occur during treatment and subside when treatment is completed. Those symptoms that persist over a longer period of time are considered chronic.

Simulation: A process in which therapy is planned and defined before actual treatment begins. It can be likened to a trial run, in which specifics of treatment can be worked out prior to using the actual radiation therapy machine.

Site: The location of the tumor.

Stage: The anatomic extent of the cancer. Cancer may exist in the organ of origin, extend locally, spread to regional tissues, then to local lymph nodes, and then to distant areas as metastases.

Systemic: Having a widespread effect on the body rather than just local tissue.

Tumor: A swelling, mass, or lump that may be either benign or malignant. Samples of tumor tissue are examined, or biopsied, when cancer is suspected.

Type: Which type of cell in a particular organ becomes cancerous. Thus, an organ, such as the skin, containing different types of cells can develop different types of cancer—for example, basal cell cancer, squamous cell cancer, and melanoma.

X-rays: Penetrating electromagnetic radiations that are usually produced by bombarding a metallic target with fast electrons.

Additional Resources

The books and websites listed below represent only a small sample of the vast resources available to cancer patients and their families. If you wish to expand your knowledge about a particular cancer and look for tips for coping with the disease and its treatments, we recommend first calling the American Cancer Society in your community. This organization has access to resources that can help patients and families, including information about peer support groups in your area. It also publishes numerous pamphlets and other helpful materials. In addition, both public and university libraries may be able to assist you with an online search for specialized information. We also note that many of the websites listed below will lead you to publications, provide links to other organizations, and introduce you to a wealth of information that may help you or your loved one understand and cope with a cancer diagnosis, treatment options, and posttreatment care.

Books

Coping with Chemotherapy, Nancy Bruning. New Garden City, New York: Avery Penguin Putnam, 2002.

Diagnosis Cancer, Wendy Schlessel Harpham, M.D. New York: W. W. Norton, 1998.

Getting Well Again, Carl O. Simonton, Stephanie Matthews, James L. Creighton. New York: Bantam, 1992.

Head First, Norman Cousins. New York: Penguin Books, 1990.

Love, Medicine, and Miracles, Bernie Siegal, M.D. New York: Perennial, 1998.

Websites

The following websites may be useful in your search for information:

General Information

American Cancer Society
cancer.org
(Well known for a variety of information and programs for patients and families, including the publication "American Cancer Society Guidelines on Nutrition and Physical Activity for Cancer Prevention.")

Coalition of National Cancer Cooperative Groups, Inc.
CancerTrialsHelp.org
(A source of information about clinical trials.)

National Comprehensive Cancer Network
nccn.org
(Includes treatment guidelines written for patients.)

National Cancer Institute
cancer.gov/search/clinical_trials
(A potential source of information on clinical trials.)

National Coalition for Cancer Survivorship
canceradvocacy.org
(A leading organization for cancer survivors.)

National Institutes of Health
www.nih.gov
(General information about cancer and specific information about research; it also will lead you to the information about clinical trials published by National Cancer Institute.)

People Living with Cancer
peoplelivingwithcancer.org
(Accurate, up-to-date information on cancer provided by the American Society of Clinical Oncology. Information can be searched by cancer type, and you can also find treatment guidelines written for patients.)

Disease Specific

Alliance for Lung Cancer Advocacy, Support, and Education
alcase.org

American Foundation for Urologic Disease
afud.org

Colorectal Cancer Network
www.colorectal-cancer.net

The International Myeloma Foundation
myeloma.org

The Leukemia and Lymphoma Society
leukemia-lymphoma.org

National Brain Tumor Foundation
braintumor.org

National Ovarian Cancer Coalition
ovarian.org

National Prostate Cancer Coalition
4npcc.org

Susan G. Komen Breast Cancer Foundation
komen.org

Other

American Pain Foundation
painfoundation.org
(Information on pain management.)

Cancer Supportive Care
cancersupportivecare.com
(Includes valuable tips about exercise for cancer patients.)

Memorial Sloan-Kettering Cancer Center
mskcc.org
(A source of general patient information, which includes a section called "About Herbs.")

National Center for Complementary and Alternative Therapy
nccam.nih.gov
(An NIH website that includes, among other things, information about complementary medicine and herbs.)

National Hospice and Palliative Care Organization
nhpco.org
(Information about end-of-life care.)

Index

Abdomen
 and CT scans, 217
 and MRI, 220
 and radiation side effects, 27–28, 41
ABVD, 121
Acoustic neuroma, 77
Actonel, 40
Addiction, 195
Adenocarcinoma, 109
Adjuvant therapy, xix, 126
Adriamycin
 and bladder cancer, 72
 and breast cancer, 90, 90–91, 96, 97
 and hair loss, 35
 and the heart, 41
 and Hodgkin's disease, 121, 123
 and myeloma, 131, 133
 and non-Hodgkin's lymphoma, 135–36,
  137
 and prostate cancer, 149–50, 153
 and uterine cancer, 162
Alcohol, 50
Allogenic bone marrow transplantation, 184, 185
Alopecia. *See* Hair loss
Alternative therapies, 227–28
American Cancer Society, 50, 59–60, 210, 235
American Society of Clinical Oncology
  (ASCO), 97
Amsterdam Criteria, 103
Androgen supplements, 54
Angiogenesis, 20, 188
Antevert, 36
Antiangiogenesis therapy, 20, 188
Antibodies, 189–90
Anticancer substances, 185–86. *See also*
  Chemotherapy
 bisphosphonates, 169, 186
 cortisone medication, 171, 180, 185–86
Anticipatory nausea, 36, 37
Antiestrogenic effect, 89
Antigens, 189
Antiprostaglandins, 191
Anxiety, 62, 65–66
Anzemet, 37
Appearance issues, 59–60
Appetite loss, 46–47

Aranesp, 31
Aredia, 150, 169, 186, 197
Arimidex, 89
Aromasin, 89
Aromatase inhibitors, 89–90, 92
Arterial venous malformation, 77
Ativan, 37
Autologous bone marrow transplantation, 184, 185
Avastin, 106, 108
Axilla, 175

Bacille Calmette–Guerin (BCG), 70–71
Barium enema, 104, 206–7
Barrett's esophagus, 109
Basal cell cancer, 154, 155, 157
BCNU, 77, 79
Benign prostatic hypertrophy (BHP), 143
Bexxar, 136, 190
Bisphosphonates, 169, 186, 197
Bladder, 152–53, 208–9
Bladder cancer, 69–75
 and chemotherapy, 71–72, 72–73, 75
 and chemotherapy side effects, 73–74
 combination treatment, 71–72, 75
 cystectomy, 71
 follow-up and outlook, 75
 and intravenous pyelogram examination
  (IVP), 208–9
 invasive, 71, 72–73
 metastatic, 72–73, 176
 multidisciplinary approach to, 72–73
 neobladder, 71
 non-organ-confined, 72
 and radiation, 71–72, 73–74, 75
 and radiation side effects, 28, 41, 73–74
 risk factors, 69–70
 and surgery, 72
 symptoms, 70
 and transurethral resections, 70
 treatment, 70–73
Blenoxane, 41
Blood-brain barrier, 79
Blood clots, 214
Blood counts, 28, 29–32, 122, 229
Blood tests, 98–99, 229

Bone marrow, 29–30, 32
  and Hodgkin's disease, 121, 122
  and non-Hodgkin's lymphoma, 135
  stem cells, 183
Bone marrow transplantation, 183–85
  age and, 185
  allogenic, 184, 185
  autologous, 184, 185
  breast cancer and, 185
  chemotherapy and, 183–84
  donor marrow, 184
  graft failure, 185
  graft versus host disease, 185
  and Hodgkin's disease, 121
  and leukemia, 183–85
  and myeloma, 131–32
  and non-Hodgkin's lymphoma, 135, 183
  peripheral blood stem cell transplant, 184
  side effects, 184–85
  testicular cancer and, 185
  types, 184
Bone pain, 132, 133, 134, 151, 167–68
Bone scans, 213
Bone x-rays, 204
Bones, metastasis to, 166–70
  bisphosphonates and, 169
  and bone pain, 167–68
  and bone scans, 213
  and bone x-rays, 204–5
  and chemotherapy, 169
  follow-up and outlook, 170
  hair loss, 172
  and orthopedic procedures, 167
  and radiation therapy, 167–69
  side effects, 169
  symptoms, 167
  treatment, 167–69
Brachytherapy, 100–101, 147
Brain, metastasis to, 170–72
  and chemotherapy, 170
  and cortisone medication, 171
  and edema, 171
  follow-up and outlook, 172
  and radiation therapy, 170–71
  side effects of treatment, 171–72
  treatment, 170–71
Brain cancer, 75–79
  blood-brain barrier, 79
  and chemotherapy, 77
  and chemotherapy side effects, 79
  CT scans and, 75, 76, 217–18
  detection of, 75–76
  drowsiness and, 78
  emotional support and, 78
  follow-up and outlook, 79

  gamma knife and, 77
  gliomas, 75
  hair loss and, 78
  MRI and, 75, 76, 220
  primary, 75
  and radiation side effects, 25, 77–79
  and radiation therapy, 76–79
  radiosurgery, 76–77
  stereotactic system and, 76
  surgery, 76
  treatment, 76–77
  types, 75
Breakthrough pain, 193, 195
Breast cancer, 79–99
  aromatase inhibitors and, 89–90, 92
  biopsies, 82
  blood tests and, 98–99
  breast-conserving therapy, 86–88
  and breast self-exams, 210
  breast size and, 83–84, 86
  and chemotherapy, 17, 90–93
  and chemotherapy side effects, 96–97
  and clinical trials, xxi
  cure rate, 225
  diagnosis, 81–85
  dose-dense treatment, 91
  ductal carcinoma in situ (DCIS), 79–80,
      84, 85
  estrogen and, 88–93
  exercise and, 57–58
  follow-up and outlook, 97–99
  genetic testing, 81
  growth factor, 91
  and hormonal therapy, 19–20, 88–93
  and hormonal therapy side effects, 94–97
  invasive, 83–84, 86–93
  locally advanced, 91
  lumpectomy, 86–87
  and lymph nodes, 80, 83–84, 90–91
  and mammocyte therapy, 87–88
  mammography, 81–82, 83, 84–85, 97–98, 209–11
  mastectomy, 80, 86–88
  metastasis to the lymph nodes, 175–76
  metastatic, 92–93, 175–76
  minimally invasive approaches, 82–84
  and MRI, 82, 98, 220–21
  needle localization, 82–83
  neoadjuvant therapy, 91
  noninvasive, 79–80, 84, 85
  pathology report, 84–85
  postexcision mammogram, 83
  prevention of, 81
  and radiation, 86–88
  and radiation side effects, 41, 93–94
  radical mastectomy, 80

risk factors, 80–81
sentinel node biopsy, 84
and sexuality, 59
specimen mammogram, 83
spread of, 79–80
surgery, 80, 82–84
as systemic, 80
tamoxifen and, 20, 81, 85, 89–90, 92, 94–95
targeted therapies and, 20
and treatment side effects, 32, 35
and ultrasound, 82, 215
Breast coil accessory, 220
Breast self-exams, 210
Bronchial irritation, 26–27

Caffeine, 50
Camptosar, 105–6
Cancer. *See also* specific types of cancer
causes, 230
contagiousness of, 224
and death, 181, 225
development of, 3–4
diagnosis. *See* Diagnostic testing
discussing, 233
drug resistance and, 5, 15
extent, 6
genes and 3–4
grade, 6
and the lymph system, 4, 165–66
and motivation for change, 64
personality traits and, 230
and quality of life, 225–26
secondary, 123
sensitivity and, 5, 15
stage, 6
stress and, 230
and treatment planning, 5–7
types of, 5, 6. *See also* specific types of
cancer
viruses and, 224
Cancer cells
cell grades, 6
differences in, 5
spread of, 4, 165–66
types of, 5, 6
Carboplatinum, 93
Cardiac ultrasonography, 215
Casodex, 149
CAT scans. *See* CT scans
Catapres, 39
Catheters, 34–35
CCNU, 77, 79
CD20, 136
CEA levels, 142
Celebrex, 191

Cells. *See also* Cancer cells
chromosomes and, 186–87
plasma cells, 129–30
types of, 6
Central nervous system, 217–18. *See also* Brain;
Spine
Cervical cancer, 99–102
and chemotherapy, 99, 101
and chemotherapy side effects, 102
diagnosis, 99
follow-up and outlook, 102
and lymph nodes, 99–100, 176
and radiation side effects, 101–2
and radiation therapy, 99, 100–101
risk factors, 99
and sexuality, 101–2
and surgery, 99
treatment, 99–101
Cheerfulness, 63–64. *See also* Positive attitude
Chemoprevention, 191
Chemotherapy, xv–xvi. *See also* Treatment
adjuvant, 126
administration of, 15–17
and alleviation of symptoms, 17–18
basics of, 15–19
for bladder cancer, 71–72, 72–73, 75
blood tests and, 229
for bone cancer, 169
and bone marrow transplantation, 183
for brain cancer, 77, 170
for breast cancer, 17, 90–93
for cervical cancer, 99, 101
for chest cancer, 173
for colorectal cancer 104–5, 105–6
combination treatment, 18–19
continuous infusion, 16
current, 22
cycles, 15
dosages, 16
doublets (two drugs), 18
for esophageal cancer, 110–11
fear of, 60–61
for head and neck cancers, 17, 114, 118
for Hodgkin's disease, 120–21
injection, 16
for leukemia, 17
limitations of, 187
for lung cancer, 125–28
and the lymph nodes, 175–76
for lymphomas, 17
metastasis and, 17–18, 166
mistakes in administering, 236
and the multidisciplinary approach, viii–xx
for myeloma, 130–32
neoadjuvant, 91, 126

for non-Hodgkin's lymphoma, 135–36
and numbness in fingertips, 19
for ovarian cancer, 138–39
and pain management, 196
and palliative treatment, xvi–xvii, 166
for pancreatic cancer, 140–41
preoperative, 17
for prostate cancer, 149–50
questions about, 21–22
and radiation therapy, 5, 17–18
for rectal cancer, 17
resistance and, 15
safety and, 16
schedules, 15
sensitivity and, 15
side effects. *See* Chemotherapy side effects
for skin cancer, 154–56
and symptom alleviation, 17–18
as a systemic treatment, 3, 15
and targeted therapies, xvii, 20
for testicular cancer, 158–59
treatment planning, 5–7
triplets (three drugs), 18
for uterine cancer, 162
venous access devices, 16–17
and work life, 58
Chemotherapy side effects, xiii, 33–40
absence of, 235
acute, 24
appetite loss, 46–47
bladder cancer and, 73–74
bone cancer and, 169
brain cancer and, 79
breast cancer and, 96–97
cervical cancer and, 102
chronic, 24
colorectal cancer and, 107–8
in common with radiation, 28–32
diarrhea, 38, 48–49
digestive tract, 37–38
dry mouth, 47
early menopause, 32–33, 38–40, 96–97
esophageal cancer and, 111–13
fatigue, 28–29, 55–56
hair loss, 227
head and neck cancers and, 118–19
the heart and, 41, 123, 137
Hodgkin's disease and, 122–24
long-term, 40–43
low blood counts, 28, 29–32
lung cancer and, 41, 129
management of, 18–19, 33–34
mouth infections, 37–38
mouth sores, 37
mucositis, 37
and nails, 40

nausea, xiii, 18–19, 36–37, 47–48, 96
neurological, 42
non-Hodgkin's lymphoma and, 137
numbness, 19, 42
ovarian cancer and, 139
pancreatic cancer and, 142
salivary changes, 47
and skin, 40
testicular cancer and, 159
tingling, 19, 42
vaginal dryness, 40
variation in, 24–25
vomiting, 18–19, 36–37
Chest, metastasis to, 173–74
follow-up and outlook, 174
side effects, 173–74
symptoms, 173
treatment, 173
Chest cancers
and CT scans, 218–19
and MRI, 221
and radiation side effects, 26–27, 41
Chest x-rays, 204–5
CHOP, 135–36
Chromosomes, 186–87
Chronic pain, 193, 194–95
Cisplatin, 101, 102, 118
Cisplatinum, 42
Clinical trials, xx–xxi, 106, 183, 190, 233–34
Phase I, xx
Phase II, xx
Phase III, xx
Collimators, 12, 13, 105
Colonoscopy, 104, 108, 207
Colorectal cancer, 102–8
barium enema, 104
and chemotherapy, 104–5, 105–6
and chemotherapy side effects, 107–8
clinical trials and, 106
colonoscopy, 104, 108
colostomy, 105
and CT scans, 104
diet and, 106–7
family history and, 102–3
and flexible sigmoidoscopy, 103
follow-up and outlook, 108
genes and, 102–3
genetic testing for, 102
hepatic artery infusion and, 108
and lymph nodes, 104–5
metastatic, 108
polyposis, 103
and radiation side effects, 106–7
and radiation therapy, 104–5
risk factors for, 102–4
screening for, 103–4

spread of, 102
surgery for, 104–5
symptoms, 103
targeted therapies and, 20
treatment, 104–6
and treatment side effects, 48
and urinary tract infections (UTIs), 107
virtual colonoscopy, 104
vitamins and, 52
Colostomy, 105
Communication
asking questions and, xxi–xii, 21–22, 63
with family members, 233
with physicians, xiv, 197–98
treatment-team concept and, xviii–xx, xxii
Compazine, 37, 112, 121, 141
Complementary therapies, 227–28
Complete blood counts (CBC), 30
Computed axial tomography scanning. *See* CT
scans
Computers, 12–13, 14
Confusion, 25
Consultations, 7–9, 197–98
Contagiousness, 224
Continuous infusion, 16
Contrast agents, 205
Coping strategies, xiii–xiv, 62–63
Cortisone medication, 171, 180, 185–86
Coughing, 26–27
Counseling, xiii, xv, 61–62
Cousins, Norman, 8
Cryosurgery, 148
CT scans (computed axial tomography scanning),
12–13, 216–19
and the abdomen, 217
and bone cancer, 205
and the brain, 75, 76, 217–18
and the central nervous system, 217–18
and the chest, 218–19
and colorectal cancer, 104
and head and neck cancers, 119, 219
and liver cancer, 216
and lung cancer, 124, 129, 218–19
and MRI, 219–21
and myeloma, 134
and nuclear scans, 213, 213–14
and the pelvis, 217
and PET scanning, 222
procedure, 216–17
and the spine, 217–18
spiral, 205
virtual colonoscopy, 104, 207
Cure rates, 225
CVP, 135–36
Cycles, 15
Cyclotrons, 171

Cystectomy, 71
Cytoxan, 35, 90, 131, 149–50

Death, 181, 225
Debulking, 138
Decadron, 37, 77–78, 96, 131, 133, 180, 185–86
Dehydration, 49
Delayed nausea, 36, 37
Dental issues, 114, 115–16
Depression, 61, 231
Diagnostic testing, xviii, 6, 201–22. *See also* CT
scans; MRI
barium enemas, 104, 206–7
blood clots and, 214
bone scans, 213
bone x-rays, 204
breast ultrasound, 215
breasts and, 209–11, 215
cardiac ultrasonography, 215
chest x-rays, 204–5
choosing, 202
colonoscopy, 104, 108, 207
during treatment, 203
echocardiogram, 215
endoscopy, 206
gastrointestinal examination, 205–6, 207–8
gynecological ultrasonography, 215–16
heart and, 215
imaging tests, 202–3
intravenous pyelogram examination (IVP),
208–9
and kidney function, 208–9
kidney ultrasonography, 216
large-bowel disease and, 206–7
liver scans, 213–14
liver ultrasonography, 216
lung scans, 214
mammography, 81–82, 83, 84–85, 97–98, 209–11
nuclear scanning, 211–14
pancreatic ultrasonography, 216
PET scanning, 221–22
posttreatment, 203
pretreatment review of test results, 202
radiation and, 3
radiologists and, 202
rectal ultrasonography, 216
small-bowel series, 207–8
types, 201, 203–22
and ulcers, 206
ultrasound, 82, 214–16
and the urinary system, 208–9
ventilation scans, 214
Diarrhea, 27, 38, 48–49
Diet, xiv, 45–55
alcohol, 50
appetite loss, 46–47

caffeine, 50
and colorectal cancer, 106–7
dehydration, 49
diarrhea and, 48–49
eating, act of, 47
esophogeal cancer and, 111–13
general tips, xiv–xv, 49–50
head and neck cancers and, 116–17
herbal supplements, 53–55
nausea and, 47–48
obesity, 50
pancreatic cancer and, 141
posttreatment, 50
vitamins, 50, 51–52
Dietary Supplement and Health Education
    Act (DSHEA), 53
Digestive tract, 37–38
Dilantin, 78
Disorientation, 25, 171–72
Ditropan, 74, 101, 107, 162
DNA, 4
Doctors. *See* Physicians
Donor marrow, 184
Dosage, calculation of, 16
Dose-dense treatment, 91
Dose-time relationship, 6
Doublets (two drugs), 18
Doxil, 93, 149–50
Drowsiness, 25, 78, 172. *See also* Fatigue
Dry mouth, 26, 47, 116
Ductal carcinoma in situ (DCIS), 79–80,
    84, 85
Duodenum, 205–6

Eating. *See* Diet
Echocardiogram, 215
Edema, 171
Effexor, 39
Elavil, 194
Ellence, 35
Eloxatin, 105
Emcyt, 149–50
Emend, 37
Emotions, xi–xii, xv, 60–64
    anxiety, 62, 65–66
    appearance and, 59–60
    coping strategies, xiii–xiv, 62–63
    depression, 61, 231
    emotional strength, 61–62
    expressing, 63–64
    false cheerfulness, 63–64
    fear of death, 225
    fear of treatment, xii–xiii, 60–61
    fears, xii–xiii, 231
    information and, 63
    at night, 56

pain and, 194
positive attitude, xiii–xiv, 62–63, 231
posttreatment, 65–66
psychological support, xii, 61–62
relaxation, 62
and sexuality, 230
spiritual support, xiii, 61–62, 65
supportive therapies, xiii–xiv
End-of-life care, 181, 234–35
Endometrial cancer. *See* Uterine cancer
Endorphins, 194
Endoscopy, 206
Enzymes, 189
Epidermal growth factors, 20, 188–89
Erbitux, 106, 108
Erythema, 156
Eschars, 155
Esophageal cancer, 108–14
    adenocarcinoma, 109
    Barrett's esophagus, 109
    and chemotherapy, 110–11, 113
    and chemotherapy side effects, 111–12
    eating and, 111–13
    esophagram, 112–13
    follow-up and outlook, 113
    gastroesophageal reflux (GERD) and,
        109
    incidence, 109
    and lymph nodes, 109, 176
    and percutaneous endoscopic gastrostomy
        (PEG), 112–13
    and photodynamic therapy, 113
    and radiation side effects, 111–13
    and radiation therapy, 110–11, 113
    risk factors, 109
    spread of, 108–9
    squamous cell carcinoma, 109
    surgery and, 110, 113
    treatment, 110–11, 113
Esophagram, 112–13
Esophagus
    examination of, 205–6
    irritation, 128
    swelling, 26
Estrogen
    and breast cancer, 88–93
    drugs, 38
Eulexin, 150
Exercise, 57–58

Facial cancer, 26. *See also* Head and
        neck cancers
Family members, xii, 22, 61–62, 102–3, 233.
        See also Genes
Faslodex, 92
Fatigue, 28–29, 55–56, 57, 178

Fear, xii–xiii, 60–61, 225, 231
Femara, 89
Fertility, 32–33, 123, 138, 159
Fibrocystic change, 210
Fibrocystic condition, 210
5-FU, 105–6, 107–8, 110, 111, 118, 141
Flexible sigmoidoscopy, 103
Follow-up, xii, 9, 11–12, 237. *See also*
    Posttreatment; specific types of cancer
Food. *See* Diet; Eating
Food and Drug Administration (FDA), 53
Fosamax, 40
Fractionation, 11
Friends, 61–62

Gamma camera, 212
Gamma knife, 13–14, 77, 171
Gamma rays, 4
Gastroesophageal reflux (GERD), 109
Gastrointestinal (GI) examination, 205–6,
    207–8
Gemzar, 35, 73, 93, 97
Gene therapy, 186–89
    and attacking abnormalities, 188–89
    and correcting abnormalities, 188
    growth factors and, 188
Genes
    and breast cancer, 81, 190–91
    and cancer, 3–4, 186–88, 190–91
    and colorectal cancer, 102–3
    definition, 187
    genetic predisposition, 190–91
    metastasis and, 187
    mutation of, 80–81, 187
    and ovarian cancer, 80–81, 140
    and prevention of cancer, 190–91
Genetic testing, 81, 103, 190–91
Germ cell tumors. *See* Testicular cancer
Ginkgo biloba, 54
Ginseng, 53–54
Gleason score, 144, 145–46
Gleevec, 20, 189
Gliadel Wafer, 77
Gliomas, 171
Graft failure, 185
Graft versus host disease, 185
Granulocyte-colony stimulating factors (G-CSF),
    122, 132–33, 137, 184
Growth factors, 122, 184, 188–89
Gynecological ultrasonography, 215–16

Hair loss, 25, 35–36, 59–60, 172, 226–27
Head and neck cancers, 114–19. *See also* Brain
    cancer
    and chemotherapy, 17, 114, 118
    and chemotherapy side effects, 118–19

and CT scans, 119, 219
and dry mouth, 116
and eating and drinking, 116–17
follow-up and outlook, 119
metastasis to the lymph nodes, 175
and MRI, 119, 219, 221
multidisciplinary approach, 114
and radiation side effects, 25–26, 42, 115–18,
    119
and radiation therapy, 114–17, 119
and skin, 118
and surgery, 114
and swallowing, 117–18
teeth and, 114, 115–16
and the thyroid gland, 119
treatment, 114–19
Head First, 8
Headache, 25
Heart
    and chemotherapy side effects, 41, 123, 137
    echocardiogram and, 215
Hepatic artery infusion, 108
Herbal supplements, xiv, 53–55, 228
Herceptin, 20, 41, 93, 189
Heredity. *See* Genes
Hereditary nonpolyposis colorectal cancer
    (HNPCC), 103
Hickman catheters, 34, 35
High-intensity iridium after-load device, 14
HIV virus, 224
Hobbies, 58
Hodgkin's disease, 119–24
    and blood counts, 122
    and bone marrow, 122
    and bone marrow transplantation, 121, 185
    and chemotherapy, 120–21
    and chemotherapy side effects, 122–24
    cure rate, 225
    follow-up and outlook, 124
    immunosuppression and, 42
    lymph nodes and, 119–20, 174
    metastasis and, 174
    origin, 119–20
    and radiation side effects, 121–22, 122–24
    and radiation therapy, 120–21
    and sarcomas, 123–24
    and secondary cancers, 123
    treatment, 120–21
    and treatment side effects, 32–33, 122–24
Hormonal therapy, 19–20
    and breast cancer, 88–93
    and metastasis, 166
    and pain management, 196
    and prostate cancer, 148–49, 150–51, 153
    side effects, 94–96
Hospice, 181, 234–35

Hot flashes, 94–95, 96
Hyperalimentation, 46

Ifex, 73
Imaging tests, 202–3. *See also* specific types of
    imaging tests
Immunocompetence, 45
Immunosuppression, 42
Immunotherapy, 19, 131, 155–56
Imodium A-D, 38, 101, 152, 162
Implanted ports, 34–35
Implants
    permanent, 14
    prostate, 223–24
    radioactive, 14, 147, 161, 223–24
Impotence, 146, 153, 229
IMRT (intensity-modulated radiation therapy), 13
    and brain cancer, 76
    and prostate cancer, 147
Incontinence, 148
Indigestion, 27
Infection, 132
Infertility, 32–33, 123, 138, 159
Information
    current, 236–37
    and emotions, 63
    Internet and, 236–37
    locating, 236–37
    seeking, 21–22, 63
    truth and, 64–65
Injections, 16, 223
    intraarterial, 16
    intralesional, 16
    intramuscular, 16
    intraperitoneal, 16
    intrapleural, 16
    intrathecal, 16
Insertion, radioactive, 161
Insomnia, 56. *See also* Sleep
Integrative therapies, 228
Intensity-modulated radiation therapy
    (IMRT), 13
Interferon, 131, 133, 156
Internet, 236–37
Intestines, 205, 206–7, 207–8
Intravenous feeding, 46
Intravenous (IV) lines, 34–35. *See also* Venous
    access devices
Intravenous pyelogram examination (IVP), 208–9
Iressa, 189
Isotopes, 212–14
IV. *See* Intravenous lines

Joints, 221
Journal writing, 63

Kidney ultrasonography, 216
Kidneys, 208–9, 216
Knowledge
    and emotions, 63
    seeking, 21–22, 63
    truth and, 64–65
Kytril, 37

Labeling, 212
Lactose intolerance, 48
Large-bowel disease, 206–7
Leukemia
    bone marrow transplantation and, 183–85
    chemotherapy and, 17
    targeted therapies and, 20
Lifestyle changes, xiv–xv, 55–60
    appearance issues, 59–60
    hobbies, 58
    motivation for, 64
    physical activity, 56–58
    rest, 55–56
    sexuality, 58–59
    sleep, 55–56
    work life, 58
Linear accelerator, 171
Liver scans, 213–14
Liver ultrasonography, 216
Local invasion, 165
Local treatment, xix, 3. *See also* Radiation therapy;
    Surgery
Localized cancer, 6
Lomotil, 38, 101, 152, 162
Low blood counts, 28, 29–32
Lumpectomy, 86–87
Lung cancer, 124–29
    categories, 125
    and chemotherapy, 125–28
    and chemotherapy side effects, 41, 129
    and chest x-rays, 204–5
    and coughing, 128
    and CT scans, 124, 129, 218–19
    diagnosis, 124–25
    early-stage, 125–26
    and esophageal irritation, 128
    follow-up and outlook, 129
    and lymph nodes, 124–25, 176
    and metastasis, 126, 129
    non-small-cell (NSCLC), 125–27
    and radiation side effects, 41, 128
    and radiation therapy, 125–28
    small-cell, 125, 126, 128
    smoking and, 129
    spread of, 126
    stages, 125–26
    and surgery, 125–26

symptoms, 125
targeted therapies and, 20
treatment, 125–28
Lung scans, 214
Lupron, 39, 149
Lycopene, 54–55
Lymph nodes, metastasis to, 174–77, 231–32
    axilla, 175
    from breast cancer, 175–76
    and chemotherapy, 175–76
    detection, 174
    from esophageal cancer, 176
    follow-up and outlook, 177
    from head and neck cancer, 175
    from lung cancer, 176
    origins, 174–76
    from other lymph nodes, 174, 176
    from pancreatic cancer, 176
    from pelvic cancer, 176
    and radiation therapy, 174–76
    side effects, 177
    treatment, 174–77
Lymph system, 231–32. *See also* Hodgkin's disease;
    Non-Hodgkin's lymphoma
    and breast cancer, 80, 83–84, 90–91
    and cervical cancer, 99–100
    and colorectal cancer, 104–5
    and esophageal cancer, 109
    and lung cancer, 124–25
    lymphatic spread, 165
    and the spread of cancer, 4, 80, 83, 165–66,
        231–32
    and testicular cancer, 158
    and uterine cancer, 161
Lymphatic spread, 165
Lymphomas
    chemotherapy and, 17
    immunosuppression and, 42
    non-Hodgkin's. *See* Non-Hodgkin's lymphoma
    targeted therapies and, 20

Magnetic resonance imaging. *See* MRI
Malabsorption, 208
Mammocyte therapy, 87–88
Mammography, 81–82, 83, 84–85, 97–98,
    209–11
Margins (specimen), 83
Mastectomy, 80, 86–88, 178, 179, 190–91
Medical history, 8–9
Medical oncologists, 7–9
    consultations with, 7–9, 237
    follow-up by, xii, 11–12, 237
    and pain management, 196
    and side effect management, 33–34
    support staff for, 21

Medical records, 8
Medication. *See also* Chemotherapy
    addiction, 195, 226
    cortisone, 171, 180, 185–86
    narcotics, 195–96
    as needed, 194
    for pain, 193, 194–96, 197, 197–98
    round-the-clock, 194–95
    and sleep, 56
Megace, 39
Melanoma, 154, 155–56, 157
Menopause, 32–33, 38–40, 96–97, 230
Menstruation 32–33
Metastasis, xvi–xvii, 4, 6, 165–81
    and bone scans, 213
    to bones. *See* Bones, metastasis to
    to the brain. *See* Brain, metastasis to
    breast cancer and, 92–93
    chemotherapy and, 17–18, 166
    to the chest. *See* Chest, metastasis to
    colorectal cancer and, 108
    and death, 181
    and end-of-life care, 181
    genes and, 187
    and hospice, 181
    and local invasion, 165
    lung cancer and, 126, 129
    to the lymph nodes. *See* Lymph nodes,
        metastasis to
    and palliative treatment, 166
    prostate cancer and, 151
    and recurrence, 166
    to the skin. *See* Skin, metastasis to
    to the spine. *See* Spine, metastasis to
    and systemic treatment, 166
Methadone, 195
Microcalcifications, 210–11
Monoclonal antibody therapy, 19, 20, 136, 137,
    189–90
MOPP, 123
Mouth infections, 37–38
Mouth sores, 37
MRI (magnetic resonance imaging), 219–21
    and the abdomen, 220
    and the brain, 75, 76, 220
    and the breast, 82, 98, 220–21
    and the chest, 221
    and CT scans, 219–21
    and diagnosis, 202
    and head and neck cancer, 119, 219, 221
    and joints, 221
    and the pelvis, 220
    procedure, 219–20
    resonance, 219
    and the spine, 220

MS Contin, 194
Mucositis, 37
Mucus production, 26–27
Multidisciplinary approach, xviii–xx
MVAC, 72–73
Myeloma, 129–34
    and bone marrow transplantation, 131–32
    and bone pain, 132, 134
    and chemotherapy, 130–32, 133–34
    and chemotherapy side effects, 132–33, 133–34
    and CT scans, 134
    diagnosis, 130
    follow-up and outlook, 133–34
    and infection, 132
    multiple, 130
    origin, 129–30
    plasma cells and, 129–30
    and radiation side effects, 132
    and radiation therapy, 130, 132, 134
    refractory, 131
    and systemic treatment side effects, 132–33
    treatment, 130–32

Nails, 40
Narcotics, 195–96, 226
National Bone Marrow Transplant Registry, 184
National Cancer Institute, 93
National Hospice and Palliative Care, 181, 235
Nausea, xiii, 18–19, 27, 36–37, 47–48
Navelbine, 35, 93, 97
Neck cancers. *See* Head and neck cancers
Needle localization, 82–83, 211
Neoadjuvant therapy, 91, 126
Neobladder, 71
Neulasta, 31, 73, 122, 137
Neupogen, 30–31, 73, 122, 137
Neurological abnormalities, 217–18
Neurological impairment, 180–81
Neurological side effects, 42
Neurontin, 39, 194
Neutropenia, 30
Neutrophils, 30
Nocturia, 143
Non-Hodgkin's lymphoma, 134–38
    aggressive, 134–35
    and bone marrow transplantation, 135, 185
    and chemotherapy, 135–36
    and chemotherapy side effects, 137
    diffuse large-cell, 135
    follow-up and outlook, 138
    immunosuppression and, 42
    indolent, 134–35
    and lymph nodes, 134–36, 174
    metastasis and, 174
    and radiation side effects, 136–37
    and radiation therapy, 135–36

    spread of, 134
    treatment, 135–36
    and treatment side effects, 33
Nonseminomatous germ cell tumors (NSGCT), 157, 158–59
Nuclear scanning, 211–14
Numbness, 19, 42
Nurse practitioners, 21
Nurses, 21
Nutrition, 45. *See also* Diet

Oat cell lung cancer, 125, 126, 128
Obesity, 50
Oncogenes, 3–4
Oncologists. *See also* Medical oncologists;
        Radiation oncologists
    consultations with, 7–9, 237
    follow-up by, 11–12, 237
    and pain management, 196
    support staff for, 21
Oncology nurses, 21
Oophorectomy, 190
Oophoropexy, 32, 233
Orthopedic procedures, 167
Osteoporosis, 186
Ovarian cancer, 138–42
    chemotherapy and, 138–39
    chemotherapy side effects and, 139
    debulking, 138
    diagnosis, 138, 215–16
    and fertility, 138
    follow-up and outlook, 139–40
    genes and, 80–81, 140
    and gynecological ultrasonography, 215–16
    recurrence, 138, 139
    surgery and, 138–39
    symptoms, 138
    treatment, 138–39
OxyContin, 194–95

Pain, xvii–xviii, 193–98
    acute, 193, 194
    alternative management strategies, 198
    assessment, 197–98
    and bisphosphonates, 197
    bone, 132, 134, 151, 167–68
    breakthrough, 193, 195
    causes, 193–94
    and chemotherapy, 196
    chronic, 193, 194–95
    communication and, 197–98, 198
    continuous, 193
    and disease treatment, 196–97
    and emotions, 194
    endorphins and, 194
    and hormonal therapy, 196

intermittent, 193
management of, xvii–xviii, 194, 196
medication for, 193, 194–96, 197, 197–98, 226
and neurosurgical procedures, 198
and oncologists, 196
and physicians, xviii, 197–98
and radiation therapy, 196
reactions to, 194
specialists, 198
and surgery, 197, 198
Pain specialists, 198
Palladium seeds, 14, 223–24
Palliative treatment, xvi–xvii, 166
Pancreatic cancer, 140–42
and CEA levels, 142
and chemotherapy, 140–41
and chemotherapy side effects, 142
diagnosis, 140, 216
eating and, 141
follow-up and outlook, 142
metastasis to the lymph nodes, 176
and radiation side effects, 141
and radiation therapy, 140–41
and surgery, 140–41
symptoms, 140
treatment, 140–41
ultrasound, 216
Paraplatin, 73
Paxil, 39
Pelvic inflammatory disease (PID), 216
Pelvis, 217, 220, 229. *See also* specific organs
Percocet, 194
Percutaneous endoscopic gastrostomy (PEG), 112–13
Peripheral blood stem cell transplant, 184
Permanent implants, 14
Personality traits, 230
PET scanning, 221–22
Photodynamic therapy, 113
Physical activity, 56–58
Physical dependency, 195, 226
Physicians. *See also* Oncologists
communication with, xiv, 197–98
consultations with, 7–9
follow-up by, 11–12
pain management and, xviii, 197–98
and treatment-team concept, xviii–xx
Physician's assistants, 21
Pituitary adenoma, 77
Plasma cells, 129–30
Plasmacytoma, 130
Platelet counts, 32
Platinol, 73
Polyposis, 103
Polyps, 103, 207

Portacath, 34–35
Portals, 8, 10–11
Positive attitude, xiii–xiv, 62–63, 231
Positron emission tomography (PET) scanning, 221–22
Postexcision mammogram, 83
Posttreatment
anxiety, 65–66
diet, 50
follow-up, xii, 9, 11–12, 237
oncologist visits, 12, 237
Prayer, xiv. *See also* Spiritual support
Prednisone, 77–78, 180, 185
Preoperative chemotherapy, 17
Prevention, 190–91, 209
Procrit, 31
Proscar, 149
Prostaglandins, 191
Prostate cancer, 13, 142–54
and benign prostatic hypertrophy (BPH), 143
biopsy and, 143–44
and bladder side effects, 152–53
brachytherapy and, 147
and chemotherapy, 149–50
and chemotherapy side effects, 38–39, 153
combination therapy, 147–48
cryosurgery, 148
and decision making, 150–51
diagnosis, 143–44
external radiation therapy and, 146–47
follow-up and outlook, 153–54
and Gleason score, 144, 145–46
and hormonal therapy, 148–49, 150–51
and hormonal therapy side effects, 153
and impotence, 146, 153
incontinence and, 148
and lycopene, 54–55
and metastasis, 151, 176
other treatments, 150
pain relief, 151
positron radiation therapy, 148
and prostate specific antigen (PSA), 143–44, 153–54
prostatectomy, 146
and prostatic intraepithelial neoplasm (PIN) number, 144
and radiation side effects, 41, 152–53
and radiation therapy, 146–48, 150, 151
and rectal side effects, 152–53
and saw palmetto, 55
seed implants and, 147, 223–24
and sexual intercourse, 59
and surgery, 146, 147, 150
symptoms, 143–44
testosterone and, 148–49
3-D conformal technique, 146

treatment, 145–51
and urinary frequency, 143, 152
and urinary urgency, 143, 152
watchful waiting, 145–46
Prostate gland, 142–43
Prostate specific antigen (PSA), 143–44,
153–54
Prostatectomy, 146
Prostatic intraepithelial neoplasm (PIN) number,
144
Prostatitis, 143–44
Proteosome inhibitors, 131
Prozac, 39
Psychological dependency, 195
Psychological support, xii, xiii, 61–62
Pulmonary scans, 214
Pyridium, 74, 101, 107, 162

Quality of life, 225–26
Questions, asking, xxi–xxii, 21–22, 63

Radiation, diagnosis and, 3
Radiation oncologists, 7–9, 21. *See also* Radiation
therapy
consultations with, 7–9, 237
follow-up by, 11–12, 237
and pain management, 196
support staff for, 21
Radiation physicists, 21
Radiation side effects, xiii, 23–33
abdominal, 27–28, 41, 46
absence of, 235
acute, 24
appetite loss, 46–47
bladder and, 28, 41
bladder cancer and, 28, 41, 73–74
bone cancer and, 169
brain cancer and, 25, 77–79, 171–72
breast cancer and, 41, 93–94
bronchial irritation, 26–27
cervical cancer and, 101–2
chest and, 41, 173–74
chronic, 24
colorectal cancer and, 106–7
in common with chemotherapy, 28–32
confusion, 25
coughing, 26–27, 128
danger to others, 224
definition, 24
diarrhea, 27, 48–49
disorientation, 25, 171–72
duration of beneficial effects, 235
dry mouth, 26, 47, 116
eating and drinking and, 116–17
esophageal cancer and, 111–13
esophageal irritation, 128

esophageal swelling, 26
fatigue, 28–29, 55–56, 128, 172
hair loss, 25, 172, 226–27
head and neck cancers and, 25–26, 42, 115–18,
119
headache, 25
Hodgkin's disease and, 121–22, 122–24
immunosuppression and, 42
indigestion, 27
lag effect, 235
long-term, 40–43
low blood counts, 28, 29–32
lung cancer and, 128
lymph nodes and, 177
mucus production, 26–27
nausea, 27, 47
non-Hodgkin's lymphoma and, 136–37
pancreatic cancer and, 141
prostate cancer and, 41, 152–53
radioactivity, 223–24
respiratory, 41
salivary changes, 26, 42, 47
on skin, 26, 28, 42, 93–94, 117, 227
skin cancer and, 156, 178–79
sleepiness, 25, 171–72
spinal cancer and, 180
on teeth, 114, 115–16
testicular cancer and, 159
on the thyroid gland, 119
tracheal irritation, 26–27
from treatment to head and chest, 25–27
from treatment to lower abdomen, 27–28
from treatment to upper abdomen, 27
on tumor cells versus normal cells, 24
urinary frequency, 28
urinary urgency, 28
variation in, 24–25
vomiting, 25
Radiation therapy, xv–xvi. *See also*
Treatment
for bladder cancer, 71–72, 73–74, 75
blood tests and, 229
for bone cancer, 167–69
brachytherapy, 100–101, 147
for brain cancer, 76–79, 170–71
for breast cancer, 86–88
for cervical cancer, 99, 100–101
and chemotherapy, 5, 17–18, 232
for chest cancer, 173
for colorectal cancer, 104–5
communication and, 11–12
computers and, 12–13, 14
current, 21–22
danger to others, 224
dosage, 11, 232
driving home from, 10

for esophageal cancer, 110–11
external, 146–47
fear of, 60
follow-up, 11–12
fractionation, 11
functioning of, 4–5
gamma knife, 13–14
for head and neck cancers, 114–17, 119
high-intensity iridium after-load device, 14
history of, 12–13
for Hodgkin's disease, 120–21
intensity-modulated radiation therapy (IMRT), 13
internal, 199
length of, 4–5, 10–11
limitations of, 187
as a local treatment, 3
for lung cancer, 125–28
and the lymph nodes, 174–76
metastasis and, 166
and the multidisciplinary approach, xviii–xx
for myeloma, 130, 132
new techniques and procedures, 12–13
for non-Hodgkin's lymphoma, 135–36
and pain management, 196
and palliative treatment, xvi–xvii, 166
for pancreatic cancer, 140–41
permanent implants, 14
positron, 148
procedures, 9–14
for prostate cancer, 146–48, 150, 151
questions about, 21–22
radiosurgery, 13–14
repeat of, 232
safety of, 234
scatter, 233
schedule, 11
seed implant, 147, 223–24
shielding body during, 232–33
side effects. *See* Radiation side effects
for skin cancer, 154–55, 157, 177–78
for spinal cancer, 180
for testicular cancer, 158
3-D conformal radiation therapy, 13, 146
treatment planning, 5–7
for uterine cancer, 161–62
and work life, 58
Radiation Therapy Oncology Group (RTOG), 110
Radical mastectomy, 80
Radioactive iodine, 14, 212, 223
Radioactivity, 223–24
Radiologists, 202
Radiosurgery, 13–14, 76–77, 171

Reconstructive surgery, 59–60
Recovery, 62–63. *See also* Posttreatment
Rectal cancer. *See also* Colorectal cancer
chemotherapy and, 17
and radiation side effects, 27
ultrasound, 216
Rectal side effects, 152–53
Recurrence, 166
of ovarian cancer, 138, 139
of uterine cancer, 163
Refractory myeloma, 131
Reglan, 37
Relaxation, 62
Religious support, xiii, 61–62, 65
Reproductive issues, 32–33. *See also* Sexuality
Research, xxii–xxiii
Rest, 55–56
Rituxan, 20, 136, 137

Salivary changes, 26, 42, 47
Salogen, 116
Sandostatin, 38
Sarcomas, 123–24
Saw palmetto, 55
Scans, 212. *See also* CT scans; Nuclear scanning
Schedules (for chemotherapy), 15
Secondary cancers, 123
Seed implants, 14, 147
Self-expression, 63
Self-hypnosis, 62
Seminoma, 157–58
Sentinel node biopsy, 84
Sexuality, 32–33, 58–59, 101–2, 229–30
Side effects, xiii, 23–43. *See also* Chemotherapy side effects; Radiation side effects
acute, 24
chronic, 24
common to chemotherapy and radiation, 28–32
early menopause, 32–33
fatigue, 28–29, 55–56, 57
fertility and, 32–33
low blood counts, 28, 29–32
reproductive and sexual issues, 32–33
treatment of, 7
variation in, 24–25
Sigmoidoscopy, 103
Simulator machine, 8
Skin
and chemotherapy side effects, 40
and radiation side effects, 26, 28, 42, 93–94, 117, 227
Skin, metastasis to, 177–79
mastectomies and, 178, 179
side effects, 178–79
treatment, 177–78

Skin cancer, 154–57
    basal cell, 154, 155, 157
    and chemotherapy, 154–56
    and chemotherapy side effects, 156–57
    cure rate, 225
    erythema and, 156
    eschars and, 155
    follow-up and outlook, 157
    immunotherapy, 155–56
    melanoma, 154, 155–56, 157
    and radiation side effects, 156
    and radiation therapy, 154–55, 157
    squamous cell, 154, 155, 157
    and surgery, 154–55
    treatment, 154–56
    types, 154
Sleep, 55–56
Sleepiness, 25, 78, 171–72. *See also* Fatigue
Small-bowel series, 207–8
Small-cell lung cancer, 125, 126, 128
Smoking, 51, 69, 129
Social workers, 61–62
Solitary plasmacytoma, 130
Specimen mammogram, 83
Sperm, 159
Spine, 217–18, 220
Spine, metastasis to, 179–82
    follow-up and outlook, 181
    neurological impairment, 180–81
    side effects, 180
    treatment, 180
Spiral CT scans, 205
Spiritual support, xiii, 61–62, 65. *See also*
        Psychological support
Spirituality, 65
Squamous cell carcinoma, 109
Stanford V, 121
Stem cells, 183
Sterility, 123. *See also* Fertility
Steroids, 54, 186. *See also* Cortisone medication;
        Decadron
Stress
    as cause of cancer, 230
    family, 62
    and immunocompetence, 45
    and nutrition, 45
    reduction, 62
Subcutaneous injections, 16
Support groups, xiii, 61–62
Support staff, 21
Supportive therapies, xiii–xiv
Surgery
    for bladder cancer, 72
    for brain cancer, 76

    for breast cancer, 80, 82–84
    for cervical cancer, 99
    for colorectal cancer, 104–5
    cryosurgery, 148
    debulking, 138
    for esophageal cancer, 110
    for head and neck cancers, 114
    for lung cancer, 125–26
    metastasis and, 166
    and the multidisciplinary approach, xviii–xx
    for ovarian cancer, 138–39
    and pain management, 197, 198
    for pancreatic cancer, 140–41
    for prostate cancer, 146, 147, 150
    radiosurgery, 13–14, 76–77, 171
    second look, 139
    for skin cancer, 154–55
    reconstructive, 59–60
    for testicular cancer, 158–59
    for uterine cancer, 160–61
Swallowing, 117–18
Symptoms. *See also* specific types of cancer
    alleviation of, 17–18
    treatment of, 18–19
Synchrotrons, 171
Systemic treatment, xix, 3, 15. *See also*
        Chemotherapy; Hormonal therapy
    antiangiogenesis therapy, 20, 188
    immunotherapy, 19, 131, 155–56
    and metastasis, 166
    monoclonal antibody therapy, 19, 20, 136,
        137, 189–90
    targeted therapies, 20, 188–89

Tamoxifen, 20, 38, 81, 85, 89–90, 92, 94–95,
    191
Tarceva, 189
Target organ, 212
Targeted therapies, xvii, 20, 188–89
Taste, 116
Taxol, 42, 73, 90–91, 93, 96, 149, 153, 162
Taxotere, 42, 73, 91, 93, 96, 149, 153
Team concept, xviii–xx, xxii
Teeth. *See* Dental issues
Temodar, 77
Testicular cancer, 157–60
    and chemotherapy, 158–59
    and chemotherapy side effects, 159
    cure rate, 225
    follow-up and outlook, 160
    and infertility, 159
    and lymph nodes, 158, 176
    nonseminomatous germ cell tumors (NSGCT),
        157, 158–59

and radiation side effects, 159
and radiation therapy, 158
seminoma, 157–58
and sperm production, 159
and surgery, 158–59
treatment, 158–59
and treatment side effects, 33
Testosterone, 148–49
Thalidomide, 131, 133, 134
Therapy. *See* Treatment; specific types of
therapy and treatment
3-D conformal radiation therapy, 13
Thyroid gland, 119
Tingling, 19, 42
Tobacco, 51, 69, 129
Tolerance, medication, 195
Tomograms, 209
Tomographic sections, 217
Tracheal irritation, 26–27
Transplantation. *See* Bone marrow
transplantation
Transurethral resections, 70
Treatment. *See also* Bone marrow
transplantation; Chemotherapy; Gene
therapy; Hormonal therapy; Radiation
therapy; Systemic treatment
adjuvant therapy, xix, 126
alternative therapies, 227–28
blood tests during, 229
clinical trials, xx–xxi, 106, 183, 190, 233–34
complementary therapy, 227–28
current, 21–22
diet and. *See* Diet
and dose-time relationship, 6
family members and, 22
follow-up, 9, 11–12
future of, 191–92
genetic testing, 190–91
herbal supplements, xiv, 53–55, 228
integrative therapies, 228
local, xix, 3
monoclonal antibody therapy, 19, 20, 136,
137, 189–90
multidisciplinary approach, xviii–xx
other anticancer substances, 185–86
and other conditions, 6, 9
and pain management, 196–97
palliative, 166
planning, 5–7, 9
portal, 8
prevention, 190–91
questions about, 21–22
research and, xxii–xxiii
side effects. *See* Side effects

and supportive therapies, xiii–xiv
systemic. *See* Systemic treatment
vitamins and, 51–52, 228
Treatment fields, 8, 10–11
Treatment-team concept, xviii–xx, xxii
Triplets (three drugs), 18
Truth, 64–65
Tumor growth factors, 20
Tumors
and angiogenesis, 20
cancerous versus benign, 165
germ cell. *See* Testicular cancer
and intralesional injections, 16
stage of, 6
Tunneled catheters, 34
Tylenol, 194
Tyrosine kinases, 189

Ulcers, 206
Ultrasound, 82, 214–16
Urinary system
diagnostic testing and, 208–9
urinary frequency, 28, 143, 152
urinary tract infections (UTIs), 107
urinary urgency, 28, 143, 152
Uterine cancer, 160–63
and chemotherapy, 162
and chemotherapy side effects, 162–63
and gynecological ultrasonography,
215–16
and hormonal therapy, 162
and hormonal therapy side effects,
162–63
and lymph nodes, 161, 176
origins, 160
and radiation side effects, 162
and radiation therapy, 161–62
recurrence, 163
and sexual intercourse, 59
spread of, 160
and surgery, 160–61
tamoxifen and, 95
treatment, 160–62

VAD, 131
Vaginal dryness, 40, 59, 230
Veins, 34–35
Velcade, 131
Venous access devices, 16–17, 34–35
Ventilation scans, 214
Viagra, 153
Vincristine, 133
Virtual colonoscopy, 104, 207
Viruses, 224

Vitamins, 50, 51–52, 228
Vocal cord cancer, 117
Vomiting, 18–19, 25, 36–37

Walking, 57
Watchful waiting, 145–46
Work life, 58

Xeloda, 35, 93, 97, 105
X-rays, 4. *See also* Radiation therapy
    abdominal, 209
    bone, 204
    chest, 204–5, 235
    and diagnostic testing, 202

follow-up, 235
kidney, 209
mammography, 81–82, 83, 84–85, 97–98,
    209–11
tomograms, 209
Xylocaine Viscous, 112, 116

Yoga, 62

Zevelin, 136, 190
Zofran, 37
Zoladex, 149
Zoloft, 39
Zometa, 150, 169, 186, 197